ANN ARBOR DISTRICT LIBRARY

D0226024

THE AFRICAN AMERICAN ENTREPRENEUR

THE AFRICAN AMERICAN ENTREPRENEUR

Then and Now

W. Sherman Rogers

PRAEGER

An Imprint of ABC-CLIO, LLC

A B C 🔹 C L I O

Santa Barbara, California • Denver, Colorado • Oxford, England

Copyright 2010 by W. Sherman Rogers

All rights reserved. No part of this publication may be reproduced, stored in a retrieval system, or transmitted, in any form or by any means, electronic, mechanical, photocopying, recording, or otherwise, except for the inclusion of brief quotations in a review, without prior permission in writing from the publisher.

Library of Congress Cataloging-in-Publication Data

Rogers, W. Sherman
  The African American entrepreneur : then and now / W. Sherman Rogers.
      p. cm.
  Includes bibliographical references and index.
  ISBN 978-0-313-35111-2 (alk. paper) — ISBN 978-0-313-35112-9 (ebook)
   1. African American business enterprises—History. 2. African American businesspeople—History. 3. African American business enterprises. 4. African American businesspeople. 5. Entrepreneurship—United States. I. Title.
  HD2358.5.U6R65 2010
  338.6'4208996073—dc22   2009041628

ISBN 978-0-313-35111-2
EISBN 978-0-313-35112-9

14 13 12 11 10   1 2 3 4 5

This book is also available on the World Wide Web as an eBook.
Visit www.abc-clio.com for details.

Praeger
An Imprint of ABC-CLIO, LLC

ABC-CLIO, LLC
130 Cremona Drive, P.O. Box 1911
Santa Barbara, California 93116-1911

This book is printed on acid-free paper ∞
Manufactured in the United States of America

To my parents,
Dr. Ernest E. Rogers and Mildred O. Rogers,
who taught me that love, and not hope of reward,
should be the motivation for service.

CONTENTS

PREFACE

Entrepreneurial firms have been responsible for creating nearly 80 percent of all new jobs in the United States over the past 20 years. President Barack Obama acknowledged the significance of entrepreneurship to job creation in a speech he gave on regulatory reform on June 17, 2009. The president, in that speech, stated in relevant part:

> I believe that jobs are best created not by government, but by businesses and entrepreneurs who are willing to take a risk on a good idea. I believe that our role is not to disparage wealth, but to expand its reach; not to stifle the market, but to strengthen its ability to unleash the creativity and innovation that still make this nation the envy of the world.

Implicit in the president's remarks is the recognition that entrepreneurs are continually discovering opportunities to provide new and innovative services, products, and methods of doing things to the consuming public. In bringing these services and products to the marketplace, the entrepreneur creates wealth for himself. Eventually, these businessmen and women hire employees as their firms grow in order to meet the increased demand for the goods and services their businesses produce.

Sometimes, the only alternative for persons who experience persistent difficulty in finding employment is to start a business and employ themselves. But many individuals lack the confidence, the capital, or the knowledge to start, operate and grow a new firm.

Part I of this book attempts to inspire readers to adopt an entrepreneurial mindset by highlighting the amazing success stories of black entrepreneurs from the 1600s to the present. It does so by charting the economic activity of these remarkable individuals in a historical, legal, political, sociological, and economic context.

Part II of the book furnishes important practical information that readers can use to improve their chances of achieving entrepreneurial success. It features, among other items, perhaps the best guide for drafting business plans that exists in America—*The Nuts and Bolts of Business Plans*, a product of the Syracuse University Department of Entrepreneurship and Emerging Enterprises at the Whitman School of Management. Part II also covers such topics as the entrepreneurial process, business basics, choosing the appropriate vehicle for doing business, business continuation agreements, intellectual property, raising capital for the business, tax matters, and estate planning considerations.

This book can be used as a primary text for courses that explore issues involving minorities and entrepreneurship. It can also be used as academic resource material for a wide variety of courses including Entrepreneurship, Political Science, American History, American Constitutional Law, Business Law, Small Business Law, Economics, Civil Rights, and other course offerings.

ACKNOWLEDGMENTS

Many thanks to Missy Scott for her brilliant organizational and technical contributions to this project.

Kudos to Jeff Olson, Senior Acquisitions Editor at Praeger Publishing, for his unswerving commitment to the production and dissemination of this book to a world-wide audience.

I would like to also express my gratitude for the words of encouragement and the helpful suggestions of Kurt L. Schmoke, Dean of the Howard University School of Law, Dr. Emory Tolbert, Warren Banfield, Loreal Andrews, Cynthia Brame, Mia Mitchell, Yvonne Gordon, and Joi Belfon Valentine.

Special thanks also to my literary agent, Sha-Shana Crichton of Crichton & Associates, Inc.

I would like to also acknowledge the many well wishes of Karen Richardson and Paul Monteiro.

Finally, special thanks to Johnetta Boseman Hardy, Executive Director of the Howard University Institute for Entrepreneurship, Leadership, and Innovation, and the other officers of the Institute, for their enthusiastic support for this project.

INTRODUCTION

This book has five overriding purposes:

1. to inspire people to develop an entrepreneurial mindset through the compelling and uplifting stories of slaves and half-free blacks who achieved a measure of financial success through business enterprise despite adverse and oppressive conditions;
2. to provide little-known information to the general public concerning the economic history of blacks in America from the 1600s to the present (with an emphasis on the black entrepreneur/business owner);
3. to explain why black Americans still lag behind their white counterparts in wealth and income;
4. to demonstrate why increased entrepreneurship in the black community is one of the most promising ways to achieve black economic parity in America; and
5. to equip the would-be entrepreneur—regardless of his/or her race or national origin—with the necessary tools to successfully launch, grow, and ultimately transfer ownership in a business venture to future generations. Accordingly, the ultimate goal of this book is to provide sufficient information and motivation to help individuals increase their economic productivity and add value to all their endeavors.

The entrepreneurial mind thrives on ideas. Sometimes they are new ideas. Sometimes they are creative approaches to old ideas that bring new innovations that breath life back into lagging projects or processes. The success of the idea or innovation hinges on the entrepreneur's ability to recognize opportunity and the courage to seize it. As the pieces fall into place, and the idea begins to take shape or go into practice, it adds value to the situation, project, or process that inspired it in the first place. Studies confirm that the pursuit of entrepreneurial endeavors plays an important role in bringing prosperity to disadvantaged groups and underdeveloped countries. The success of various microenterprise programs and innovative efforts, such as the Prison Entrepreneurship Program, serve to buttress these findings.

Statistics clearly show that nations that vigorously protect the individual property rights of their citizens and encourage the pursuit of private profit by entrepreneurs have the highest standard of living in the world. In the United States, for example, from 1993–1996, fast-growth emerging companies created about two-thirds of all new jobs.[1] And the Small Business Administration reported in 2007 that entrepreneurial firms contributed over 50 percent of the United States' gross domestic product and created about 78 percent of all new jobs every year for the past twenty years.[2] Additionally, small entrepreneurial firms are responsible for 67 percent of all innovations and 95 percent of radical innovations since World War II.[3] Part II of this book provides information to assist individuals in achieving multi-generational business success.

In view of these statistics, some social scientists and economists maintain that an increase in entrepreneurship in the African American community is one of the most promising routes for blacks to achieve economic parity in America. Moreover, these commentators increasingly state that the economic dislocation and job insecurity caused by the new global economy mandates that all Americans—including those employed by large corporations—develop an entrepreneurial mindset if they are to economically survive international competition for their jobs.[4] But exactly who is an entrepreneur and what is entrepreneurship?

This book uses the term "entrepreneur" in a generic way to refer to the process by which an individual pursues opportunities (whether for profit or nonprofit purposes) without regard to resources he or she may currently control. "An entrepreneur recognizes an opportunity to make a profit, raises the money to open a business, and eventually hires managers to run the business."[5] Entrepreneurs are innovators, agents of change, and risk takers who establish their ventures regardless of whether they currently have the financing they need.

Not all start-up businesses are entrepreneurial firms. Academicians categorize new businesses as one of three types of organizations—entrepreneurial firms, salary substitute firms, or lifestyle firms. True entrepreneurial firms—unlike salary substitute firms (e.g., hairstyling salons, law firms, dry cleaners, restaurants, etc.) or lifestyle firms (e.g., tour guides, golf pros, etc.)—rely, as mentioned, on a process of creativity, innovation, opportunity discovery, and risk evaluation to bring new products and services to the market. This process is the essence of the entrepreneurial mindset. The new products and services that result from the entrepreneurial process always add value to situations, projects, activities and organizations. Thus, entrepreneurs provide a significant contribution to society by developing new and better products, services, and technologies. These new products and services invariably make the current ones obsolete—a process that one economist referred to as the process of creative destruction.[6] The process of creative destruction is also involved when entrepreneurs create new pricing strategies, new distribution channels, and new retail formats. The new products, technologies, and techniques increase consumer demand and stimulate economic activity.

Salary substitute firms and lifestyle firms, in contrast, are not particularly innovative nor do they usually produce new products, services, or business methods. Notwithstanding these notable differences between true entrepreneurial firms and salary substitute and lifestyle firms, the book will refer to any person who attempts to establish a start-up business—regardless of whether it is a salary substitute or life-style firm—as an "entrepreneur."

History has largely ignored the stirring success stories of black entrepreneurs, inventors, and other black innovators who achieved so much in the face of great adversity and oppression. Consequently, the world has been deprived of valuable lessons to be learned from studying the lives of these extraordinary individuals. The achievements of black businessmen and women during the 1600s, slavery, reconstruction, segregation, and even the post-civil rights era are not widely known to Americans of any race. Therefore, an informational gap exists regarding the combined effect of law, politics, economics, sociology, and other factors in charting the economic circumstances of black people at all historical stages of their journey from slavery to freedom. This book historically explores the economic condition of black people in America from the date of their arrival to the present time. In doing so, the book continues a trend to preserve and disseminate this information for current and future generations.

Additionally, the book examines various sociological and economic theories that attempt to explain the lower economic status of blacks in America. It also discusses the impact of judicial decisions and federal and state legislation on the economic aspirations of black Americans, and it analyzes the views of selected black thought leaders such as Booker T. Washington, W. E. B. Du Bois, and others.

The historical role of the black church in promoting the development of black businesses is also an important topic. Accordingly, the book covers the important role of the black church in stimulating black economic development and in providing basic support, security, and a social outlet to the black community during the dark days of slavery and segregation. It also provides selected examples of the black church's current economic activities in the 21st century.

However, this book is far more than a history book on blacks in business. To the contrary, it contains practical information that prospective entrepreneurs can use in successfully starting and growing a business enterprise. To this end, the book provides information on how to write a business plan, legal considerations in choosing the right type of business organization to pursue the business venture, and various ways to finance and market an emerging business. It also discusses innovative programs, such as the Prison Entrepreneurship Program and various microenterprises that are designed to develop entrepreneurial thinking in members of society who need a helping hand in becoming productive citizens.

Entrepreneurial ability is considered by economists to be one of the four scarce means of production toward the satisfaction of human wants (the others being land, labor, and capital). Why is this the case? The answer is simple. "Not everyone can set up a successful business. Proof of this lies in the fact that three out of every five new businesses in the United States fail within the first two years."[7] For these reasons, all prospective entrepreneurs, and especially those who are African Americans, should be exposed to the essential considerations in establishing a viable business. To meet this need, the book attempts to explain the important role of corporate law, agency law, business organizations law, intellectual property law, small business administration law, tax law, franchise law, estate planning law, and the law governing a firm's efforts to raise capital. The budding entrepreneur must understand the interplay of these legal subjects if he or she wishes to increase the odds of successfully launching, growing, and ultimately transferring ownership in a new business venture to future generations.

Unfortunately, the United States has excluded black people from participation in the American economic system of capitalism for most of its history. Nevertheless, there have been astonishing, but little known, success stories of black entrepreneurs beginning as early as the 1600s. And the fabulous success of the so-called Black Wall Street of the early 1900s—which consisted of the segregated black business districts in Durham, North Carolina and Tulsa, Oklahoma—provided some idea of how black businesses could prosper when allowed to sell their goods and services outside of the black community; a phenomenon rarely encountered during the era of slavery and segregation in America.

How, then, has the United States excluded black persons from full participation in the American capitalistic economic system? According to Robert Heilbroner and Lester Thurow in *Economics Explained*, there are at least four ways:[8]

First, in order to be a part of a capitalistic system, the government must allow everyone the right to own private property. The United States denied virtually all black persons the right to own private property from the Colonial period until the Civil War by classifying black people themselves as property. Moreover, black people still do not have equal access to the ownership of property despite passage of anti-discrimination laws.

Second, to be a participant in a capitalistic system, prospective employees must be legally free to contract their labor as they choose. This was not an option for black persons through much of American history because the government forced black persons to work for others during slavery and limited the choices of free black persons in significant ways even after it ended slavery.

Third, a capitalistic system requires that there must be a market system in which persons are able to freely respond to the opportunities and discouragements of the marketplace, unrestricted by the routines of tradition or the dictates of someone's command. American law, however, permitted others to exclude black people from the general market system in which all others could participate during slavery. American law also continued to limit the full participation of blacks in the free market system during the years of legally enforced racial segregation. Therefore, the dictates of government largely relegated black persons to find a business market among other black people.

Fourth, a capitalistic system requires that the market, which we just discussed, be one in which lenders finance a company's investment in capital to help the business grow. American history, however, reveals that banks and other lenders have historically discriminated against otherwise qualified black persons in awarding loans.

The hallmarks of capitalism, therefore, consist of government protection of the freedom of economic contract, government protection of the right of all people to own private property, government protection of an individual's freedom to choose whether to make business decisions free of the dictates of others or the routines of tradition, and non-discriminatory access to loans. Government-sanctioned slavery of blacks, government approval of the segregation of black persons from the rest of society, private and governmental discrimination against blacks in employment, housing, contracting, borrowing, and other aspects of life make clear that America excluded black Americans from fully participating in the benefits of the economic system of capitalism.

Interestingly, the dominant culture did not consider black people of African descent to be legally capable of being "American" during a substantial portion of this nation's history. The United States Supreme Court's decision in *Dred Scott v. Sandford*,[9] is the clearest, most emphatic (and troubling) statement of this view. Indeed, it was not until the states ratified the Fourteenth Amendment to the United States Constitution in 1868 that black persons officially became undisputed American citizens.

The multi-disciplined comprehensiveness of this book is what makes it different from others of this genre. Significantly, the book chronologically covers the business activities of black people in America during every notable period of American history—the pre-civil war era, the civil war era, the reconstruction era, the era of legally imposed segregation, and the civil rights and post-civil rights eras. Additionally, the book covers the same business concepts treated in standard texts on entrepreneurship. Thus, the author's goal in writing this book is to provide both historical and practical information to inspire and assist all entrepreneurs in launching, growing, and ultimately, transferring ownership in a business venture to future generations. As Dr. Martin Luther King, Jr. often said, "the cause of economic justice is the cause of social justice."[10]

Notes

1. Bruce R. Barringer and R. Duane Ireland, *Entrepreneurship* (Upper Saddle River, NJ: Pearson Prentice Hall, 2006), 16.

2. Jeff Cornwall, "Growing Firms in the Entrepreneurial Economy," *Entrepreneurial Mind*, October 25, 2007, http://www.drjeffcoenwall.com

3. Bruce R. Barringer and R. Duane Ireland, *Entrepreneurship* (Upper Saddle River, NJ: Pearson Prentice Hall, 2006), 15.

4. Marshall Goldsmith, "We're All Entrepreneurs," *Business Week*, (August 25, 2008) 46. Mr. Goldsmith, according to the article, has a "new book" on the market entitled *What Got You Here Won't Get You There*. In his book, Mr. Goldsmith expands on his thesis that "in the new era of uncertainty, we all need to think like entrepreneurs." Ibid.

5. Steve Slavin. *Economics: A Self Teaching Guide* (Hoboken, NJ: Wiley & Sons, Inc., 1999), 35.

6. Joseph Schumpeter, *The Theory of Economic Development* (Cambridge, MA: Harvard University Press, 1934).

7. Steve Slavin. *Economics: A Self Teaching Guide* (Hoboken, NJ: Wiley & Sons, Inc., 1999), 33–35.

8. Robert Heilbroner and Lester Thurow. *Economics Explained* (New York: Simon & Schuster, 1998), 11–17.

9. 60 U.S. 393 (1856).

10. Charles Steele, Jr., "The Color of Credit," *Washington Post*, June 23, 2008, sec. A15.

PART I

FOUNDATIONS OF EXCELLENCE: THE AFRICAN AMERICAN ENTREPRENEUR FROM SLAVERY TO THE PRESENT

CHAPTER 1

ENTREPRENEURSHIP AS A KEY FACTOR IN THE BLACK QUEST FOR ECONOMIC PARITY

A stunning array of statistical, legal, historical, and sociological data chronicle the African American quest for economic liberty. The role that law has played in the economic progress of African Americans, however, lies near the core of any meaningful discussion. It was law that enslaved, freed, segregated, and ultimately provided a window of hope for the economic aspirations of black people in the United States.[1] However, greed and fear, the twin engines of capitalism,[2] are the primal forces that underlie every manifestation of significant and persistent economic disparity between groups.[3] This book attempts to explain the lower economic status of black Americans in comparison to the white population in light of legal, historical, sociological, political, and economic considerations related to America's legacy of slavery, segregation, and rampant discrimination against blacks.

As we begin, it is important to note that the term "black" (without the capital "b") is used to refer to "African Americans" in many, if not most instances throughout this book. This is because the dominant culture did not consider black people of African descent to be legally capable of being "American" during a substantial portion of this nation's history. The United States Supreme Court expressed this view in the case of *Dred Scott v. Sandford.*[4] Consequently, black people did not unequivocally become citizens of the United States until the states ratified the Fourteenth Amendment to the Constitution in 1868. Accordingly, it is somewhat awkward to refer to black people as "African Americans" in some parts of this book. Additionally, not all black persons permanently residing in the United States are "Americans." The term "black" is therefore a much more inclusive description of persons of African descent.

Background and Overview

Adam Smith, capitalism's founding philosopher, acknowledged in his landmark book *Wealth of Nations* that a self-interested desire for gain drives capitalism and that this self-interest could be beneficial to everyone. The great British economist, John Maynard Keynes, also noted, somewhat sarcastically, that "capitalism is the extraordinary belief that the nastiest of men, for the nastiest of reasons, will somehow work for the benefit of us all." [5]

The United States has the largest economic disparity between rich and poor of any industrial nation in the world.[6] The richest 1 percent of U.S. households controls 40 percent of the nation's wealth, and the poorest 20 percent of the population earns just 5.7 percent of total after-tax income.[7] In Finland, the most egalitarian nation, the income of the top 10 percent was 2.7 times greater than the total income of the bottom 10 percent. In Norway it was 2.8 to 1; in the Netherlands, it was 2.9 to 1; in Canada, it was 3.8 to 1; in the United States, it was 5.7 to 1.[8] The ever-present hope of Americans of achieving wealth and riches, however, largely explains why Americans—both black and white—are willing to tolerate the huge gap in economic equality between rich and poor. Accordingly, most Americans tolerate a government that provides a less generous system of social services in exchange for lower taxes and reduced regulation. This in turn allows for a greater investment in capital to produce wealth, which will supposedly benefit all.[9] Indeed, 55 percent of Americans under 30 believe they will become rich, and by a six-to-one margin believe that poverty is due to personal flaws.[10]

Fear, however, has often caused greedy, self-interested persons who benefit most from the American capitalistic system to consider the negative consequences that can occur when great economic disparities exist between persons in society. Fear of societal upheaval has, undoubtedly, been an unspoken factor in the passage of legislation that benefits the poor and minorities. Some commentators have noted that Congress passed Social Security and other financial assistance programs during the great depression of the 1930s in part because of fear of "social revolution" and "social upheaval" by the masses.[11]

Professor Marcellus Andrews, then an Associate Professor of Economics at Wellesley College, argues in his book, *The Political Economy of*

Hope and Fear: Capitalism and the Black Condition in America,[12] that "black people were completely unprepared for, and unable to take advantage of, the shift in structure of the American economy toward a knowledge and technology driven system," which offers huge rewards for brains over brawn. This, he maintains, is because black people largely remain an industrial labor force in a post-industrial country.

He also asserts that in the post-industrial society of competitive capitalism and globalism, the preference of the wealthy in "controlling the unwanted classes and the coming black rebellion" is for incarceration and prison growth rather than the old policies of income redistribution and race-based redress. He maintains that the old policies are no longer tenable in an age of competitive capitalism, globalism, budget deficits, and capital mobility.[13]

A snapshot of black America today reveals the following groups: a burgeoning population of college-educated, middle-class, and upper-middle-class blacks who live in fear that those who control the levers of power may roll back programs that helped them to achieve their current status; an insecure group of lower-middle-class blacks who lack college educations and who work as cooks, truck drivers, secretaries, janitors, mail delivery personnel, factory workers, and similar positions; and a shrinking, but persistent, impoverished black underclass that comprises approximately 28–33 percent of all black Americans. Recent studies indicate that the black lower middle-class and the so-called black underclass were unprepared for the shift in the American economy from an industrial labor economy to a knowledge- and technology-driven system spurred by competitive capitalism, globalism, and the off-shoring of jobs.[14] The new economy, unlike the industrial labor economy, is one that values brains and education over brawn.

Suggested solutions for narrowing the economic gap between black and white Americans include programs to increase black entrepreneurship, community-based empowerment programs, vigorous enforcement of the anti-discrimination laws, better schools, and a concerted effort to encourage and fund blacks in obtaining college and specialized degrees. However, education is the key to the economic advancement of black Americans. A recent study by the Washington D.C. Fiscal Policy Institute indicates that the ever-widening gap between the richest and poorest households in America is largely based on the level of one's educational attainment. The study also noted a disturbing trend in the economy "in which people without college educations will be stuck at the bottom."[15] Since 1973, the real wages of the least educated American workers have declined between 20–30 percent.[16]

Historical data reveals African American entrepreneurial activity at the incipient stages of the nation's development in the 1600s. *Before the Mayflower*,[17] *The Negro As Capitalist*,[18] and *The African American Almanac*[19] set forth the first documented entrepreneurial activity by a black person in America. The individual in question, a man by the name of Anthony Johnson, originally came to this country in 1620 or 1621 as an indentured servant from England.

One historian determined that a conservative estimate of the collective wealth of the nearly 500,000 free African Americans on the eve of the Civil War was approximately $50 million.[20] Citing statistics from *Target Market News*,[21] two articles—one in the January 2003 issue of *Black Enterprise*[22] and the other in the February 5, 2003, edition of the *Washington Post*[23]—indicate that in 2001, African Americans earned a whopping $601 billion.[24] This figure is, however, only 5.96 percent of the U.S. gross domestic product. The percentage of total black earning power as a percentage of the United States gross domestic product has held steady during the intervening years as the United States gross domestic product has increased. This figure is well *under* the percentage of black Americans in the population, which is approximately 12 percent.[25] By 2006, the earnings of African Americans had increased to $744 billion.[26] This figure exceeds the gross domestic product of all but 15 nations of the 192 independent countries in the world.[27]

African Americans have achieved these economic gains under difficult circumstances. American law freely allowed for others to enslave black people; segregate black people from the general economic marketplace; segregate black people from attending any establishment owned by whites; prohibit black individuals from having any social relationships with white persons; and discriminate against black persons in employment, ownership of property, and all other benefits, privileges, terms, and conditions afforded to persons of the dominant culture.[28]

While in Senegal, Africa in July 2003, President George W. Bush acknowledged the effect of these practices on black Americans today. He boldly and clearly stated that "Racial bigotry fed by slavery did not end with slavery or with segregation. And many of the issues that still trouble America have roots in the bitter experience of other times."[29] The American legal system's long tolerance of such practices, both legislative and judicial, and the subtle continuation of these practices partially explains why African Americans remain mired at the bottom of the economic ladder today.

Black individuals, when compared to their white counterparts, experience twice the rate of unemployment, have substantially lower personal and family income, are three times more likely to live in poverty, and possess only one-fifth of the net worth of whites.[30] Additionally, 75 percent of black children are born to unwed mothers; 33.33 percent of black men are under judicial supervision;[31] black men constitute a majority of incarcerated persons although black Americans constitute only 12 percent of the population;[32] and only 12 percent of black persons in high school are proficient in reading and math.[33] "Conventional economists ... forget that human beings will do almost anything to avoid viewing themselves as failures, even at the risk of destroying themselves and their communities." Moreover, a cost/benefit analysis partially explains why some members of the black underclass who have experienced multiple generations of damage to their self-esteem turn to crime to win acceptance, achieve wealth, and gain prestige.[34]

However, statistics indicate that the median income of black families comprised of married couples is significantly closer to that of similarly situated whites than any other comparison. The gap between black family income as a percentage of white family income increases from 64.3% to 87% when one compares black families without two parents and black families with two parents. This strongly supports the conclusion that the traditional family unit composed of two parents "remains the cornerstone of societal structure"[35] and demonstrates that "it is statistically verifiable that marriage has a powerful wealth-building effect." Children of single-parent families are "five times more likely to be poor, four more times more likely to engage in criminal behavior, and three times more likely to become welfare recipients when they reach adulthood."[36] However, the two-parent black family has declined from 67% in 1960 to 33% in 1995. The white marriage rate has declined from 91% to 76% during the same time frame. Black persons have the lowest marriage rate of any group in America.[37]

Interestingly, the family instability that plagues today's black family was essentially unknown among black migrant communities in the 20th century. "In 1925 Harlem, 85[%] of black families were intact and single teenaged mothers were a rarity."[38] Although it would be "absurd" to suggest that the failure to marry will result in poverty, the research clearly shows that "[g]etting married and maintaining a healthy union in which both partners communicate well about money can be financially beneficial."[39]

The Role of the Courts

The wide economic and related disparities that exist between blacks and whites today may have been substantially narrowed if, in the years following the Civil War, the U.S. Supreme Court had demonstrated that it valued true racial equality above maintenance of the status quo, and if Congress had continued its efforts to bring blacks into the mainstream notwithstanding the Court's decisions. During this period, the Reconstruction Era, "emancipated slaves giddy with optimism opened businesses, banks, funeral homes, insurance companies, schools, and newspapers."[40] However, in several instances, the U.S. Supreme Court undermined congressional efforts to achieve equality between black and white Americans by either invalidating federal laws or restrictively interpreting federal and state laws aimed at seeking the equality of black people. In *The Civil Rights Cases*[41] and *United States v. Reese*[42] the U.S. Supreme Court invalidated important civil rights statutes. Moreover, Congress did nothing to amend these statutes to make them pass constitutional muster.

In *The Slaughter-House Cases*[43] and in *United States v. Cruikshank*[44] the Supreme Court weakened federal laws to the extent that they had little or no value in protecting the federal rights of U.S. citizens, and especially the recently freed slaves whom these laws were primarily intended to protect. Additionally during this time period, the Supreme Court overturned a state anti-discrimination law enacted to prevent the segregation of blacks in *Hall v. De Cuir*.[45]

The Court, in *Plessy v. Ferguson*[46] ultimately crushed the economic aspirations of black people near the end of the 19th century by allowing states to exclude blacks from any interaction with the white population, a phenomenon directed exclusively to African Americans.[47] Moreover, Congress did nothing to legislatively "fix" the statutes the Court had struck down or had greatly weakened, nor did Congress take steps to protect blacks from rampant discrimination by private businesses and individuals in view of the changed political climate. In 1894, for example, Congress repealed the most important Reconstruction civil rights legislation that the Supreme Court had not previously invalidated. This legislation included the suffrage protections of the Enforcement Act and the Force Act.[48] Consequently, private companies were free to blatantly discriminate against blacks in every conceivable way.

The United States has excluded blacks from participation in the American economic system of capitalism for most of its history. To include a group in a capitalistic system, the following elements must exist: (1) the government must legally accord the right of ownership of private property to all persons; (2) prospective employees must have the legal right to work or not to work as they choose; (3) there must be a market system "in which economic activities are left to men and women freely responding to the opportunities and discouragements of the marketplace, not to the established routines of tradition or the dictates of someone's command"; and (4) the market must allow for a regular flow of wealth into production through a flow of savings and investment organized through banks and other financial companies in which borrowers pay interest as the reward for using the lenders' wealth.[49]

Accordingly, the hallmarks of capitalism consist of government protection of the freedom of economic contract, government protection of all persons' rights to own private property, government protection of an individual's freedom to choose whether to make business decisions free of the dictates of others or the routines of tradition, and a nondiscriminatory system of bank financing.[50] However, government-sanctioned slavery of blacks, government approval of the segregation of black persons from the rest of society, and private and governmental discrimination against blacks in employment, housing, contracting, borrowing, and other aspects of life make clear that America excluded black Americans from fully participating in the benefits of the economic system of capitalism.

The U.S. Supreme Court continues to have a significant role in either assisting or frustrating the long-delayed inclusion of black Americans into all aspects of the American economic system. For example, in *Grutter v. Bollinger*,[51] the Court decided that an educational institution's use of racial diversity as a factor in the admissions' process is constitutional in light of the reality that blacks are still recovering from the racial caste system the Court endorsed in 1896 and only overturned in 1954 in *Brown v. Board of Education*.[52] The Court also based its decision on the observation that admission to selective, elite institutions of higher education "is a prelude to power, and that a racially and ethnically mixed leadership . . . is essential to the public's support of American institutions."[53]

The majority in *Grutter* recognized that racial discrimination has not ceased and that the playing field is not level. This recognition was manifested by Justice Sandra Day O'Connor's hope that affirmative action would not be necessary 25 years from the date of the decision.[54] Justice Ginsburg elaborated on this point in a separate concurring opinion in *Grutter* and stated "one may hope, but not firmly forecast, that over the next generation's span, progress toward nondiscrimination and genuinely equal opportunity will make it safe to sunset affirmative action."[55] Speaking more pointedly in her dissent in the companion case of *Gratz v. Bollinger*,[56] she noted that blacks "historically have been relegated to inferior status by law and social practice" and that the affirmative action measure in the *Gratz* case was designed to "hasten the day when entrenched discrimination and its aftereffects have been extirpated."

Additionally, the extent to which private and public entities may use affirmative action in the employment process and the award of government contracts remain hot-button issues. The desire for economic prosperity and security underlie both. For example: with regard to persons employed by state and local governments, in *Wygant v. Jackson*[57] the Supreme Court ruled 5-4 that a public school board's desire to maintain a sufficient number of minority teachers as role models did not justify a policy of laying off white teachers with more seniority than minority teachers who kept their jobs. With regard to persons employed by private companies, the United States Supreme Court, in *United Steel Workers v. Webber*[58] upheld a collective bargaining agreement that set a quota on promotions for black aluminum plant workers. The Court held that the Civil Rights Act of 1964 did not prohibit voluntary private agreements to help blacks when the agreements were temporary, not designed to maintain racial balance, and necessary to eliminate a manifest racial imbalance in traditionally segregated job categories.[59]

In the government contracts arena at the state and local levels, the U.S. Supreme Court, in *City of Richmond v. J.A. Croson Co.*[60] struck down a Richmond, Virginia, affirmative action plan that set aside 30 percent of city contracts for minority firms. The Court held that state and local race-conscious programs to benefit minorities must face the same "strict scrutiny" under the Constitution as discrimination against minorities.[61] However, in *Metro Broadcasting v. FCC*[62] a case involving a federal affirmative action program, the Court held that, in order to ensure diversity on the air waves, the federal government may take race into account in federal affirmative action programs such as the FCC's program for determining the distribution of broadcast licenses. The Court held, however, that only an intermediate scrutiny should apply to federal affirmative action plans authorized by Congress in the exercise of its powers to remedy discrimination under Section 5 of the Fourteenth Amendment. However, a more conservative Supreme Court, in *Adarand Constructors, Inc. v. Pena*[63] (Justice Thomas having replaced Justice Marshall on the Court), overruled the *Metro Broadcasting* decision to the extent that the *Adarand* Court held that "strict scrutiny" applies to federal affirmative action programs to the same extent that it applies to state and local affirmative action programs such as the one involved in *City of Richmond v. J.A. Croson Co.*[64] We will discuss these and other cases further in Chapter 7.

The Ongoing Journey to Equality

During the 1800s and well into the 20th century, economists, using Western European and American whites as the standard, assumed that genetic inferiority was the reason for the low economic status of African Americans, Eastern Europeans, and other minorities. Institutional economists such as Gunnar Myrdal dismantled these commonly held assumptions during the 20th century by showing that a culture of poverty, discrimination, and oppression were the primary cause of the lower economic status of African Americans.[65]

However, the genetic inferiority theory persists. There are some economists today who believe that laws prohibiting race discrimination are unnecessary and inefficient in a free market system. They believe that, absent government compulsion as in the pre-1964 South, unrestricted market forces alone are all that are necessary to generate economic progress for blacks.[66]

A chorus of critics, both black and white, has increasingly come to view African Americans and black culture as the primary cause of the ongoing economic disparity between blacks, whites, and others.[67] Some even argue that an inferior black culture is the reason for all the social problems facing many poor African Americans and that segregation was a well-intentioned system created to "protect" blacks from the real racists.[68] Additionally, middle- and upper-income blacks, who compromise approximately two-thirds of all blacks, have increasingly become more vocal in their criticisms of the behavior and attitudes of blacks of lower socio-economic status.[69] However, many middle- and upper-income blacks do not believe this criticism is justified, contending that competitive capitalism, globalism, and racism have combined to limit the access of poor blacks to education, good jobs, health care, and good lives.[70]

Some commentators believe that the most effective way for African Americans to achieve true economic liberty is by assimilating more completely into the dominant culture.[71] For example, Gunnar Myrdal, who wrote in the late 1930s and early 1940s concerning the plight of blacks during the tough days of segregation, noted the importance of improving the educational level of blacks. To Myrdal, however, "Education mean[t] an assimilation of white American culture. It decrease[d] the dissimilarity of the Negroes from other Americans." Myrdal noted "there is no magic either in mixed schools or segregated schools" and emphasized that blacks needed good schools regardless of their race.[72] Walter R. Allen and Joseph O. Jewell, in *An American Dilemma Revisited: Race Relations in a Changing World*, noted that Myrdal "like most of the social scientists of his era, believed in assimilation as the 'final solution' to the race problem. Myrdal did not anticipate the black political cultural movement of the 1960s and 1970s, which not only advocated community control of educational institutions but also questioned the validity of the broader American culture and its relevance for black students." They also note that Myrdal's study relative to education "failed to anticipate the intractability of American racial prejudice and discrimination."[73] Today, statistics indicate that black students who attend black colleges are more likely to graduate than those who attend white institutions. Accordingly, black colleges remain a significant avenue of social and economic mobility for black Americans.[74]

Others believe the ultimate solution for black economic equality is through entrepreneurship.[75] The proponents of this approach believe that entrepreneurship will bring financial independence, transmission of black wealth to successive generations of black persons, and is more likely to create a class of professionally educated offspring.[76] A third position suggests that a blending of the assimilation and entrepreneurial theories is the better approach.[77] Perhaps this position is the most realistic alternative. Although black people attempt to engage in entrepreneurial activities at a greater rate than their white counterparts,[78] the reality is that "three out of every five new businesses in the United States will fail within the first two years of operation."[79] Nevertheless, black entrepreneurship remains underdeveloped in America when compared to the majority population.[80] Therefore, existing efforts to increase the number of thriving black-owned businesses should remain a priority. In Chapter 7, The Civil Rights Era, we will look closely at programs designed to help blacks and other minorities succeed in establishing, maintaining, and growing their business enterprises.

This book canvasses the legal, historical, and other considerations that help to explain the current economic condition of African Americans in this country. The legal issues, however, are at the bottom of any analysis of this topic, whether it be issues of sociology, economics, history, political science, or other disciplines. This book maintains that any decision by the U.S. Supreme Court or any other entity with decision-making power that suggests the history of pervasive racial discrimination in the United States has ended will only prolong the day of economic liberty for many African Americans. Until African Americans and other disadvantaged groups become more connected to the American economic system, increases in the crime rate, continued social imbalance, and racial distrust should be expected.

The benefits flowing from the civil rights movement have not been distributed evenly among the entire black community. However, innovative federal initiatives such as the Empowerment Zone and Enterprise Community Program[81] have helped inner cities and their residents outpace the nation between the 1990 and 2000 census in population growth, household income, housing unit growth, high school graduates, college graduates, home ownership, and poverty reduction.[82]

Nevertheless, competitive capitalism, globalism, and racism have combined to limit the access of poor blacks to education, health care, and good jobs. Accordingly, this book also contends that the American brand of capitalism must be modified to lessen the gap between rich and poor. This goal can be accomplished through innovative efforts to improve and provide access to the education system and the continuation of programs to assist blacks in employment, business development, and community-based empowerment programs. Research demonstrates a clear relationship between investments in education and economic well-being. Thus, education is ultimately the key. Moreover, studies indicate that the inflation-adjusted wages of young high school graduates declined by 18 percent from 1963–1992. In contrast, the inflation adjusted wages of college graduates rose 8 percent during this general period, while the wages of male high school graduates of all ages fell by 40 percent. Thus, "For better or worse, university education is a gateway to authority in a complex, hierarchical, technology-driven society that distributes power and prestige on the basis of achievement."[83]

Capitalism for all its virtues is not a perfect system and frequently requires government intervention. For quite a few years now, markets have been largely unregulated, and while it has had its benefits, it also has drawbacks. Steven Pearlstein, writing in the *Washington Post*, noted that:

> But what Americans have also come to realize is that the same model is less adept at providing other things we value highly—things like safety, fairness, economic security, and environmental sustainability. [84]

He noted that the U.S. health care system is a good example of the downside of privatization:

> . . . it has become one of the least efficient and effective, with extraordinary high costs, mediocre results, and a large and growing pool of working families with little or no insurance and inadequate care.[85]

He points to the 2008 crash of the housing and financial sectors as yet another example:

> These bubbles had their roots in deregulated credit markets that were hailed as models of innovation and market-driven efficiency. Now that the bubbles have burst, it is more than a bit ironic that government has had to

step in to rescue the markets from their excesses and prevent a meltdown of the financial system.[86]

Accordingly, the government still has an important role to play in providing an economic safety net for workers and innovative programs for prospective entrepreneurs that a free-market economy has not provided, and will not provide.

Innovative Programs That Foster Entrepreneurship

Innovative programs that foster entrepreneurship play a key role in the black quest for economic parity. Let's look at some examples.

Micro-Enterprise Programs

The success of various micro-enterprise programs and innovative efforts such as the Prison Entrepreneurship Program buttress the numerous findings that the pursuit of entrepreneurial endeavors plays an important role in bringing prosperity to disadvantaged groups and underdeveloped countries.

Micro-enterprises are "programs or businesses that offer a combination of credit, technical assistance, training, and other business services to disadvantaged people for the purpose of helping them launch small self-employment projects."[87] An inspirational story on the subject is detailed in an article by Elaine Lee entitled, "Do Good, Get Rich" (Social Warriors Start Businesses That Improve the Lives of African Women).[88] The article discusses micro-lending, micro-business ventures, and provides the definition of micro-enterprises set forth earlier.

The article is primarily about the story of how an African American social entrepreneur, E. Aminata Brown, has made a difference in the lives of a small group of female porters (kayayoo) in Ghana. These Ghanaian women carry loads up to 100 pounds on their heads or backs in the stifling heat for as little as $1.00 per day. Ms. Brown, 36, a Los Angeles resident working in Ghana as a freelance management consultant, decided that she had to do something.

Ms. Brown invested $30,000 of her own money to start a business in Ghana called BaBa Blankets to make a profit and to better the lives of these women. Ms. Brown hired skilled tailors to train some of these Ghanaian women how to make blankets, table runners, and other products. BaBa Blankets' annual net sales have grown from $30,000 in 2006, its first year of operations, to $150,000 in 2007. BaBa Blankets is on track to clear $300,000 in sales by the end of 2008. The girls and women of

BaBa blankets went from making an average of $1.00 a day to become seamstresses and businesspeople joining together in a collective that brings in $1,000 to $6,000 per month. Ms. Brown sells products made by BaBa Blankets at African American festivals and churches, folk art and bedding shows, via the internet (www.wondala.com), and other venues.

In 2007, BaBa Blankets contributed $150,000 to the women and girls. And the article notes that "Ms. Brown's goal is to support 50 girls' educations by the 2008–2009 school year."

These programs are an outgrowth of a "nascent lending program created by Muhammad Yunus, a Bangladeshi economist who won the 2006 Nobel Peace Prize for developing the Grameen Bank, which uses micro-loans to help eradicate poverty in developing nations."[89] Yunus started the micro-loan program in 1974 by making tiny loans to micro-entrepreneurs, mostly women in businesses such as street vending and farming with "transformative results." The Grameen Bank has since disbursed $6 billion in tiny loans to about 7.4 million Bangladeshi micro-entrepreneurs.

Mr. Yunus recently established Grameen America, which offers loans from $500 to $3,000. In the first three weeks of February, 2008, Grameen America authorized 36 loans worth a total of $100,000 to small businesses, including the following types: salons, clothing, jewelry, handbags, candy, catering, tailoring, cleaning, doll-making, printing, and day care.

The Prison Entrepreneurship Program

Another innovative social entrepreneurship program is Catherine Rohr's Prison Entrepreneurship Program, a nonprofit organization based in Houston, Texas. Ms. Rohr, a former venture capitalist in California and New York, decided to start the program after she heard a story about a graduate of Charles Colson's prison ministry program leaving prison after eight years and starting a general contracting business that made $1.7 million in sales in 18 months. Ms. Rohr created a business curriculum consisting of more than 350 hours of class time that is taught by 100 business executives. The program pairs prisoners with Harvard and Texas A&M students, who work with the prisoners online or in person and help edit their business plans. As of 2006, Ms. Rohr stated that the Prison Entrepreneurship Program graduated 220 participants and 21 former inmates had started to operate small businesses.[90]

Other Programs

There are several other helpful programs designed to encourage entrepreneurship and help aspiring entrepreneurs grow their businesses. Here are a few examples.

Small Business Administration Programs—The Section 8(a) Program for Small Disadvantaged Businesses; Small Business Development Centers; Section 7(a) Loan Guaranty Program; Microloan Program; and the Section 504 Certified Development Company Program.

These programs provide entrepreneurs with technical guidance and/or financial assistance in a variety of ways. We will discuss these programs in Chapter 7.

Other Government Programs—HUD's Community Development Block Grant Program; The Community Reinvestment Act; The New Markets Tax Credit Program; HUD's Renewal Communities; Empowerment Zones, and Enterprise Community Programs.

These programs provide financial incentives and other types of assistance to entrepreneurs who seek to establish businesses in low-income and underdeveloped communities. We will discuss these programs in chapter 7 of the book.

The Historic Role of the Black Church in Black Economic Development, Past and Present

Many scholars have argued that the black church is the most important social institution within the black community aside from the family.[91] The self-made men who founded the independent black church in the 1700s were the first to introduce bootstrap economics to the black American experience. These men formed independent black churches as a protest to the segregationist polices of the institutionalized white church. The black independent church soon became a nationwide network of social, economic, and political activism.[92]

Men such as Richard Allen and Absalom Jones, pooling the scanty resources of runaway slaves and free blacks to purchase land and a building, heralded the beginning of the black church. It is the oldest and most enduring black institution in America. The black church was, generally, the only strategically located major building owned by blacks in their community. As such, the church edifice became the focal point of black life. The black church's earliest concern was in establishing mutual aid societies that provided services and resources to the excluded and oppressed black population who made up its membership. Bill Alexander, in the *The Black Church and Community Empowerment*, writes:

> Black entrepreneurship gained its legs through this church-led process of aggressive self-determination. Insurance companies, banks, publishing

houses, newspapers, and a host of small businesses owe their existence to the economic muscle of the black church.[93]

Church-backed mutual assistance societies as early as the 1700s provided sick benefits, death benefits, and assistance to black families. The Philadelphia Free African Society, founded by Richard Allen and Absalom Jones in 1778, is the earliest example of note. The mutual assistance societies were centers of religious worship, secular and fraternal interest, and a source of financial aid. These organizations were necessary because it was clear that the dominant society did not accept former slaves as the social equals of whites and did not welcome them to assimilate into the social life of the general community.[94]

Black churches helped to organize mutual assistance societies to generate capital. This in turn led to the development of private lending businesses, which were the precursors to efforts to organize black banks. As the fraternal organizations and societies increased in number, there was a corresponding increase in the capital, investments, and subsidiary businesses developed by these organizations. The increasing asset basis of these organizations led to the formation of the first banks organized and administered by blacks after the Civil War.

Tens of thousands of African Americans seeking a better life left the South following the Civil War, including 50,000 who settled in Kansas from 1878–1881 referred to as "Exodusters."[95] Nevertheless, at the turn of the 20th century, nine out of every ten blacks still lived in the rural South.

World War I witnessed a mass migration of blacks from the rural South to the urban North. This movement reached epic proportions around 1915 when the escalation of the war in Europe spurred an economic boom in the United States. This economic boom created many new industrial jobs in the Northern cities. In 1910, 75 percent of African Americans had lived in rural areas and nearly 90 percent still resided in the South. By 1960, more than 75 percent of African Americans lived in cities and only 60 percent remained in the South.

The World War I era witnessed the establishment of new religious and quasi-religious groups to cater to the needs and frustrations of this massive influx of people to the Northern cities. Marcus Garvey, for instance, held his first public meeting in this country at the historic Bethel African Methodist Episcopal Church in Philadelphia.

George Baker, (a/k/a Father Divine), like Garvey, lulled a disoriented black population away from the established church with the promise of free food, free lodging, and guaranteed employment. His Peace Mission

Movement attracted both blacks and whites from all social classes. Beginning in 1919, he began buying farms and buildings so his organization could produce its own food and provide shelter for its followers. Additionally, he created and staffed businesses such as dry cleaners, laundries, and restaurants. During the depression of the 1930s, Father Divine's organization provided meals for the unemployed and working poor.

Similarly, Bishop C.M. (Daddy) Grace's United House of Prayer for All People invested heavily in real estate, capitalized small businesses, and also set up a manufacturing and distribution network during this general time period. The United House of Prayer has continued to prosper long after the death of its founder. Its most ambitious activities involve the construction of low to moderate income housing. The church has attempted to build better urban communities by providing affordable, decent housing. As the 1990s approached, the United House of Prayer had invested $20 million in housing construction from its own resources. The church had 145 churches in 22 states at that time.[96]

Additionally, the Black Muslims (Nation of Islam) at the height of their influence provided a positive entrepreneurial model for the black community. The Black Muslims, under their economic system of self-support, established bakeries, dry cleaners, restaurants, a fishing fleet, and a well-equipped, state-of-the art publishing house that published the largest-selling black newspaper in the country at the time.

Between the 1960s and the 1990s, black churches began to move beyond traditional support programs and engaged in greater activities to empower the black community. Economic development with an emphasis on community reinvestment became the dominant theme. Additionally, interdenominational conference alliances, such as the Congress of National Black Churches, represented a giant leap toward community empowerment and self-reliance on a nationwide scale. From small community credit programs to multi-million dollar national economic networks, the black church escalated its efforts to marshal its resources to improve the quality of life in the black community.

Among the activities of the black church during the period from the 1960s to the 1990s include the establishment of: credit unions; computer training schools; community based employment and skills training programs for youth; employment agencies; adult education programs; in-school tutoring programs; full-scale adult education programs; and classes on family budgeting, taxation, minority business issues, financial planning, and mutual fund investment. Black churches also began to increasingly build apartments for senior citizens and individuals with low and moderate incomes. They also began to establish commercial ventures such as drug stores, grocery stores, thrift shops, restaurants, barber and beauty shops, and dry cleaners. In some notable instances, black churches also financed small minority businesses.

The Spirit of Faith Christian Center in Temple Hills, Maryland, a Washington, D.C. suburb in Prices George's County, is an example of the growing trend of some 21st century black churches toward establishing, owning, and operating for-profit businesses. In 1995, the church, which then had a membership of 300, came up with the down payment to purchase, for $850,000, a dilapidated, crime-ridden, empty shell strip mall in Temple Hills that was known to attract drug dealers and graffiti. By 2004, the church's 60,000 square foot strip mall, renamed Faith Plaza, employed 100 persons, had a beauty salon, upholstery shop, private school, bookstore, computer training center, a Bible institute, a teen arcade called Hang Time, and housed the church, which had grown to 3,000 members. The beauty salon alone has made more than $500,000 dollars in the seven years since it opened in 1997. The Church's assets also include Faith Flight II, a small jet the pastor uses to fly around the country to various Christian conventions. As of 2004, the church was attempting to acquire 500 acres—tied up by zoning regulations—to establish a development called Faith City. The church wants to use the property for a senior citizens home, a battered women's center, a clothing store, a grocery store, and other businesses.[97]

The beauty salon, called Divine Design, as of 2004 had ten stylists, a barber, and two manicurists who all attend the church. The salon boasts a profit-sharing plan in which a percentage of the salon's earnings are returned to the stylists through bonuses or months of free booth rent. There is a board of elders to oversee the church's affairs. However, a nonprofit organization, Hosanna Enterprises, Inc., operates the businesses. Profits from the church's business enterprises have paid overdue bills for church members and funded other good works.[98]

The Church's pastor and founder, Michael A. Freeman, is a fourth-generation preacher. Freeman's ancestors in the ministry are and were members of established denominations. His father is a member of the evangelical Free Will Baptist denomination; and his grandfather and great-grandfather were Methodists. Freeman, however, decided to start his own nondenominational church. A few black churches in Prince George's county own credit unions and many operate nonprofit community centers and child day-care centers. Only a few, however, are opening for-profit businesses.

This trend toward church ownership of for-profit ventures is taking the role of black churches to another level. In the 1990s, The First African

Methodist Episcopal Church in Los Angeles started a small business loan center that helped bring a Disney Store to the central city, churches in Philadelphia and Oakland invested in grocery stores, and a black Baptist church in Houston opened a McDonald's restaurant on its 111 acre property. Preston Williams, a retired Harvard divinity school professor, notes that these churches must make sure the theological mission is the driving force of the church and not their business operations.[99]

The black church, however, continues to engage in traditional support programs. The rise of the African American megachurch—roughly defined as churches with more than 2,000 worshippers—with its large congregations and tremendous resources has witnessed the black church's continued involvement in a wide variety of significant social missionary work. According to Wallace D. Best, a professor of African American religious studies at Harvard University, the megachurch is the predominant model now; the standard to which other churches aspire with regard to their ability to provide a wide array of social programs. These outreach efforts include, among others, the provision of meals and shelter for the homeless, free clothing, household goods, books, and payments for dentistry and other medical services.[100] The black church, however, will likely continue the trend toward opening for-profit businesses to generate additional revenues to support its social outreach programs.

Why Entrepreneurship Is a Key to Greater Black Prosperity

The Small Business Administration reported in 2007 that entrepreneurial firms contributed over 50 percent of the United States' gross domestic product and created about 78 percent of all new jobs every year for the past 20 years.[101] Additionally, small entrepreneurial firms are responsible for 67 percent of all innovations and 95 percent of radical innovations since World War II.[102]

For these and other reasons, this book strongly suggests that African Americans must attempt to become economically independent, preferably as entrepreneurs, to the greatest extent possible regardless of the likelihood of business failure. The statistics suggest that the families of entrepreneurial African Americans fare better than those who assimilate into the job structure of the dominant culture. Additionally, persons who experience difficulty finding jobs have the option of establishing a business. This book takes the position that taking a chance in starting a business is probably better than never testing the waters.

We shall next explore the economic journey of black people in the United States from the 1600s, when black people first arrived in this country, until the Civil War. The activities of black entrepreneurs in securing a measure of economic security during the era of enforced slavery in the United States is an important aspect of American history with which all should be familiar. The lives of these early entrepreneurs will hopefully serve to inspire those who are pondering the establishment of a business enterprise.

Notes

1. Thurgood Marshall, "The Constitution: A Living Document," *Howard University Law Journal*, 30 (1987): 623.

2. Albert B. Crenshaw, "Fear, Greed the Players in Pension Debate: Middle Ground Could Prove Elusive as Congress Considers Reforms After Enron," *Washington Post*, Feb. 8, 2002, sec. E.

3. Paul Farhi, "Feeding the Beast: The Greed That Lives (and Seems to be Thriving) in Us All," *Washington Post*, Mar. 3, 2002, sec. F1.

4. 60 U.S. 393 (1856).

5. Paul Farhi, "Feeding the Beast: The Greed That Lives (and Seems to be Thriving) in Us All," *Washington Post*, Mar. 3, 2002, sec. F1.

6. Robert Heilbroner and Lester Thurow. *Economics Explained* (New York: Simon & Schuster, 1998), 193.

7. Joseph Matthews and Dorothy M. Berman. *Social Security, Medicare & Government Pensions* (Berkeley, CA: Nolo Press, 2002), 2.

8. Robert Heilbroner and Lester Thurow. *Economics Explained* (New York: Simon & Schuster, 1998), 193.

9. John Derbyshire, "Attack of the Wealth Eaters," *National Law Review*, Sept. 25, 2000, 39, 2000 WL 11593985.

10. Peter Engardio, "Nice Dream If You Can Live It," *Business Week*, (Sept. 13, 2004), 22.

11. Joseph Matthews and Dorothy M. Berman. *Social Security, Medicare & Government Pensions* (Berkeley, CA: Nolo Press, 2002), 3.

12. Marcellus Andrews. *The Political Economy of Hope and Fear: Capitalism and the Black Condition in America* (New York: NYU Press, 1999).

13. Ibid., 126–28, 138–39, 142, 152–57, 160, 175–84.

14. Ibid., 17–26, 28–31.

15. D 'Vera Cohn, "D.C. Gap in Wealth Growing: Uneducated Suffer Most Study Shows," *The Washington Post*, July 22, 2004, sec A.

16. Marcellus Andrews. *The Political Economy of Hope and Fear: Capitalism and the Black Condition in America* (New York: NYU Press, 1999), 176.

17. Lerone, Bennett Jr. *Before the Mayflower* (New York: Penguin Books, 6th Rev.Ed. 1993), 37–38.

18. Abram L. Harris, *The Negro As Capitalist* (Chicago: Urban Research Press, Inc., 1992, originally published in 1936, American Academy of Political Science).

19. *The African American Almanac* (Farmington Hills, MI: Gale Research Inc., 1997).

20. Abram L. Harris. *The Negro As Capitalist* (Chicago: Urban Research Press, Inc., 1992, originally published in 1936 by the American Academy of Political Science), 10–11.

21. http://www.targetmarketnews.com/publications.htm

22. Lee Ann Jackson, "Not Just For a Rainy Day, Getting African Americans to Start Saving One Dollar at a Time," *Black Enterprise*, Jan. 2003, 87.

23. Krissah Williams, "Radio One Branches out So Blacks Will Tune In," *Washington Post*, Feb. 5, 2003, sec. E.

24. Krissah Williams, "Radio One Branches out So Blacks Will Tune In," *Washington Post*, Feb. 5, 2003, sec. E.

25. *The World Almanac and Book of Facts 2003.* (New York: The Rosen Group, 2003), 400.

26. The Buying Power of Black America in 2007, *Target Market News* (2007). Staff reporters.

27. *The World Almanac and Book of Facts 2003.* (New York: The Rosen Group, 2003), 108.

28. Lerone, Bennett Jr. *Before the Mayflower* (New York: Penguin Books, 6th Rev.Ed. 1993), 255–96.

29. Colbert I. King, "Happy Talk on Holiday," *Washington Post*, July 12, 2003, sec. A.

30. Robert L. Wallace. *Black Wealth, Your Road to Small Business Success* (Indianapolis, IN: Wiley Publishing, Inc., 2002), 5–8, 9–10.

31. Clint Bolick, "Rule of Law: So Far, Clinton Can't Kick His Quota Addiction," *Wall Street Journal*, June 12, 1996, sec. A.

32. N. Taifa, "Criminal Sentencing," *University of Memphis Law Review* 12, (1996), 21, 158, 160.

33. Clint Bolick, "Rule of Law: So Far, Clinton Can't Kick His Quota Addiction," *Wall Street Journal*, June 12, 1996," 21.

34. Marcellus Andrews. *The Political Economy of Hope and Fear: Capitalism and the Black Condition in America* (New York: NYU Press, 1999), 82, 176.

35. Robert L. Wallace. *Black Wealth, Your Road to Small Business Success* (Indianapolis, IN: Wiley Publishing, Inc., 2002), 8.

36. Michelle Singletary, "Many Marriages Would Benefit from Sound Family Financial Plans," *The Washington Post*, Apr. 25, 2002, sec. E (referring to statement made by Matt Daniels, Executive Director for the Alliance for Marriage).

37. Abigail Thernstrom and Stephen Thernstrom. *America in Black and White, One Nation Indivisible* (New York: Simon and Schuster, 1997) 237–38.

38. Glenn C. Loury, "Making It All Happen" in *On the Road to Economic Freedom, An Agenda for Black Progress* (Washington, DC: Regnery Gateway, Robert L. Woodson, ed., 1987), 118.

39. Michelle Singletary, "Many Marriages Would Benefit from Sound Family Financial Plans," *The Washington Post*, Apr. 25, 2002, sec. E (referring to statement made by Matt Daniels, Executive Director for the Alliance for Marriage)

40. Teresa Wiltz, "BET a Case of Selling Out or Selling Up? But Has the Network Sold a Bit of its Soul?" *Washington Post*, Nov. 4, 2000, sec. C1.

41. 109 U.S. 3 (1883).

42. 92 U.S. 214 (1876).

43. 83 U.S. 36 (1873).

44. 92 U.S. 542 (1876).

45. 95 U.S. 485 (1878).

46. 163 U.S. 537 (1896).

47. *See Plessy v. Ferguson*, 163 U.S. 537 (1896).

48. Laurence H. Tribe. *Constitutional Law Treatise* (New York: West Publishing Company, 2000), 922.

49. Robert Heilbroner and Lester Thurow. *Economics Explained* (New York: Simon & Schuster, 1998), 11–17.

50. Ibid., 16–17.

51. 539 U.S. 306 (2003).

52. 347 U.S. 483 (1954).

53. *Grutter*, 539 U.S. at 332.

54. Ibid at 343.

55. *Grutter*, 539 U.S. at 346 (Ginsburg, J., concurring).

56. *Gratz*, 539 U.S. at 301–03.

57. 476 U.S. 267 (1986).

58. 443 U.S.193 (1979).

59. 443 U.S. 193 (1979).

60. 488 U.S. 469 (1989).

61. 488 U.S. 469 (1989)

62. 497 U.S. 547 (1990).

63. 515 U.S. 200 (1995).

64. 515 U.S. 200, citing to *City of Richmond v. J. A. Croson Co.*, 488 U.S. 469 (1989).

65. Robert Cherry, "The Culture of Poverty Thesis and African Americans: The Work of Gunnar Myrdal and Other Institutionalists," *Journal of Economic Issues* 29, (1995), 1119.

66. Micheal J. Zimmer et al., "Are Antidiscrimination Laws Necessary," *Cases and Materials on Employment Discrimination* (New York: Aspen 5th Ed. 2000), 35, 35–55.

67. John H. McWhorter, *Losing the Race: Self-Sabotage in Black America*. (New York: The Free Press, 2000), and Marcellus Andrews, *The Political Economy of Hope and Fear: Capitalism and the Black Condition in America* (New York: NYU Press, 1999), 38–45.

68. Koteles Alexander, "Adarand: Brute Political Force Concealed as a Constitutional Colorblind Principle," Howard University Law Journal 39, (1995), 367, 380. (Taking issue with the position in the text as espoused by Dinesh D'Souza).

69. Jonetta Rose Barras, "United We Stood, but Divisions Now Show; Cosby Ignited a Debate About Class, We Need to Keep Talking," *Washington Post*, June 27, 2004, sec. B, and Hamil R. Harris, "Some Blacks Find Nuggets of Truth in Cosby's Speech, Others Say D.C. Remarks About Poor Blacks Went Too Far," *Washington Post*, May 26, 2004, sec. B.

70. Marcellus Andrews. *The Political Economy of Hope and Fear: Capitalism and the Black Condition in America* (New York: NYU Press, 1999), 1–6, 26–29, 48, 53, 138–39, 152–57; Jonetta Rose Barras, "United We Stood, but Divisions Now Show; Cosby Ignited a Debate About Class, We Need to Keep Talking," *Washington Post*, June 27, 2004, sec. B and Hamil R. Harris, "Some Blacks Find Nuggets of Truth in Cosby's Speech, Others Say D.C. Remarks About Poor Blacks Went Too Far," *Washington Post*, May 26, 2004, sec. B.

71. E. Franklin Frazier. *Black Bourgeoisie* (New York: Simon & Schuster, 1997); Gunnar Myrdal. *An American Dilemma: The Negro Problem and Modern Democracy* (New York: Harper & Brothers, 1944, in 1998 reprinted edition); and Lateef Mtima, *African American Economic Empowerment Strategies for the New Millennium—Revisiting the Washington–Du Bois Dialectic*, Howard University Law Journal 42, (1999), 400.

72. Gunnar Myrdal. *An American Dilemma: The Negro Problem and Modern Democracy* (Harper Brothers, New York, 1944), 879.

73. Walter R. Allen and Joseph O. Jewell, "The Miseducation of Black America: Black Education Since an American Dilemma," in *An American Dilemma Revisited: Race Relations in a Changing World* (New York: Russell Sage Foundation Publications, 1996), 181–82, 185.

74. Abigail Thernstrom and Stephen Thernstrom. *America in Black and White, One Nation Indivisible*, (New York: Simon and Schuster, 1997), 194.

75. John Sibley Butler. *Entrepreneurship and Self-Help Among African Americans, a Reconsideration of Race and Economics* (New York: State University of New York Press, 1991); Robert Wallace, *Black Wealth, Your Road to Small Business Success*; John Sibley Butler, "The Negro in Business, the Professions, Public Service, and Other White Collar Occupations" in *An American Dilemma Revisited Race Relations in a Changing World* (New York: Russell Sage Foundation, 1996), 142–45, 164–65.

76. John Sibley Butler, "The Negro in Business, the Professions, Public Service, and Other White Collar Occupations" in *An American Dilemma Revisited Race Relations in a Changing World* (New York: Russell Sage Foundation, 1996), 63, 142–45, 164–65; 574–77.

77. Lateef Mtima, *African American Economic Empowerment Strategies for the New Millennium — Revisiting the Washington–Du Bois Dialectic*, Howard University Law Journal 42, (1999), 393.

78. John Sibley Butler. *Entrepreneurship and Self-Help Among African Americans, a Reconsideration of Race and Economics* (New York: State University of New York Press, 1991), 311.

79. Steve Slavin. *Economics: A Self Teaching Guide* (Hoboken, NJ: Wiley & Sons, Inc., 1999), 35.

80. Jean Saddler, "Black Entrepreneurship: The Next Generation, Young Black Risk Takers Push the Business Envelope," *Wall Street Journal,* May 12, sec. B.

81. *African American Desk Reference* (New York: Stonesong Press and New York Public Library, 1999), 245.

82. Aaron Bernstein, "An Inner City Renaissance," *Business Week,* (Oct. 27, 2003): 64.

83. Marcellus Andrews. *The Political Economy of Hope and Fear: Capitalism and the Black Condition in America* (New York: NYU Press, 1999), 72–75, 147, 170.

84. Steven Pearlstein, "Farewell to Free- Market Capitalism: Wave Goodbye to the Invisible Hand," *Washington Post,* August 1, 2008, sec. D1. and 8.

85. Ibid

86. Ibid., 8.

87. Elaine Lee, "Do Good, Get Rich," *Black Enterprise,* (May 2008), 73.

88. Ibid.

89. Robin Shulman, "After Success in Poor Nations, Grameen Tries New York," *Washington Post,* March 10, 2008, sec. A3.

90. Sylvia Moreno, "As Release Nears, These Inmates Are All Business" (Street Smarts Are Put to Good Use in Tex. Program), *Washington Post,* November 3, 2006, sec. A3.

91. Obie Clayton, "The Church and Social Change: Accommodation, Modification, or Protest," in *An American Dilemma Revisted, Race Relations in a Changing World* (New York: Russell Sage Foundation Publications, 1996), 191 (Obie Clayton, ed.).

92. Bill Alexander, "The Black Church and Community Empowerment," in *On The Road to Economic Freedom, An Agenda for Black Progress* (Robert L. Woodson, ed., 1987), 45.

93. Ibid., 45.

94. Abram L. Harris. *The Negro As Capitalist* (Chicago: Urban Research Press, Inc., 1992, originally published in 1936 by the American Academy of Political Science), 25–26, 57.

95. *African American Desk Reference* (New York: Stonesong Press and New York Public Library, 1999), 101.

96. Bill Alexander, "The Black Church and Community Empowerment," in *On The Road to Economic Freedom, An Agenda for Black Progress* (Robert L. Woodson, ed., 1987), 53, 62–63.

97. Krissah Williams, "Church Reaches Out Through Small Businesses," *Washington Post,* March 2, 2004, sec. E1, E9.

98. Ibid., E9.

99. Ibid., E1, E9.

100. Philip Rucker, "Megachurches Migrating to Charles: Boon Mirrors Population Growth," *Washington Post,* December 12, 2006, sec. A1 and A4.

101. See Jeff Cornwall, "Growing Firms in the Entrepreneurial Economy," *Entrepreneurial Mind,* October 25, 2007, http://www.drjeffcoenwall.com (search growing firms), and Small Business Administration, Office of Advocacy "*How*

Important are Small Businesses to the U.S. Economy?" March 4, 2004. See Frequently Asked Questions, http://www.sba.gov/advo/stats/sbfaq.pdf http://www.sba.gov/advo/stats/sbfaq.pdf

102. Bruce R. Barringer and R. Duane Ireland, *Entrepreneurship* (Upper Saddle River, NJ: Pearson Prentice Hall, 2006), 15.

CHAPTER 2

THE BLACK ECONOMIC JOURNEY FROM THE 1600s TO THE CIVIL WAR

As we begin our journey through the history of black entrepreneurship in America, it is important to keep in mind the profound role that legal principles have played in determining the economic, political, social, and legal condition of black people. The late U.S. Supreme Court Justice, Thurgood Marshall, in a significant 1987 speech, observed that it was law that enslaved, emancipated, disenfranchised, and segregated blacks. It took a bloody Civil War, constitutional amendments, and the lapse of approximately 100 years subsequent to the Civil War before the United States took steps to provide blacks with such basic rights as the right to equality in education, housing, employment, voting, and public accommodations.[1]

Justice Marshall noted that, contrary to popular opinion, the founding fathers, in drafting the Constitution, created a flawed document. In Justice Marshall's view, the founding fathers' foresight and sense of justice was troubling and not particularly profound. He noted that economic interests of the Northern and Southern states led the Constitution's framers to a compromise that allowed the Southern states to continue importing slaves to the United States until 1808. The first three words of the Constitution's preamble, "We the People," did not include black people, although they were counted for representational purposes as three-fifths of a white man. Moreover, nearly seven decades after the Constitutional Convention, the Supreme Court made clear that the founding fathers never intended persons of African descent to be citizens of the United

States. Justice Marshall, citing the Supreme Court's decision in *Dred Scott v. Sandford*, noted that the framers of the Constitution considered blacks to be no more than "an article of property" and had "no rights which the white man was bound to respect."[2]

The true miracle of America, Justice Marshall stated, was not the birth of the Constitution. The true miracle, which resulted in the America we know today, was the evolution of the Constitution as a living document and the laws passed pursuant to it after much suffering, struggle, bloodshed, and sacrifice.[3]

The First Black Entrepreneurs: Pre-Civil War

Non-black scholars have not discussed the historical roots of black entrepreneurship in their research on how distinct ethnic groups have adjusted to American capitalism through entrepreneurial endeavors. This is unfortunate because there is a tremendous volume of work that pre-dated their research. We'll examine some of that work more closely in Chapters 4 and 6. In any case, an understanding of the early history of black enterprise and the considerable obstacles that black business persons had to overcome provides valuable information and perspective to the population of black Americans who seek to adjust to the American capitalistic economy through entrepreneurship. Additionally, exposure to this information removes a cloud of ignorance and misunderstanding with respect to the general population as to why black people remain in a catch-up stage in establishing business enterprises in the 21st century.

The first group of black indentured servants arrived in colonial America in 1619. These black indentured servants had approximately identical economic opportunities as their white counterparts after fulfilling the terms of their indentures. Colonial documents indicate that they engaged in entrepreneurial activities, voted, and participated in public life. It is interesting to note that Virginia did not deny blacks the right to vote until many years later.[4]

The first black entrepreneur was probably Anthony Johnson. Mr. Johnson arrived in Jamestown, Virginia, in approximately 1620 or 1621 as an indentured servant from England. Mr. Johnson worked out the term of his indenture, accumulated property, had black and white servants, and established one of America's first black communities. Official records of the 1650s document this entrepreneurial activity.[5]

Both free blacks and slaves engaged in business enterprise prior to the civil war.[6] John Baptiste Du Sable, Paul Cuffe, Emmanuel, who is known to historians by the single name only, Thomas Downing, and Robert

Bogle are notable examples of black persons who engaged in entrepreneurial activities in America during the 1700s and early 1800s.

John Baptiste Du Sable was a black pioneer, entrepreneur, and capitalist. Du Sable was a leader in the Westward movement and the founder of Chicago in the 1770s. He built the first home and opened the first business there. Some commentators have suggested there are "indications" that white settlers, in keeping with the prevalent racial attitudes of that time, isolated Du Sable.[7]

Paul Cuffe, born near Dartmouth, Massachusetts, in 1759, engaged in entrepreneurial activities from the 1770s to approximately 1817 as a ship builder, ship captain, builder, and African colonizer. "Mr. Cuffe, in 1797, built a wharf and warehouse on the Westport River in Massachusetts. By 1806, he owned one ship, two brigs, and several smaller vessels."[8] Mr. Cuffe commanded black crews that made voyages to Europe, Russia, Africa, and the West Indies.

In 1811, Mr. Cuffe traveled to Sierra Leone "attending to missionary duties . . . and exploring the country to determine what opportunities it offered the free Negroes for trade and colonization. He hoped to encourage trade relations between Sierra Leone and America and England."[9] Mr. Cuffe, aware of the sentiment held by some blacks that white America would never change, carried 38 blacks to Sierra Leone in his ship in 1815. Interestingly, it was anti-black and pro-slavery whites, not blacks, who were behind the movement to resettle free blacks to Liberia in the wake of the Gabriel Prosser slave uprising in Virginia. Apparently, most free blacks believed that a mass exodus of blacks would strengthen slavery in America and deprive slaves of support and sustenance from free blacks. Cuffe never migrated to Africa and died in Massachusetts in 1817. He was the forerunner of a large number of black Americans who attempted to mix their entrepreneurial efforts with racial progress.[10]

Free blacks engaged primarily in small service businesses. In the North, free blacks ran popular eating and drinking establishments that, in the 1700s and early 1800s, catered to a white clientele. For example, in the middle 1700s, an emancipated slave named Emmanuel established the first oyster and ale house in Providence, Rhode Island. Emmanuel was the forerunner of a large number of black saloon keepers, restaurant owners, and caterers who followed in the next century. Emmanuel, at his death in 1769, left an estate valued at 539 pounds and 10 shillings.[11]

In 1800, Thomas Downing, in the footsteps of Emmanuel, established and operated a restaurant near Wall Street in New York. Downing's restaurant served New York's professional and commercial classes at this location for over 30 years. George Bell, George Alexander, and Austin

Steward operated similar businesses in nearby neighborhoods. Similarly, in the early 1800s, caterers Prosser and Minton served the leading citizens of Philadelphia.[12] The restaurant industry was a significant source of business for black people throughout the North during this period.[13]

Free blacks in the South had practically no competition in operating personal service enterprises "where their social position had long habituated them to the obsequiousness and humility necessary for conducting this type of business."[14] Black entrepreneurs operating barbershops, livery stables, and tailoring shops provided a source of considerable income for free blacks in the South prior to the Civil War.[15] Moreover, blacks had virtually cornered the market for providing skilled trades in the South, such as carpentry, the blacksmith trade, and shoemaking.[16] This was largely because white masters forced their servants to become proficient carpenters, blacksmiths, shoemakers, and tailors to avoid the expense of obtaining white labor to perform these skilled services.

In the North, free blacks did not engage in the skilled trades to the same extent as in the South.[17] However, in 1840, free blacks in New York City "were publishing a Newspaper, *The Colored American* . . . operating two first class restaurants in the downtown financial district, six boarding houses, a hairdressing establishment, two dry good stores, two coal yards, four pleasure gardens, a confectionery, and a fruit store."[18]

Free blacks in the North did, however, enter into businesses that represented virtually every sector of the business community. For example, Henry M. Collins of Pittsburgh, Pennsylvania, was engaged in real estate brokerage and development. Samuel T. Wilcox, a merchant in Cincinnati, Ohio built a wholesale grocery store in 1850 and soon became the largest dealer in provisions in the city; he invested heavily and profitably in real estate and had a fairly sizeable net worth upon his death.[19]

In the 1840s, Stephen Smith of Columbia, Pennsylvania, was one of the wealthiest black men in the country before the Civil War. He and William Whipper engaged in the coal and lumber business. Smith individually owned approximately 50 houses in the city of Philadelphia, and several more in Lancaster and Columbia, Pennsylvania. By 1864, statisticians placed Smith's net worth at $500,000.[20]

Henry Boyd, who was in the manufacturing business, was born a slave in Kentucky on May 14, 1802, and learned cabinetmaking from one of his masters. In 1826, at the height of his trade, he settled in Cincinnati, formed a partnership with a white man, manufactured all types of furniture, and hired 20–50 black and white workmen. Boyd also invented a machine for turning the rails of a bed but failed to obtain a patent. His factory was equipped with improved machinery, and the Boyd Bedstead had a national market.[21] Unfortunately, his success was not appreciated by everyone and he was burned out four times. He kept rebuilding until the fourth fire, when his insurance company refused to cover it. John Sibley Butler wrote:

> The experiences of Henry Boyd are more than interesting. They alert us to a very important aspect of competition within the American business world—namely, the tendency of Euro-Americans to view significant profits in an enterprise to be reserved for themselves. Their reaction to Boyd's success repeats itself systematically in the literature on race and business experience.[22]

James Forten of Philadelphia, who lived between 1766 and 1841, operated a major manufacturing firm that made sails. By 1829, his manufacturing operations employed approximately 40 black and white employees. Scholars state that sources placed Forten's worth at $100,000 in 1832. Forten's enterprise, however, faced great odds in adjusting to steam transportation, which was already proving itself to be adaptable to river and ocean commerce.[23]

Liberal masters, in some instances, allowed enterprising slaves to engage in business ventures. Due to their status, these slaves could not become true entrepreneurs. They did, however, use what earnings they generated to purchase freedom for their families and themselves. Lunsford Lane, Robert Gordon, Robert Clark, and Free Frank are examples of slaves who used tips from providing services to whites to purchase their freedom and start business enterprises.

Portrait of an Entrepreneur: Lunsford Lane

The story of Lunsford Lane is a particularly illuminating example of the ingenuity and resourcefulness of slaves who used their tips to purchase their freedom and pursue entrepreneurial endeavors. Lane's experiences also portray the difficulties these men faced in achieving a degree of economic security during the era of slavery before the Civil War.

Lane was born in 1803 on the enormous Haywood Plantation near Raleigh, North Carolina. His parents were house servants at the mansion, a position that Lane would also assume when he got older. His first experience at making money came when he was just a youngster when he sold a basket of peaches his father had given him. He quickly began making more money running errands and doing other small chores suitable for a little boy. As he grew older and joined the house staff, he collected tips from the master's guests. He also cut and sold wood, cleaned stores, and ran errands for townspeople when he wasn't on duty at the house. He had good business sense.

Lane purchased practically all of the food that the household required. Often he secured bargains on his own account when goods were exceptionally cheap and these he resold later at a profit to himself.[24]

He "struck gold" when the legislature was in session, and he was able to serve the legislators in various ways. His first official business, however, was tobacco.

With the help of his father, Lane sold pipes and developed a special tobacco with a "peculiarly pleasant flavor." In Raleigh, state legislators soon sought out the "Edward and Lunsford Lane" brand; eventually customers in Fayetteville, Chapel Hill, and Salisbury bought it. This achievement is extraordinary considering Lane worked primarily as a slave by day and for profit only at night.[25]

Business boomed and it soon required more time. Because it was so profitable, Lane came up with a plan.

Lane hired his time from his master at a rental of from $100 to $120 a year. Within eight years he was selling tobacco throughout the state and had accumulated a surplus of $1,000 over the rental that he paid his master.[26]

He used that $1000 to buy his freedom, but it couldn't be made official because North Carolina law held that slaves could only be freed for meritorious service. Undaunted, he traveled to New York to complete the paperwork. Once back in Raleigh, he opened a general store and a wood yard. He also bought a house, and bought the freedom of his wife and children.

During this time Lane was exceptional in his public conduct, trying at all times to retain the friendship of the slave owners. His steady progress, however, did not go unnoticed. Sentiment began to grow against him. Finally a group composed of "poor whites" and the younger sons of slave owners rose up demanding his expulsion from the state. In consequence, Lane, who had been legally freed in New York, was expelled from the state on the basis of a statute that forbade free blacks from other states to take up residence in North Carolina. Lane then went to Philadelphia and finally to New York, where he was engaged to lecture on southern slavery.

In 1842 he requested the written permission of the Governor of North Carolina to allow him to return to that state for the final settlement of his accounts. The governor was powerless to grant this request but advised Lane to come on anyway on the chance that he would not be molested.

Shortly after arriving, Lane was arrested on the charge of making aboli-
tionist speeches in Massachusetts. The case was dismissed by the mayor.
In spite of the precautions of the police he was seized by a mob at night-
fall, tarred and feathered, and driven from the state.

Upon returning North he attempted to recoup his business losses by
placing upon the market a proprietary herb medicine that he called Dr.
Lane's Vegetable Pills. But this as well as his real estate investments
turned out poorly. When last heard from, he was working as head steward at a Union hospital in 1863. Fortunately for historians, he left behind
a rich narrative of his life, which he self-published in 1842. The *Narrative
of Lunsford Lane*, in its entirety, can be found at http://docsouth.unc.edu/
neh/lanelunsford/menu.html.

As seen in the story of Lunsford Lane, the situation for free blacks was
not much better than the circumstances of slaves. Prior to America's
independence from Britain, the colonies enacted laws to limit the rights
of free blacks. Some of the colonies denied free blacks the right to vote,
carry weapons, or serve as witnesses in court cases against white persons. In the 1800s, some of the states in the newly independent United
States of America enacted laws that restricted the rights and movements
of free blacks, established higher property and residency requirements
for blacks as a precondition for them to vote, denied free blacks the right
to vote, prohibited free blacks from meeting in groups of more than five
persons, required the deportation of free blacks, attempted to expel free
blacks because of complaints from white businessmen that free black
laborers and entrepreneurs monopolized some of the service industries,
and prohibited whites from teaching the free black children to read.[27]

Prior to the Civil War, free blacks in the 1700s and the 1800s laid the
foundation for the black business tradition. White hostility and intense
racism forced blacks into entrepreneurial undertakings as a means of
economic survival. Historically, black business development has been
greatest when racism, discrimination, and poverty have been at their
highest levels.[28]

Black entrepreneurs prior to the Civil War were self-starters with no
form of government assistance. They developed restaurants, catering,
and tavern businesses that served a white clientele outside of the black
community. In these personal service enterprises, the free blacks had
practically no competition because whites tended to avoid such businesses because of their servile status. These businesses flourished until
the large influx of Europeans immigrated to the United States.[29] These
immigrants effectively ended black entrepreneurs' unimpeded access to
this white clientele.

Wealth of the 500,000 Free Blacks Prior to 1860

Many persons reading this book may be surprised to learn about the economic achievements of free blacks as well as slaves prior to the Civil War. There is much that today's generation of blacks, whites, and other groups can learn from this bit of American history in terms of the benefits of entrepreneurship and ownership in a capitalistic economy. In *The Negro as Capitalist*, the black scholar Abram Harris stated that a conservative estimate of the wealth of free black persons prior to the Civil War was approximately $50 million, but that $75 million would be a more realistic figure.[30]

Sources of Black Wealth Prior to the Civil War

Real Estate—Free blacks did not own much real estate during the colonial years of U.S. history. Their holdings increased, however, between the Revolutionary War and the Civil War. This is illustrated by the growth in real estate holdings by free blacks in Pennsylvania, New York, and Ohio. Free blacks in slave states also acquired real estate. Approximately 3,777 blacks also owned slaves as personal property by 1830. Benevolent motives seemed to be an important factor in such purchases. However, some black slave owners seemed motivated by economic gain in purchasing other blacks as slaves.[31]

Stocks, Bonds, and Annuities—Free blacks' ownership of stocks, bonds, and annuities was negligible due to restrictions prohibiting blacks from becoming stockholders and depositors. However, they were able to own securities and other investments in some jurisdictions where these prohibitions were not rigorously enforced.[32]

Business Pursuits of Free Blacks and Slaves Prior to the Civil War

The business enterprises owned by blacks prior to the Civil War included barber shops, livery stables, tailoring and clothing businesses, cooking, catering, restaurant and drinking establishments, farming enterprises, real estate brokerage and development companies, merchandising, retailing and commercial undertakings, manufacturing and building, water transport, and trade businesses. Additionally, free blacks began their first activities in banking and money lending businesses prior to the Civil War.[33]

These free black entrepreneurs faced numerous obstacles in growing their businesses. Some of these obstacles included difficulty in obtaining credit, mob violence by whites who resented successful black business persons, prohibitions against black ownership of certain types of property, and denial of the right to sue.

By far, the biggest hurdle was the difficulty of borrowing money. As early as 1789, records show that blacks found it difficult to borrow money. There are, however, many explicit references in the historical records that indicate some enterprising blacks were able to obtain loans. The enterprising blacks of Charleston, South Carolina, Solomon Humphries of Macon, Georgia, Stephen Smith and William Whipple of Pennsylvania, and Samuel Wilcox of Ohio were able to borrow from white institutions to finance their business enterprises.[34] In response, free black persons formed mutual assistance organizations and began their first attempts to engage in banking and money lending businesses. In the decade prior to the Civil War, free blacks in New York and Philadelphia held meetings to discuss the establishment of a bank, but the talks came to nothing.[35]

The wealth of free black persons prior to the Civil War is impressive when viewed in light of the obstacles confronting them. However, because of the hostility and numerous obstacles they faced, "only a pitifully small number of free blacks could be considered wealthy even when judged by the business standards of that day."[36] It was these obstacles that prevented free blacks from developing large business enterprises and a wealthy class of black businessmen prior to the Civil War.

Why Pre-Civil War Black Entrepreneurial Activities are Utterly Amazing

When one examines the social and political attitudes toward black people before the Civil War, one has to wonder how any aspiring entrepreneur could make any headway at all. This was particularly true in the South.

The South's Preoccupation in Maintaining Slavery

The political climate was particularly hostile to black people prior to the Civil War. The Southern states were politically committed to the indefinite enslavement of black people as part of the operation of the Southern economy. Therefore, the economic accomplishments of black persons during this period are somewhat astonishing. However, the Northern states had effectively recognized the immorality of slavery prior to the Civil War. By 1804, all of the states north of the Mason-Dixon Line had enacted laws prohibiting slavery or phasing it out. The Mason-Dixon Line is the boundary line between Pennsylvania on the north and Maryland on the south. The Mason-Dixon Line is the line celebrated as the line of demarcation between the slave and free states.[37]

Massachusetts became the first state to legalize slavery in 1641. The Massachusetts Supreme Court, however, abolished slavery in 1783 and granted blacks, in taxable categories, the right to vote. New York abolished slavery on July 4, 1827. The number of slaves in the English colonies in 1700 was approximately 28,000. Approximately 23,000 of these slaves, however, resided in the South. Upon New Jersey's passage of an emancipation law in 1804, all states north of the Mason-Dixon Line had enacted laws forbidding slavery or laws that set dates when slavery would end.[38]

The Southern states, however, were preoccupied with legal maneuvering in Congress to maintain slavery at all costs during the time that free blacks were attempting to achieve a measure of economic security in the United States. The economic importance of maintaining slavery in the South was clear, and ultimately led to a war that claimed more American lives than all other wars combined, excluding World War II.[39] The continued legal recognition of slavery and the status of black persons as property clearly delayed the economic emancipation of black persons in the United States.

Nevertheless, in some instances free blacks were achieving fairly remarkable economic progress and gaining financial solidarity in the late 1700s. The Southern states' preoccupation with ensuring the continuance of slavery, however, was playing itself out in Congress to the detriment of both free and enslaved blacks. Slavery and the role of black people in this country were at the root of every significant piece of legislation that led to the Civil War. For example, the Northwest Ordinance of 1787, which Thomas Jefferson drafted, barred slavery from the territory that became the states of Ohio, Indiana, Illinois, Michigan, and Wisconsin, to insure that the number of free and slave states would be equal as the United States spread westward. Similarly, the U.S. Congress' admission of Kentucky, Tennessee, Alabama, Mississippi, and Louisiana to statehood was done in a manner to ensure that the number of free and slave states remained equal.[40]

Other significant legislation that followed witnessed a nation focused on matters other than economic and social liberation of enslaved and free black people in America. The Missouri Compromise, enacted in 1820, provided that Missouri would enter the Union as a slave state and Maine would enter as a free state. This scheme allayed fears that the South would gain more influence in the U.S. Senate. The South agreed to outlaw slavery north of "36°30'" latitude, a line extending west from Missouri's southern border. The compromise made the new territory of Arkansas, which is present day Oklahoma and Arkansas, open to slavery, but barred slavery from the remainder of the Louisiana Purchase. Accordingly, under the Missouri Compromise, the United States barred slavery in the areas consisting of present day Kansas, Nebraska, Colorado, Minnesota, Iowa, Montana, Wyoming, North Dakota, and South Dakota.[41]

The Compromise of 1850 attempted to address the issue of slavery's expansion as a result of the U.S. victory in the Mexican-American war. The territory covered land that would become the states of California, Nevada, Utah, New Mexico, and Arizona. The Compromise of 1850 provided that the United States would fulfill the following requests: admit California as a free state; organize the rest of the territories without restrictions on slavery; outlaw the slave trade in Washington, D.C. (but not slavery itself); and enact a tougher Fugitive Slave Act.[42]

Congress enacted the Kansas-Nebraska Act in 1854 because Southern senators foresaw that, under the Missouri Compromise, slavery would be prohibited in each state carved out of Nebraska Territory and some parts of Kansas territory. The Act repealed that part of the Missouri Compromise that prohibited slavery in the territory above "36° 30' latitude" in favor of allowing "popular sovereignty" to determine the issue.[43] Battles between pro-slavery and anti-slavery forces attempting to settle Kansas became known as "Bleeding Kansas."[44]

In 1857, the U.S. Supreme Court, in *Dred Scott v. Sandford*,[45] attempted to resolve the question of slavery in the territories in one comprehensive decision. The Supreme Court's consideration of the case was set against the backdrop of mounting tensions surrounding "Bleeding Kansas," which threatened to draw the nation into open warfare. The case involved a slave, Dred Scott, who argued that his stay in territory above the "36° 30'" latitude made him a free man after his owner died. The Supreme Court held that the Missouri Compromise was unconstitutional, and noted, among other things, that the Constitution's reference to "citizens" and the Preamble's reference to "We the People" did not include blacks of African descent; that Congress had no power under the Constitution to keep slavery out of any territory; and that the case should not have been heard in the first place because slaves of African descent were not citizens of the United States.[46] The case was certainly a surprise to many free blacks who were legal citizens in several Northern states.[47] The *Dred Scott* case was clearly one of the driving forces leading to the Civil War.

By 1859, there were 15 free states and an equal number of slave states. On December 20, 1860, South Carolina voted to repeal its 1788 ratification of the U.S. Constitution. Ten other states voted, in convention, to secede from the United States of America in 1861: Mississippi (January 9), Florida (January 10), Alabama (January 11), Georgia (January 19), Louisiana (January 26), Texas (February 1), Virginia (April 17), Arkansas (May 6), Tennessee (May 7), and North Carolina (May 21).

On February 8, 1861, seven southern states voted to form the Confederate States of America and named Jefferson Davis of Mississippi as provisional President. These states adopted a provisional Constitution for the Confederate States of America. On March 11, 1861, the Confederate states adopted a permanent Constitution that abolished the African slave trade, but did not bar interstate commerce in slaves. On July 20, 1861, the Confederate Congress moved to Richmond, Virginia. In October 1861, the Confederate Congress elected Jefferson Davis as the permanent President and inaugurated him on February 22, 1862.

The Civil War began on April 12, 1861, when the Confederates fired upon Fort Sumter in Charleston, South Carolina, and captured it on April 14, 1861. The Civil War ended on April 9, 1865, when General Robert E. Lee surrendered 27,800 Confederate troops to General Ulysses S. Grant at Appomattox Court House in Virginia. The Civil War resulted in more American deaths than any war except World War II. No other war in which Americans have fought, except World War II, even comes close to the number of Americans, 214,938, killed during the Civil War. The combined American deaths of all other wars, excluding World War II, do not exceed this number.[48] Matters of race have always been near the center of American life.

Many Whites Did Not Consider Blacks to Be Fully Human

The Declaration of Independence's statement in 1776 of universal equality did not apply to blacks. Under the U.S. Constitution ratified in 1787, blacks counted as "three-fifths of all other persons for political representation purposes." The Constitution also prevented Congress from prohibiting the slave trade until 1808 and sought to ensure that "escaping" slaves would be returned to their owners.[49] Interestingly, the Constitution never uses the words slave, black, African, or any other racial labels.

In *Prigg v. Pennsylvania*,[50] the Supreme Court made it clear that any state effort to prevent individuals from capturing and returning slaves to their owners was preempted by the Fugitive Slave Act of 1793.[51] In *Dred Scott v. Sandford*, the Court gave the clearest exposition on the attitude of white Americans toward blacks. The Court stated that white people regarded blacks of African origin as no more than an article of property;

that the white race considered blacks to be of an inferior order and alto-gether unfit to associate with the white race; that blacks had no rights that the white man was bound to respect; and that whites could lawfully reduce blacks to slavery for the benefit of blacks because whites deemed blacks too stupid to make wise decisions.[52] These statements and legal enactments emanating from the majority race indicate that the economic achievements of black persons who lived during this era were truly remarkable.

Notes

1. Thurgood Marshall, "The Constitution: A Living Document," *Howard University Law Journal*, 30 (1987), 627.

2. Ibid., 624–26.

3. Ibid., 627.

4. Lerone Bennett Jr. *Before the Mayflower* (New York: Penguin Books, 6th Rev.Ed. 1993), 37–38.

5. *The African American Almanac* (Farmington Hills, MI: Gale Research Inc., 1997); 4; Lerone, Bennett Jr. *Before the Mayflower* (New York: Penguin Books, 1982), 37; John Sibley Butler, *Entrepreneurship and Self-Help Among African Americans, a Reconsideration of Race and Economics* (New York: State University of New York Press, 1991), 35–36.

6. John Sibley Butler, *Entrepreneurship and Self-Help Among African Americans, a Reconsideration of Race and Economics* (New York: State University of New York Press, 1991), 36.

7. Lerone Bennett Jr. *Before the Mayflower* (New York: Penguin Books, 6th Rev.Ed. 1993), 84–85.

8. Ibid., 78–79, 446.

9. Abram L. Harris. *The Negro As Capitalist* (Chicago: Urban Research Press, Inc., 1992), 24.

10. Ibid., 25 and Lerone Bennett Jr. *Before the Mayflower* (New York: Penguin Books, 6th Rev.Ed. 1993), 145–46,

11. Abram L. Harris. *The Negro As Capitalist* (Chicago: Urban Research Press, Inc., 1992), 1–14.

12. Ibid.

13. John Sibley Butler, *Entrepreneurship and Self-Help Among African Americans, a Reconsideration of Race and Economics* (New York: State University of New York Press, 1991), 42.

14. Abram L. Harris. *The Negro As Capitalist* (Chicago: Urban Research Press, Inc., 1992), 12.

15. Ibid., 12–13.

16. Butler, John Sibley, *Entrepreneurship and Self-Help Among African Americans, a Reconsideration of Race and Economics* (New York: State University of New York Press, 1991), 44.

17. Abram L. Harris. *The Negro As Capitalist* (Chicago: Urban Research Press, Inc., 1992), 11.

18. Ibid., 11.

19. Abram L. Harris. *The Negro As Capitalist* (Chicago: Urban Research Press, Inc., 1992), 17, 19–28.

20. John Sibley Butler. *Entrepreneurship and Self-Help Among African Americans, a Reconsideration of Race and Economics* (New York: State University of New York Press, 1991), 39; and Abram L. Harris. *The Negro As Capitalist* (Chicago: Urban Research Press, Inc., 1992), 27.

21. Abram L. Harris. *The Negro As Capitalist* (Chicago: Urban Research Press, Inc., 1992), 22.

22. John Sibley Butler. *Entrepreneurship and Self-Help Among African Americans, a Reconsideration of Race and Economics* (New York: State University of New York Press, 1991), 43.

23. Abram L. Harris. *The Negro As Capitalist* (Chicago: Urban Research Press, Inc., 1992), 7, 21.

24. Abram L. Harris. *The Negro As Capitalist* (Chicago: Urban Research Press, Inc., 1992), 17.

25. http://northcarolinahistory.org/encyclopedia/18/entry. (Last Accessed 1/10/09)

26. Abram L. Harris. *The Negro As Capitalist* (Chicago: Urban Research Press, Inc., 1992), 17.

27. *The African American Almanac* (Farmington Hills, MI: Gale Research Inc., 1997), 6, 11–15, 17.

28. John Sibley Butler. *Entrepreneurship and Self-Help Among African Americans, a Reconsideration of Race and Economics* (New York: State University of New York Press, 1991), 42–43, 46, 77, 292.

29. Ibid., 40, 62, 72–73, 294.

30. Abram L. Harris. *The Negro As Capitalist* (Chicago: Urban Research Press, Inc., 1992), 10–11.

31. Ibid., 4–9.

32. Ibid., 10.

33. Ibid., 12–30.

34. John Sibley Butler. *Entrepreneurship and Self-Help Among African Americans, a Reconsideration of Race and Economics* (New York: State University of New York Press, 1991), 40–41 and Abram L. Harris. *The Negro As Capitalist* (Chicago: Urban Research Press, Inc., 1992), 28.

35. Abram L. Harris. *The Negro As Capitalist* (Chicago: Urban Research Press, Inc., 1992), 29–30.

36. Ibid.

37. *Black's Law Dictionary* (New York: Thomson West, 1983), 503.

38. *The African American Almanac* (Farmington Hills, MI: Gale Research Inc., 1997), 4–5, 9, 11, 13.

39. Laura Stanton and Seth Hamblin, "Remembering the Fallen," *Washington Post*, May 26, 2003, sec. A.

40. Jonathan, Earle. *The Routledge Atlas of African American History* (New York: Routledge, 2000), 35, and *The World Almanac and Book of Facts 2003* (New York: The Rosen Group, 2003), 364, 370–72, 374, 376.

41. *The World Almanac and Book of Facts 2003* (New York: The Rosen Group, 2003), 366, 371–73, 375–77, 381, 385, 389; and *The African American Almanac* (Farmington Hills, MI: Gale Research Inc., 1997), 12, and Jonathan, Earle, *The Routledge Atlas of African American History* (New York: Routledge, 2000), 54.

42. *The World Almanac and Book of Facts 2003* (New York: The Rosen Group, 2003), 365–66, 378-79, 386, and *The African American Almanac* (Farmington Hills, MI: Gale Research Inc., 1997), 15.

43. *The World Almanac and Book of Facts 2003* (New York: The Rosen Group, 2003), 16.

44. Jonathan, Earle. *The Routledge Atlas of African American History* (New York: Routledge, 2000), 58.

45. 60 U.S. 393 (1856).

46. Ibid., 404–07, 410–11, 449–52, 454.

47. Jonathan, Earle. *The Routledge Atlas of African American History* (New York: Routledge, 2000), 59.

48. Laura Stanton and Seth Hamblin, "Remembering the Fallen," *Washington Post*, May 26, 2003, sec. A.

49. *The African American Almanac* (Farmington Hills, MI: Gale Research Inc., 1997), 411–12; and United States Constitution, art. I. § 9, cl. 1, and United States Constitution, art. IV. § 2.

50. 41. U.S. 539 (1842).

51. *The African American Almanac* (Farmington Hills, MI: Gale Research Inc., 1997), 412.

52. 60 U.S. 393 (1866) 407–08.

CHAPTER 3

THE RECONSTRUCTION ERA: 1867–1877

The United States probably would not need affirmative action today if Congress had continued its progressive legislative course during the Reconstruction era following the Civil War. Reconstruction Era politics represented "the expression of a profound economic change" in the United States and Western Europe—"the triumph of capitalistic finance and industry over agrarianism and the plantation economy."[1] The ascendance of capitalism was accompanied by "new political ideals" stressing "legal equality and universal suffrage for men."[2] The goal of equal citizenship was a middle-class conception that carried with it the right to vote, hold office, acquire property, and achieve economic independence.

In this context, Congressman Thaddeus Stevens and the radical Republicans viewed equal citizenship for the recently freed slaves and all blacks as the best means of assimilating black people into the American mainstream. Both conservative and radical Republicans believed that opportunities for blacks to obtain education, wealth, and political equality were necessary attributes of full citizenship. In the first decade after the Civil War, Congress proposed and obtained passage of constitutional amendments and statutes providing civil liberty and equality for blacks. During this period, the federal government and states were instrumental in establishing universities for blacks. On March 3, 1865, Congress chartered the Freedman's Bank.[3]

Conservative Republicans supported the radicals, in part, to get the support of the black vote to further their economic interests. After achieving their economic goals, the conservative Republicans tacitly accepted the disenfranchisement and segregation of blacks in the new South.[4]

The eventual rift in attitudes between the radical and conservative Republicans led to "two separate and antagonistic approaches" for blacks to achieve equality and economic liberty.[5] Abram Harris, a black scholar writing in the 1930s, referred to the first approach as the "militant civil libertarian" program of W. E. B. Du Bois and the second approach as Booker T. Washington's "program of conciliation, thrift, and industry."[6]

The Du Bois approach led to the dismantling of governmentally enforced segregation of blacks and the enactment of congressional legislation seeking to affirmatively assist black businesses, which had been long excluded from the ability to compete in the general American economy under the separate but equal doctrine of *Plessy v. Ferguson*. The Du Bois approach also led to congressional legislation prohibiting racial discrimination by private and governmental entities in employment, housing, and public accommodations.

Washington's approach, that blacks could achieve wealth through business ownership and thrift notwithstanding the vicious system of enforced racial segregation, is often dismissed because of Washington's passive acceptance of the system of legal segregation as just a sad fact of life. However, Washington's approach arguably leads to greater wealth and self-determination for blacks assuming an equal playing field in the economic market.

Military Reconstruction Legislation

Congress enacted the military reconstruction legislation because of its perception that President Lincoln and President Johnson were being too lenient with the conquered South. The Civil War established the supremacy of the federal government over the states and ended the doctrines of nullification and secession. The Civil War also destroyed the influence of Southern planters in national government and gave dominance to Northern industrialists. Consequently, businessmen carried the nation into a new period of industrialization and Western expansion.[7]

President Lincoln's plan for bringing the defeated states of the Confederacy back into membership in the United States imposed very few restrictions. Lincoln's plan provided that each of the formerly rebellious states could establish its own government if 10 percent of its respective citizens who voted in 1860 swore to faithfully defend the Constitution of the United States and to abolish slavery. In response, the radical Republicans passed the Wade-Davis Bill, a much harsher plan that required that a majority of white males in the former Confederate states swear to have never supported the Confederacy, abolish slavery, and repudiate debts and acts of secession.[8]

President Johnson asserted that the reconciliation policy was an executive branch decision. He demanded that the reorganized states repudiate Confederate debts and acts of secession, and legally end slavery by ratifying the Thirteenth Amendment. President Johnson stated that he would grant a full pardon to anyone, including former Confederate officials, who swore allegiance to the U.S. Constitution. All the former Confederate states except Texas met President Johnson's demands by December 1865.[9]

The South Enacted the Black Codes in Spite of the Thirteenth Amendment

The reorganized states ratified the Thirteenth Amendment but did not intend to give equal rights to the newly freed blacks, whom people referred to as freedmen. As the reorganized states drew up their new state laws, they incorporated a number of pieces of legislation called Black Codes. The Black Codes relegated freedman to social, economic, and political inferiority. They forbade blacks from carrying arms, governed their employment, and imposed curfews upon the freedmen. Additionally, legislators gave "masters" the right to whip "servants" under the age of 18. Whites could punish blacks for "insulting gestures," "seditious speeches," and the "crime" of walking off the job.[10] These legislative acts further postponed the inclusion of African Americans into the economic fabric of America.

The Reconstruction Act of 1867

Congress passed legislation creating the Freedmen's Bureau on March 3, 1865. The Freedmen's Bureau was the first federal welfare agency. The Bureau gave direct aid, established hospitals, day schools, night schools, industrial schools, institutes, and colleges. Congress renewed the Freedmen's Bureau and extended its powers to protect blacks in February 1866. President Johnson vetoed this legislation. Congress, as it had done with other legislation of this era, passed a new version in July and overrode Johnson's veto.[11]

Similarly, in April 1866 Congress passed the Civil Rights Act, declaring freedmen citizens entitled "to full and equal benefits of the laws." President Johnson, on the grounds of states' rights, vetoed this legislation. Congress promptly overrode President Johnson's veto. Congress, fearing that the Supreme Court might agree with President Johnson, proposed the Fourteenth Amendment to the Constitution. President Johnson objected to the Fourteenth Amendment as an invasion of states' rights and advised the southern states not to ratify it. However, without the Fourteenth Amendment, the pronouncement in *Dred Scott v. Sandford* that persons of African descent were not citizens of the United States would arguably remain the law of the land.[12]

Republicans who opposed President Johnson in the congressional elections of 1866 won overwhelmingly. Congress quickly passed the Reconstruction Act of 1867 over Johnson's veto. Moreover, Congress made clear that the former Confederate states would not be readmitted to the Union unless they ratified the Fourteenth Amendment.

Neither President Lincoln nor his successor, President Johnson, came to grips with the plight of blacks. As discussed earlier, they both wanted to readmit southern states upon 10 percent of the pre-war electorate taking an oath of allegiance. Moreover, President Johnson appointed conservative provisional governors with pro-slavery biases.[13] It was these governments that enacted the infamous Black Codes. The attitudes expressed in such legislation clearly indicated that the executive branch of the federal government had no thought of proposing any programs that would provide for the economic equality of black Americans. On the other hand, the executive branch was content on leaving the plight of black Americans to their recently conquered slave masters under the rationale of states rights, the same basis set forth by the Southern states for the Civil War.

Congress instituted military reconstruction for several reasons: the Black Codes, which placed blacks virtually in a position of servitude; the officially sponsored killings and rapes of black persons; the burnings of black churches; and the failure of the President Johnson to do anything to prevent these atrocities from happening.[14]

A joint congressional committee of 15 reported on proposed legislation that put the South under military control and authorized new elections in which all males, irrespective of race, could participate. The tally of qualified voters indicated that black voters outnumbered whites in five states: Mississippi, South Carolina, Louisiana, Alabama, and Florida. The statistics further indicated that blacks outnumbered whites by majorities of seven, eight, and nine to one in some counties.[15]

Senator Charles Sumner and Representative Thaddeus Stevens were the driving forces behind this Reconstruction legislation. Sumner and Stevens were also responsible for pushing the Fourteenth and Fifteenth Amendments through Congress and the enabling legislation that sent military troops to the South to protect the rights of blacks.[16]

The Four Supports of Economic Rights of Blacks

The economic rights of blacks depended on four major pieces of legislation subsequent to the Civil War: the continued military presence of the federal government in the South pursuant to the Reconstruction Act; the Fourteenth Amendment to the U.S. Constitution; the Fifteenth Amendment to the U.S. Constitution; and the Civil Rights Act of 1875.

The Military Districts—The Reconstruction Act divided the South into five military districts, each under the control of a military commander. "The [military] commander was to register the voters, exclude prominent Confederate leaders, and include all other male citizens 'of whatever race, color, or previous condition of servitude.'"[17] Voters were to elect a state convention to frame a state constitution. Pursuant to the Reconstruction Act, Congress would readmit the states to the union if Congress was satisfied with the terms of these newly drafted state constitutions and if the state legislatures ratified the Fourteenth Amendment. By 1871, all former Confederate states had reorganized and had been readmitted to the Union.

The Fourteenth Amendment—The Fourteenth Amendment to the Constitution, ratified by the states in 1868, makes all persons born or naturalized in the United States citizens of the United States and of the state where they reside. The Fourteenth Amendment also prohibits the states from enforcing any law that abridges the privileges or immunities of citizens of the United States; from depriving any person of life, liberty, or property without due process of law; and from denying any person within the jurisdiction of a state the equal protection of the laws.

The Fifteenth Amendment Gave Blacks the Right to Vote—The Fifteenth Amendment to the Constitution provides that the rights of citizens of the United States to vote shall not be denied or abridged by the United States or by any state on account of race, color, or previous condition of servitude. The relationship between politics and the economic advancement of African Americans in this country is fairly obvious. The entire post-Civil War legislative agenda, which consisted of the passage of civil rights statutes and proposed constitutional amendments, was the result of a massive change in the political landscape accompanying the victory by the North over the South. Similarly, the Civil Rights legislation of the 1960s and the 1970s could not have occurred in the absence of a changed political climate.

Congress' introduction and passage of the Fifteenth Amendment meant that blacks now had the right to vote. The new black vote was directly responsible for the election of a notable number of black politicians to state and federal offices. White northerners who had moved to the South following the war (called carpetbaggers) and southerners who had remained loyal to the Union during the Civil War and supported Reconstruction (called Scalawags) were exerting power in state governments. A group of disgruntled whites formed the Ku Klux Klan to end black participation in political elections through force, intimidation, and murder. Congress enacted the Force Act of 1870 and the Ku Klux Klan Act in 1871 to outlaw the activities of the Ku Klux Klan.[18]

The Civil Rights Act of 1875—The Civil Rights Act of 1875 provided that all persons within the jurisdiction of the United States were entitled to the full and equal enjoyment of "the accommodations, advantages, facilities, and privileges of inns, public conveyances on land or water, theatres, and other places of public amusement, subject only to the conditions and limitations established by law and applicable alike to citizens of every race and color, regardless of any previous condition of servitude."[19]

Success in starting and operating a business requires access to the general population and the ability to commingle freely with the entire population. The hallmarks of capitalism consist of government protection of the freedom of economic contract, government protection of all persons' rights to own private property, and government protection of an individual's freedom to choose whether to make business decisions free from the dictates of others or the routines of tradition. The Civil Rights Act of 1875, along with earlier legislation guaranteeing blacks equal rights in contracting and in property transactions, sought to bring blacks into the economic mainstream.

Benefits of Reconstruction

The Reconstruction era benefited blacks in many ways. Following are the most significant areas that set the scene for future gains for blacks in general, and black entrepreneurs in particular.

More Blacks Were Elected to Statehouses and Congress

Freedmen voted for the first time in the elections held in 1867–1868. "[T]wenty-two blacks [from Southern states] served in the U.S.

Congress" and "794 blacks served in Southern legislatures" during the Reconstruction Era. Most of the black politicians in Congress had more formal education than Abraham Lincoln, and some have been described as brilliant. Mississippi and Louisiana each elected two U.S. Senators during reconstruction, but the Senate refused to seat the two elected from Louisiana. One black served as a state governor; blacks in three states served as lieutenant governor. Blacks also served as state supreme court judges, education superintendents, state treasurers, judges, and major military generals.[20] These developments were also economically beneficial to African Americans.

Blacks and Whites Were Interacting With Each Other More

Blacks and whites were attending school together, riding on public transportation together, and engaging in other interpersonal relationships protected by the by Civil Rights Act of 1875. The South Carolina House of Representatives had a black majority. Additionally, blacks and whites were cohabiting together in and out of wedlock. There were black postmasters, black lawyers, black jurors, and black judges. All of these improbable events took place during the Reconstruction Era.[21] If these developments had continued, African Americans could have perhaps achieved economic equality before the 21st century. Thus, if America had stayed the course, the United States might well have become the color-blind society it is still seeking to become today.

Some Blacks Made Substantial Economic Progress

A small number of blacks were able to economically benefit from the unprecedented change in political and social circumstances during the first 10 years following the Civil War. Some laborers were able to ascend to the artisan class. Some black farmers acquired relatively large plots of land. Additionally, a few black politicians made small fortunes as cotton farmers. They also served as directors of railroads, steamship companies, oil corporations, and banks.[22] As is true today, many of the benefits of political and legislative change did not reach a large segment of the black population.

Major Black Colleges Sprang Up

Black organizations and other entities established several black institutions of higher education during the period generally referred to as the Reconstruction Era. These colleges and universities include: Atlanta University and Virginia Union in 1865; Fisk and Lincoln (Missouri) in

1866; Talladega, Howard, Morgan, and Morehouse in 1867; Hampton in 1868; Clark, Dillard, Tougaloo and Claflin in 1869; Allen, Benedict, and Le Moyne in 1870; Alcorn in 1872; Bennett in 1873; Knoxville in 1875; and Meharry in 1876.[23] Education has undoubtedly been the key to economic advancement for African Americans.

Beneficial Legislation

Congress passed the Fourteenth and Fifteenth Amendments to the U.S. Constitution and enacted the Civil Rights Acts of 1866, 1871, and 1875 during the Reconstruction Era. The state legislatures, with a majority of black legislators in some instances, established a public school system in a region hostile to public education that benefited all citizens and public works programs of an unprecedented nature.[24]

The End of the Reconstruction Period

The North began losing interest in the rights of black Americans as other events began to transpire. One momentous event was the death of Pennsylvania congressional representative Thaddeus Stevens of Pennsylvania in 1868. Government corruption under President Grant's administration became the new hot button issue. Virtually all of the black population still resided in the South during this time. The black population's hopes for economic, social, and political justice were grounded, in large measure, on the military presence of the North in the South. Military presence was explicitly based on the perception of the South as a conquered people and provided protection and assurance to the recently liberated black population.[25] In the Compromise of 1877, the Republicans agreed to end the military presence in the South in order to secure the presidency of Rutherford B. Hayes in an election virtually too close to call. The Republicans only controlled four states by 1874. The South almost immediately began a vicious process of suppressing the social and civil rights of the black population with indirect assistance from the United States Supreme Court.[26] We'll take a much closer look at all that transpired on that front in the next chapter.

Why the North Lost Interest in Equal Justice for Blacks

The North's new focus on political corruption in President Grant's administration was only one of several reasons contributing to the North's loss of interest in pursuing the goal of equal justice for black persons in America. Other reasons include the North's interest in the conquest and dispossession of Native Americans from their ancestral homelands during the westward expansion; the North's drive to become an imperialist power in the Philippines, the Caribbean, and other areas inhabited by people of color; and Europe's diminished persuasiveness on the issue of equality for blacks in America due to Europe's preoccupation with imperialism in Africa, India, South America, and other parts of the globe.[27]

Additionally, in the fifty years following the Civil War, industrial expansion completely changed the United States from a rural and agricultural nation to a nation that was urban and industrial. From 1870–1920, approximately 25 million immigrants came to the United States and the native-born population grew from 38 million to 106 million. The United States became an imperialist nation, acquiring control of foreign countries inhabited by non-whites. Examples include U.S. activity in the Philippines, the Caribbean, Hawaii (which the United States annexed in 1898), Alaska (which the United States purchased in 1867), and the Spanish-American War of 1898.[28] It was an age of innovative and resourceful industrial leaders, and ingenious investment bankers who found creative ways to raise capital.

Underlying these events was the unprecedented rise in productivity due to technological advances. Scientific theories established during the period between Reconstruction and 1927 laid the foundation for much of the technology utilized during the United States' industrial growth during this period and throughout the 20th and 21st centuries. To some extent, many of these scientific theories changed the world's concept of reality and encouraged sinister ideas of world domination by leaders in certain countries through the misuse of these theories.

Greed and fear, the two elemental forces of American capitalism, led those in control of legislative policy to rationalize the segregation of blacks from the core of American society and its economy. The U.S. Supreme Court's rationalization for permitting state governments to allow the segregation of all American black people from American society and the general American economy continues to have lasting repercussions to this day.

Notes

1. Abram Harris. *The Negro As Capitalist*, (Chicago: Urban Research Press, Inc., 1992, originally published in 1936 by the American Academy of Political Science), 31.

2. Ibid., 31.

3. Ibid., 32, 34–56.

4. Ibid., 31.

5. Ibid., 32.

6. Ibid.

7. Reconstruction," in 2 *The Volume Library* (Nashville, TN: The Southwestern Company, 1995), 1728.

8. Ibid.

9. Ibid.

10. Lerone Bennett. *Before the Mayflower,* (New York: Penguin Books, 6th Rev.Ed. 1993), 224–25, and "Reconstruction," in 2 *The Volume Library* (Nashville, TN: The Southwestern Company, 1995), 1728.

11. Ibid., and "Reconstruction," in 2 *The Volume Library* (Nashville, TN: The Southwestern Company, 1995), 1728.

12. "Reconstruction," in 2 *The Volume Library* (Nashville, TN: The Southwestern Company, 1995), 1728.

13. Lerone Bennett. *Before the Mayflower,* (New York: Penguin Books, 6th Rev.Ed. 1993), 224.

14. Ibid.

15. Ibid., 223, 226, 233–34 (charts).

16. Ibid., 223, 226, 230.

17. "Reconstruction," in 2 *The Volume Library* (Nashville, TN: The Southwestern Company, 1995), 1728.

18. *Ibid.,* 1729.

19. Lerone Bennett, *Before the Mayflower.* (New York: Penguin Books, 6th Rev.Ed. 1993), 260.

20. Ibid., 214–15, 233, 234.

21. Ibid., 215, 216.

22. Ibid., 252–54.

23. Ibid., 218.

24. Ibid., 253–54.

25. John Sibley Butler. *Entrepreneurship and Self-Help Among African Americans, a Reconsideration of Race and Economics* (New York: State University of New York Press, 1991), 64.

26. Lerone Bennett. *Before the Mayflower,* (New York: Penguin Books, 6th Rev.Ed. 1993), 250–52.

27. Ibid., 261–62.

28. "Coming of Age," in 2 *The Volume Library* (Nashville, TN: The Southwestern Company, 1995), 1730, 1733–34.

Chapter 4

Government-Imposed Segregation: Jim Crow Dances with the U.S. Supreme Court

As you learned in Chapter 3, the Reconstruction Era brought many positive steps to ensure economic parity for blacks. Those gains, however, quickly began to evaporate once the Northern military presence was gone and the attention of the federal government turned to other things. It was the beginning of a rapid slide into perhaps the deepest period of darkness our country has even known other than slavery itself.

The Jim Crow Laws

The laws passed during the era of legalized racial segregation are often referred to as "Jim Crow laws." Greed and fear were the underlying motives behind these laws. More specifically, these motives included: the elimination of competition, economic exploitation of blacks, and prevention of the twin taboos of interracial marriage and dining. The states also intended for these laws to serve as a means for isolating, subordinating, disciplining, controlling, punishing, and humiliating blacks. Moreover, private companies and individuals were free to explicitly discriminate against blacks in employment and virtually any other aspect of life.[1]

During this era, there were white jobs and black jobs. Employers created rules that put strict limits on the relations between black and white factory workers. States passed laws that prohibited blacks and whites from eating together; forbade white nurses from treating black males;

prohibited white teachers from teaching black students; made it a crime for black and white cotton mill workers to look out the same window; required separate textbooks for white and black students; mandated separate telephone booths for whites and blacks; required separate public drinking fountains and restrooms; and required that black and white witnesses swear upon separate bibles in court.[2]

There was no relief from the higher courts, even the U.S. Supreme Court. If anything, the Court only made matters worse.

Role of the U.S. Supreme Court

Between the end of the Civil War and the turn of the 20th century, the U.S. Supreme Court judicially silenced virtually every major effort by Congress to achieve true equality of opportunity for blacks and all Americans. The U.S. Supreme Court arguably did more to crush the economic aspirations and self-esteem of black people than any other institution during the post-Reconstruction era. The Court's infamous decision in *Plessy v. Ferguson* in particular has had lasting effects that have not been totally eradicated. The Court created legal barriers that undermined the efforts of African Americans to participate equally in the American economic system of capitalism.

The Slaughter-House Cases

The *Slaughter-House Cases*,[3] decided in 1873, consisted of three suits started in response to Louisiana law that required all butchering of animals in New Orleans to be done at a facility specified in the statute. The law seriously inconvenienced butchers who slaughtered animals on their own property. The law also affected butchers who had formed trade associations that operated slaughterhouses. The effect of the law was to mandate that these butchers now undertake their business at a distance from the city, at a single center, and required that they pay fees to the facility. The butchers argued that the Louisiana law, by interfering with their right to labor, denied them privileges and immunities of citizens of the United States.[4]

In the *Slaughter-House Cases*, the Supreme Court held that the Fourteenth Amendment's prohibition against state enforcement of any law abridging the privileges and immunities of citizens of the United States did not protect a U.S. citizen's right to be free from fundamental civil rights violations not protected by state law. Instead, the Court held that it was incumbent upon the states to protect their citizens from asserted violations of law such as the one alleged by the butchers and slaughterhouses in the case before the Court. The Court then held that the only rights protected under the Privileges and Immunities Clause of the Fourteenth Amendment were a group of vaguely defined rights of national citizenship. Those rights of national citizenship included free access to seaports, federal protection when on the high seas or within the jurisdiction of a foreign government, and a few other limited rights.[5]

The Court's decision made the Fourteenth Amendment's Privileges and Immunities Clause irrelevant in protecting United States citizens from state infringement of their fundamental rights secured by the Constitution's Bill of Rights. This limited view of the amendment has prevailed to this day. The Supreme Court's post *Slaughter-House* listing of rights of national citizenship include the right to travel from state to state, to petition Congress for redress of grievance, to vote in national elections, to enter federally-owned lands, to be protected while in the custody of a U.S. Marshall, and to inform U.S. authorities of violations of federal law.[6] The Amendment remains limited to a few rights of national citizenship.

The Supreme Court's decision in *The Slaughter-House Cases*, which relied on the state to protect its citizens from civil rights violations, certainly did not advance the prospect of African Americans becoming equal participants in the American capitalistic economic system. Indeed, it was the Southern states, where nine out of ten African Americans resided, that were most determined to exile blacks to their own communities and to exclude blacks from associating with the rest of American society.[7] However, *The Slaughter-House Cases* were only an omen of what was to come.

United States v. Cruikshank

The Supreme Court's decision in *United States v. Cruikshank*[8] in 1876 paralyzed the federal government's attempt to punish those who violated the civil rights of black citizens. The decision, "in effect, shaped the Constitution to the advantage of the Ku Klux Klan."[9] The government's failure to protect the civil rights of a distinct group of individuals effectively excludes them from the economic system of capitalism.[10]

The case arose out of a federal prosecution of nightriders responsible for the Colfax massacre of 1873 in Grant Parish, Louisiana. Several hundred armed whites besieged a courthouse where hundreds of blacks were holding a public assembly. The attackers burned down the building and murdered about 100 people. The United States tried Cruikshank and others involved in the massacre and convicted three for violating § 6 of the Force Act of 1870. That statute, which survives as § 241 of Title 18 of the United States Code, is a general conspiracy statute. The statute makes it a federal crime for two or more persons to conspire to injure or intimidate any citizen with the intent of hindering a citizen's free exercise of any right or privilege guaranteed him by the Constitution or laws of the United States. The indictment claimed Cruikshank violated the federal rights of the victims to peaceably assemble, the right to bear arms, the right to be secure in one's person, life and liberty, and the right to vote.[11]

The Court, in a unanimous opinion by Chief Justice Morrison R. Waite, ignored the statute and focused on the indictment to ascertain whether federal law granted or secured the rights of the black victims. The Court, reasserting the theory of dual citizenship advanced in the *Slaughter-House Cases*, concluded that the states, not the federal government, had jurisdiction to secure the rights that plaintiffs claimed Cruikshank had violated.[12]

The Court, examining each right listed in the indictment, found that each right was solely within the jurisdiction of the states to provide protection. The Court determined that none of the asserted rights were a federal right of national citizenship. The Court held that the right to peaceably assemble predated the Constitution and remained subject to state jurisdiction. The Court stated Congress could not infringe it nor protect it because the right to peaceably assemble was not an attribute of U.S. citizenship. The Court's rationale was the same with respect to the right to bear arms and the right to be secure in one's person, life, and liberty. Accordingly, the Court held that Congress could not punish violence perpetrated by private persons such as Cruikshank. As for the right to vote under the Fifteenth Amendment, the Court held that the Fifteenth Amendment protected voters against discrimination based on race. The Constitution did not confer the right to vote on anyone. Thus, the Court held that the right to vote was not an attribute of national citizenship. The Court, by such reasoning, held that that the indictment did not show that the conspirators had hindered or prevented the enjoyment of any right granted or secured by the Constitution.[13] Therefore, no conviction based on the indictment could be sustained. Consequently, the Court ordered the defendants discharged.

The conspiracy statute remained impotent until revived during the Civil Rights Era of the 1960s. It was not until 1966 that the U.S. Supreme Court in *United States v. Guest*[14] and *United States v. Price*[15] upheld the first convictions under the Force Act and diminished the sweep of *Cruikshank*.

United States v. Reese

The Supreme Court's decision in *Reese*[16] in 1876 was the first voting rights case under the Fifteenth Amendment. The *Reese* decision crippled the federal government's legislative efforts to protect the rights of blacks to vote by making it constitutionally possible for states to circumvent the Amendment through facially nonracial voting qualifications intended to prevent otherwise qualified blacks from voting. The Court's decision in *Reese*, along with its decisions *Dred Scott v. Sandford, United States v. Cruikshank*, and *Plessy v. Ferguson*, ranks as one of the Court's worst decisions ever.

Reese involved a federal prosecution of two state election officials who refused to allow a black citizen to pay his poll tax and vote in a municipal election. The United States prosecuted the election official under a congressional statute that prohibited election officials from refusing to qualify eligible voters or not allowing them to vote. Part of the statute specified denial on account of race and another part did not. For example, one section provided for the punishment of any person who prevented any citizen from voting or qualifying to vote.[17]

The Court, in an eight-one decision written by Chief Justice Waite, held the congressional statute unconstitutional because it swept too broadly. Two sections did not "confine their operation to unlawful discriminations on account of race, etc." The Court noted that the Fifteenth Amendment provided that the right to vote should not be denied because of race. Congress, however, had overreached its powers by seeking to punish the denial on any ground. The Court voided the whole statute because it said that the statute's sections were inseparable. However, the Court inexplicably refused to broadly construe the stated sections in terms of those sections that explicitly prohibited election officials from denying persons the right to vote because of their race.[18]

The Court, by its narrow interpretation of the Fifteenth Amendment, made it constitutionally possible for states to deny the right to vote on any ground except race. As a result, the states created a number of facially neutral devices to ensure that whites would be able to vote, but not blacks. Some of the devices used by states to achieve the disenfranchisement of blacks while ensuring that white voters would not be excluded included poll taxes, literacy tests, good character tests, understanding clauses, and grandfather clauses.[19] The *Reese* decision had a negative impact on the efforts to fully include African Americans in the political and economic fabric of the United States. The relationship between politics and the economic advancement of African Americans has been amply demonstrated in American history. We will take a closer look at how that evolved in Chapter 7, The Civil Rights Era.

The Civil Rights Cases

In *The Civil Rights Cases*[20] of 1883, the U.S. Supreme Court invalidated the Civil Rights Act of 1875, which prohibited private persons from denying, on the basis of race, any individual's equal access to any place of public accommodations (for example, hotels, public transportation, theatres). The Supreme Court held that the Fourteenth Amendment only prohibited state action. The Court also ruled that the Thirteenth Amendment was inapplicable because private individuals refusing entry to blacks did not constitute a badge of slavery. In 1968, the Court overruled that portion of its decision concerning the inapplicability of the Thirteenth Amendment to private conduct. The Court held that Congress had the power under the Thirteenth Amendment to rationally determine the badges and incidents of slavery when passing legislation to prohibit racial discrimination by private individuals.[21]

Hall v. de Cuir

In *Hall*,[22] in 1878, the U.S. Supreme Court ruled that the Commerce Clause prevented a state from prohibiting segregation on a common carrier. The Court held that a Louisiana law prohibiting racial segregation could not be applied to steamboat operations on the Mississippi River because of the burden it would impose on steamboat operators if other states along the river enacted laws requiring segregation. The Court implicitly held, by negative implication, that states legally could require segregation of the races without violating the federal policy underlying the Fourteenth Amendment. Otherwise, the Court would have been compelled to hold, as it did 85 years later, that a state cannot interfere with interstate commerce by banning segregation because the Constitution prohibits both state and federal governments from requiring racial discrimination.[23] The decision in *Hall* paved the way for the Supreme Court's decision in *Plessy v. Ferguson*, in which the Court permitted state governments to legally separate black people from the rest of the population.

Plessy v. Ferguson

In *Plessy*,[24] in 1896, the Supreme Court legalized state-enforced segregation of the races so long as states provided separate but equal accommodations for blacks. The Court held that the Fourteenth Amendment could not have been intended to abolish distinctions based on color, or to enforce social equality or a commingling of the two races upon terms unsatisfactory to either.[25] The Supreme Court's decision in *Plessy* sanctioned the racial caste system endorsed by the Southern states that allowed the states to separate African Americans from the general population. The *Plessy* decision effectively doomed the aspirations of African Americans to participate equally in the American capitalistic economic system.

The Social Aftermath

From 1878–1898, whites lynched approximately 10,000 persons, most of whom were black. From 1890–1900, whites lynched approximately 1,217 persons, most of whom were black.[26]

Additionally, during this era, states systematically disenfranchised blacks through violence, massacres, and a variety of legal devices such as literacy tests, property tests, poll taxes, understanding clauses, and grandfather clauses. The problem the South faced was how to keep blacks from voting without denying the right to poor whites as well. In *Before the Mayflower*, Lerone Bennet says the South soon found a solution:

> The answer the South came up with was a wall with holes in it. The wall was made of literacy and property tests and poll taxes. The holes, designed especially for illiterate and property-less poor whites, were "understanding clauses" and "grandfather clauses." If a man's ancestors voted on or before a selected date in, say 1866—a date on which unfortunately there were no black voters—then he could escape the other provisions. Or he could escape through the holes of "good character" or the "understanding" clause. If he couldn't read or write and if he was white, surely he could understand and explain an article of the Constitution. But if he was black, the "read and write" and "understanding" clauses were unbridgeable walls that no amount of literacy could bridge.[27]

At the turn of the century, nine out of every ten blacks lived in the rural South and four million freedmen had grown to eight million. In 1901, George H. White, the last black congressman elected in the 1800s from the South, ended his last term in congress.[28] Clearly, many of the advantages blacks had gained during Reconstruction quickly evaporated.

The Economic Aftermath: The Theory of Economic Detour

The idea of economic detour is that black people, following Reconstruction, were restricted from operating their businesses in the open market through laws that restricted their interaction with whites. The government forced blacks, unlike any other ethnic group in this country, to operate in a segregated market during the era when blacks were socially and economically segregated from the general population. The institution of segregation laws involved the interference of government into the normal operation of the marketplace. This was not true for any other race or minority group. The U.S. Commerce Department acknowledged that there was a separate African American economic market apart from the general open market. In doing so, the Commerce Department conceded that the general open marketplace was closed only to blacks and no other minorities.[29]

The Chinese in Mississippi and the Japanese in California, for example, were able to enter the open market and compete, although they often encountered hostility. When the Japanese had to rely solely on a Japanese market, their businesses were not successful. Similarly, blacks were more likely to be successful when they were able to develop a business clientele outside of the black community.[30]

Why the Black Economic Journey Was Different from Minority Immigrants

The sociology of entrepreneurship examines the tendency of ethnic minorities to engage in business enterprise because of their exclusion from positions of political influence and subordination to a group of rulers. It is the sociology of self-help through entrepreneurial activities. Max Weber laid the foundation for studies examining the sociology of entrepreneurship. Weber observed that national or religious minorities who are in a position of subordination to the ruling class are likely to be driven into economic activity because of their exclusion from positions of political influence.[31]

Underlying the sociology of entrepreneurship is the theory that presupposes that ethnic minorities adjusting to a new country have access to the general consumer market. Even though they may have faced discrimination, prejudice, or open hostility, they often found economic security in the role of middlemen—rent collectors, labor contractors, money lenders, and brokers. Even though they may have operated on the fringes of the economic system, they still had access to a broad range of clientele that was not available to blacks.[32]

Contemporary scholars treating the sociology of entrepreneurship and race relations fail to acknowledge the works of black authors and thought leaders like Booker T. Washington and W.E.B. Dubois, whose ideas and findings predate their own similar ideas. Yet these black scholars as early as 1898 had demonstrated how free blacks during the 1700s had engaged in business enterprises even though they possessed half-free status. They make no mention of the entrepreneurial activities of persons such as Anthony Johnson in the 1600s, Jean Baptist Du Sable in the 1700s, the black-owned businesses during the 1700s, the variety of enterprises established by blacks prior to the Civil War, and the many black inventors during slavery and after it was abolished.

Similarly, the cities of Durham, North Carolina, and Tulsa, Oklahoma—referred to as the Black Wall Street—prospered during the first decades of the 20th century, in part because blacks were able in some instances to earn money from selling to whites in the white parts of town, although the segregation laws in effect at the time did not allow blacks to spend their money in white areas.[33] Scholars estimate that "the dollar circulated 36 to 1000 times, sometimes taking a year for the currency to leave the black community."[34] These entrepreneurial enclaves benefited from those who saved and used their black dollars to do business inside the district. The key point, however, is that these black entrepreneurs had some access to the entire market.

Economic Detour Forced Blacks Out of Mainstream Markets

The majority culture largely excluded blacks from professional opportunities in non-minority businesses during the years prior to the passage of Title VII of the 1964 Civil Rights Act. Private companies providing public accommodations such as hotels, restaurants, and other services were free to openly treat blacks with contempt, disdain, and hostility because they were not required by law to provide services to blacks on the same terms as to whites and other groups.

Black professionals, including businesspeople, medical doctors, dentists, and lawyers, had virtually no opportunity to use their professional expertise in the larger society. Similarly, the dominant culture largely excluded black wage-earners from many skilled trades. Black workers, however, always struggled to enter these skilled professions. Thus, white society relegated black workers to the status of laborers.[35]

Gunnar Myrdal, a Swedish institutional economist, provided a detailed account of the status of black business persons, professionals, and other workers in his groundbreaking book *An American Dilemma: The Negro Problem and Modern Democracy.*[36] Myrdal gave the book its name in view of the "moral contradiction of a nation torn between allegiance to its highest ideals and awareness of the base realities of racial discrimination."[37] Chapter fourteen, entitled *The Negro in Business, the Professions,*

Public Service and Other White Collar Occupations, provided an in-depth study, replete with statistical analysis, highlighting the majority culture's exclusion of blacks from the larger white economy during the years 1910–1940.

Myrdal's considerable research indicated that black businesspeople and other black professionals were outside the overall American economy. Myrdal observed:

> ... while the Negro community gives places for a fair number of Negro preachers, teachers, and neighborhood storekeepers, it does not offer much chance for civil engineers and architects ... the latter have to work in the white economy, which does not want Negroes in such positions ... the Negroes' representation among managers of industry, if anything, is still smaller.[38]

As former Republican congressman Jack Kemp stated in response to the Supreme Court's decision in *Grutter v. Bollinger,*[39] which upheld the University of Michigan Law School's use of racial diversity as a factor in its admissions process:

> Blacks were removed from the mainstream economy, denied access to education, job opportunities, and access to capital and ownership.[40]

The overwhelming majority of all black workers served the general white-dominated economy in low-paying subservient positions. Nevertheless, most black businessmen, professionals, and white-collar workers were either dependent on the segregated black community for their market or served in public institutions like schools and hospitals set up exclusively for the use of blacks. Some civil service employees were the only significant exception. This exclusion from the larger white-collar economy meant that very little opportunity existed for inclusion of blacks in the American ideal of attaining middle-class status.

This restriction of economic choice resulted in an almost nonexistent black middle and upper class, and skewed the occupational distribution in those classes. The distribution of blacks resulted in a fair number of black preachers, teachers, and neighborhood storekeepers, but offered little chance for successful black engineers, architects, and other advanced professions. Industries catering to black customers, however, presented a virtual monopoly for blacks. Nonetheless, the monopoly of the black market presented a host of societal and ideological issues. Commenting on this point, Myrdal noted:

. . . on one hand, blacks find that the caste wall blocks their economic and social opportunities while . . . on the other hand, they . . . have a vested interest in racial segregation because it gives them what opportunity they have.[41]

Teresa Wiltz, writing for the *Washington Post,* noted that despite the indignities and horrors heaped upon black people during this era, there was "another side" to the "segregation drama:"

> Much is made of the horrors of the pre-civil rights South, the rigidity of Jim Crow regulations, the lynchings, the indignities of living life etched sharply in black and white. Those horrors were real . . . and yet . . . there was another side, a far more complicated side to the segregation drama, a side where black folks of means recreated the world in their own colored image. A colored world that was by necessity populated with "Negro" educators, teachers hell-bent at uplifting the race at "Negro" universities, "Negro" lawyers, "Negro" newspapers, "Negro" hospitals.[42]

In Chapter 5, we'll take a look at the economic world that black entrepreneurs created and populated successfully. They faced enormous odds, and often outrageous challenges, yet carved out an economic niche for themselves that paved the way for successful entrepreneurs of the future.

Notes

1. Lerone Bennett. *Before the Mayflower* (New York: Penguin Books, 6th Rev.Ed. 1993), 255–58.

2. Ibid., 256–58, 289.

3. 83 U.S. (16 Wall. 1873), 36.

4. Kermit L. Hall (Editor), Michael Les Benedict (Contributor), "Slaughter House Cases," *The Oxford Guide to United States Supreme Court Decisions* (New York: Oxford University Press, Inc., 1999), 286–89.

5. Stephen E. Emmanuel. *Constitutional Law* (Larchmont, NY: Emmanuel Publishing Corp, 1997), 403.

6. Ibid., 404.

7. Robert Heibroner and Lester Thurow. *Economics Explained* (New York: Simon and Schuster, 1998),12–14, and Lerone Bennett, Jr. *Before The Mayflower* (New York: Penguin Books, 6th Rev. Ed., 1993), 295.

8. 92 U.S. 542 (1876).

9. Leonard W. Levy, "Cruikshank" in *Encyclopedia of the American Constitution* (New York: Macmillan, 1986), 527.

10. Robert Heibroner and Lester Thurow. *Economics Explained* (New York: Simon and Schuster, 1998), 11–17.

11. *United States v. Cruikshank,* 92 U.S. 542, 544–45 (1876), and Leonard W. Levy, "Cruikshank" in *Encyclopedia of the American Constitution* (New York: Macmillan, 1986), 527.

12. 92 U.S. 542, 549, 551–59.

13. Ibid., 549–59.

14. 383 U.S. 745 (1966).

15. 383 U.S. 787 (1966).

16. 92 U.S. 214 (1876).

17. Reese, 92 U.S. at 215–18.

18. Ibid., 220–21.

19. Lerone Bennett. *Before the Mayflower* (New York: Penguin Books, 6th Rev.Ed. 1993), 275–76.

20. 109 U.S. 3 (1883).

21. *Jones v. Alfred H. Mayer Co.,* 392 U.S. (1968), 409, 413, 440.

22. 95 U.S. 485 (1878).

23. *Colo. Anti-Discrimination Comm 'n v. Cont 'l Airlines, Inc.,* 372 U.S. 714 (1963).

24. 163 U.S. 537 (1896).

25. Ibid., 544.

26. Lerone Bennett. *Before the Mayflower* (New York: Penguin Books, 6th Rev.Ed. 1993), 258, 271.

27. Ibid., at 265–77.

28. Ibid., 295–96.

29. John Sibley Butler. *Entrepreneurship and Self-Help Among Black Americans: A Reconsideration of Race and Economics* (New York: State University of New York Press, 1991), 71–73.

30. Ibid., 71–72.

31. Ibid., 2.

32. Ibid., 4–5, 7–8.

33. The Black Wall Street, Wikipedia, http://en.wikipedia.org/wiki/The-BlackWall_Street, 1 (Accesssed 3-27-07).

34. See Davey D's Hip Hop Corner, Black Wall Street, http://www.daveyd.com/blackwallpolitic.html,3 (Accessed 3-27-2007).

35. John Sibley Butler. *Myrdal Revisited, Race Relations in a Changing World* (New York: Russell Sage Foundation Publications, 1996), Obie Clayton, ed., 139.

36. Gunner Myrdal. *An American Dilemma: The Negro Problem and Modern Democracy* (New York: Harper & Brothers, 1944, in 1998 reprinted edition), 304.

37. Ibid.

38. Ibid., 304.

39. 539 U.S. 306 (2003).

40. Michael A. Fletcher & Lee Hockstader, "U-Mich. Rulings Spur Strategic Scramble: Affirmative Action's Backers and Foes Ponder Response to High Court's Decision," *Washington Post,* June 25, 2003, sec. A9.

41. Gunner Myrdal. *An American Dilemma: The Negro Problem and Modern Democracy* (New York: Harper & Brothers, 1944, in 1998 reprinted edition), 304–05.

42. Teresa Wiltz, "BET, A Case of Selling Out or Selling Up? But Has the Network Sold a Bit of Its Soul?," *Washington Post*, November, 2000, sec.C1.

CHAPTER 5

BLACK ECONOMIC ENCLAVES UNDER GOVERNMENT-IMPOSED SEGREGATION

Gunnar Myrdal's studies[1] reviewed, among others, the employment of blacks in the following twelve businesses and occupations from 1910–1940: retailers and restaurant owners; undertakers, barbers, and beauticians; builders and manufacturers; bankers and financiers; life insurers; teachers; clergy; medical professionals; legal professionals; government employees; performing artists; and the black underworld. Let's take a look at each of them in turn.

Retail Trade and Restaurants

Black persons in the retail trade businesses had difficulty competing with white businesses, having only 5–10 percent of the total trade with black consumers in the retail and restaurant businesses. They had difficulty competing with whites because of the small size and high cost of operating such establishments, the greater difficulty blacks had securing credit for their businesses, and social and economic factors barring black persons from establishing retail businesses in the "main shopping districts," which were predominantly white. Accordingly, the black retailer's prices tended to be higher than the white retailers, or if the black businessman kept his prices down, his profit margins would be smaller than those of his white counterpart. Consequently, black owners of these businesses often failed to have a large enough variety of goods in stock to supply their customers' needs. The relatively low level of black purchasing

Vendehorst's Shoe Store, Jacksonville, Florida. From the Emory J. Tolbert Collection

power, the higher prices charged by the black entrepreneur for his goods, the lack of product variety, the inability to generate any business from the white community, and minimal success in attracting black customers combined to create a vicious cycle that kept black entrepreneurs in the retail and restaurant businesses from achieving financial success.

The "don't buy where you can't work" campaign in the North was an effort to get white-owned businesses in black neighborhoods to hire blacks in their establishments. This movement found more of a home in the more politically open North than in the South. Nevertheless, in spite of the political opportunity for dissent in the North, the black community witnessed little impact from this freedom movement.

Undertakers, Barbers, and Beauticians

The "real business group" was the pool of about 3,000 black undertakers, making up nearly 10 percent of all undertakers. Black undertakers had a monopoly in this line of business because white undertakers did not want to touch the bodies of deceased blacks. This was especially true in the South. Black undertakers were successful, even though they never handled white funerals, because black people tended to spend lavishly on funerals irrespective of their economic plight.

The family grocery and delicatessen, A. H. Underdowns's Store, Washington, D.C. From the Emory J. Tolbert Collection

Black barbers, beauticians, and hairdressers tended to be successful for the same reasons. In 1930, there were 34,000 black entrepreneurs and employees in this line of work, constituting about 10 percent of all such workers in the country.

Undertaking and hair-care businesses were the only businesses in which blacks were protected from white competition. Blacks were able to retain only a small portion of the black market in other business endeavors of any consequence and seldom succeeded in keeping a substantial white market.

Building Trades and Manufacturing

In the South, there were more skilled black workers than skilled white workers in the building trades prior to the Civil War. Black contractors soon lost their footing in the industrialized South after the Civil War because of the need for capital and white society's refusal to extend credit to blacks in this field. Whites, who imposed great restrictions on black efforts to obtain employment as wage earners, were even more unwilling to risk their money on black entrepreneurial efforts in the building and manufacturing areas. Compounding these factors was the poor self-image held by post-emancipation blacks. Additionally, feelings of inferiority and lack of adequate training were enhanced by the black would-be-entrepreneur's slavery background.

Banking and Finance

The first black bank opened shortly after the Civil War and many more followed in the years to come, as did savings and loan establishments. The Freedmen's Savings Bank and Trust Company, established on May 16, 1865, was the first notable attempt to assist blacks in establishing a bank that would cater to the needs of the black community. President Lincoln signed an Act of Congress incorporating the Freedmen's Bank and Trust Company on March 3, 1865, the same day on which he signed the Act creating the Freedmen's Bureau. Congress did not incorporate the bank as a government institution. Congress did, however, view the bank as a philanthropic venture that would safeguard the savings of the freedmen and encourage them to be thrifty. From 1866–1871, the bank established a total of 34 branches, 32 of which were in the South. The bank ultimately had branches in 36 cities, and by 1874, total deposits of $57 million.[2]

The National Bankers Association. From the Emory J. Tolbert Collection

The Freedmen's Bank and Trust Company aimed to train black businessmen and to encourage blacks in the acquisition of property. The bank employed few blacks when it was first established. Nonetheless, an increasing number of blacks obtained positions after 1870. Abram Harris notes in his book, *The Negro as Capitalist*, that:

> ... in Richmond and Norfolk, Virginia, as well as in Washington District of Columbia, Negro businessmen and property holders were members of the advisory councils and the board of trustees. Many were also employed as clerks, tellers, and bookkeepers at the central office and at numerous branches.[3]

Unfortunately, the bank, though covered by U.S. securities, made unwise use of reserve deposits and failed during the Depression of 1874. Harris notes, however, that the bank's speculative and dishonest management group caused the bank's failure by "its investments in overcapitalized and speculative ventures, ... its high operating costs and heavy investments in fixed assets."[4] The Freedmen's Bank, although mismanaged, accomplished its purpose of "implanting certain social and economic ideals in Negro life" including "respectability."[5] Nevertheless, the Freedmen's Bank failure, with a loss of $4 million that was not replaced, caused much distrust among blacks inclined to save.

In the 1880's, black leaders began to call for the development of black businesses in increasing numbers. They also called upon the black population to form banks to assist black businesses in acquiring credit and capital. In 1888, 15 years after the failure of the Freedmen's Bank, blacks established the first banks that were actually organized and administered by blacks. The growth of black banks thereafter was remarkable. Blacks organized no fewer than 28 banks from 1899–1905.[6]

These banks followed in the wake of the expansion of fraternal insurance and burial societies that took place in the first 20 years after the Civil War. The black church and ministry were largely responsible for the establishment of the fraternal insurance and burial societies. These fraternal insurance and burial societies were necessary because it was clear that the dominant society did not accept former slaves as the social equals of whites and did not welcome them to assimilate into the social life of the general community. As the fraternal organizations and societies increased in number, there was a corresponding increase in the capital, investments, and subsidiary businesses developed by these organizations. The increasing asset basis of these organizations led to the formation of the first banks organized and administered by blacks.

Blacks organized at least 134 banks from 1888–1934. The greatest number of black bank failures occurred from 1928–1931 during the Great Depression. The total number of black banks during this period decreased by 50 percent. There were 30 black banks in 1927, 28 in 1928, and 21 in 1929. In 1934, there were 12 black banks in existence. The most significant failures of black banks took place in Virginia, the District of Columbia, Maryland, Pennsylvania, and Illinois.[7]

During the era of segregation, most black banks were small. The characteristic of being small was one that invariably increased operating costs. Because of their small size, these banks tended to invest in more secure, low-yielding government securities. Bank investments in black-owned property produced dismal results because segregation produced a restricted market for black-owned property. A large percentage of black borrowers, compared to white borrowers, used loans for consumption rather than investment and production purposes. Additionally, very few black families had any money for savings or checking accounts.

Blacks began to establish building and loan associations because they were unable to obtain loans from white institutions to build their own homes. Blacks formed the first black-owned building and loan association in Virginia in 1883. By 1930, blacks had established approximately 70 savings and loan associations with assets totaling $6.6 million. This was less than one percent of the total assets of all American building and loan associations.[8] Some of the more successful savings and loan associations had a partly white clientele providing larger business and greater diversification of risks. Most black savings and loans, compared to their white counterparts, were small, had higher costs, and charged somewhat higher rates of interest.

Life Insurance

Black entrepreneurs had greater business success in the life insurance industry. The reasons included the differential treatment afforded black customers by white insurance companies in the form of higher premiums and the fact that even the poorest black families had some form of insurance. The life insurance business, however, provided little real protection to anyone other than black undertakers. In 1939, there were 67 black insurance companies with 1,677,000 policies, a total income of $13 million and about 8,000 workers.[9] The black insurance business, like other black financial institutions, grew out of the black church, lodges, and benevolent associations. Nevertheless, the black-managed insurance company, like the black banks of this era, could not escape the fact that they thrived on a poor, segregated community that could not offer these businesses any range of investment opportunities to minimize their risks.

Teachers

Teaching was the principal black profession during the era of segregation when Myrdal did his research. A black person's chance of getting a job was much higher in the segregated South than in the North. Black teachers were able to monopolize the teaching field in the South. The open field of segregated classrooms in the South did not mean, however, that black teachers were paid on the same scale as their white counterparts. Blacks constituted 4.9 percent and 5.2 percent of all teachers in the United States in 1910 and 1930, respectively.[10]

Clergy

The black clergy constituted the second-largest group among black professionals. They "enjoy[ed] a complete monopoly behind the caste wall of segregation."[11] This did not mean, however, that the profession provided sufficient income for that population to survive. Many ministers had very small, very poor congregations and were forced to have second jobs to survive. The ministry was the only profession in which blacks had greater representation than their percentage of the general population.[12]

Black clergymen constituted 14.8 percent and 16.8 percent of all such professionals in the United States in 1910 and 1930, respectively. Myrdal stated that probable reasons for the high percentage of black ministers in the profession were that opportunities were restricted for blacks in other fields, more blacks attended church than whites, and the religious interests of blacks were more divided than whites.[13]

Medical Profession

During the segregation era, most whites would not go to a black doctor due, at least in part, to racial prejudice. There were some questionable exceptions to this general practice. White patients who wanted to conceal venereal diseases and pregnancy from their white friends, and some low-income whites who had problems getting treatment from white doctors would visit black doctors. The black doctor, in spite of his secret white clientele, still had difficulty succeeding. The black doctor had to rely heavily on his black patients, who had little income to expend on health care, and white patients who were equally poor. Additionally, black doctors had to convince their white patients to trust them.[14]

The hospital setting provided an even greater challenge for black doctors. Harlem Hospital in New York City was one of the few hospitals in the country where white and black doctors practiced together under a system of equality. Moreover, the growth of public health facilities limited the employment opportunities for black physicians. This is because they faced the prospect of losing all their patients unless the public health organizations gave them a place in the new public health system. Loss of patients and minimal opportunities for training and specialization at hospitals fueled the perception that black physicians and surgeons were not as qualified as their white counterparts. Howard University in Washington, District of Columbia, and Meharry University in Nashville, Tennessee, trained the majority of all black doctors during this time period. The students at these schools passed the state medical boards at approximately the same percentages as graduates of white schools. Black medical doctors constituted 2 percent and 2.4 percent of all members of that profession in 1910 and 1930, respectively.[15]

The medical profession treated black nurses similarly to black doctors. The nursing profession was even harsher, resulting in an even smaller number of blacks in this profession. Nurses had to depend on the public health system for employment because they could not count on income from private practice. Black nurses occupied a peculiar place in the health system because white nurses treated black patients directly but had black nurses do all the "dirty work." Black nurses constituted 3 percent and 1.9 percent of all nurses in the United States in 1910 and 1930, respectively.[16]

Black dentists fared only a little better than doctors and nurses. There were very few black dentists in rural areas. Thus, rural blacks went to white dentists whether they wanted to or not. The black dentist, like the black doctor, had to resort to other outside jobs to survive. Black dentists constituted 1.2 percent and 2.5 percent of all dentists in the United States in 1910 and 1930, respectively.[17]

Legal Profession

Blacks constituted less than one percent of all attorneys licensed to practice law in the United States in 1910 and 1930. Almost two-thirds of black lawyers lived outside the South and were the product of white law schools in the North. The majority of black lawyers in the South had some other occupation to support themselves. Black attorneys during this era rarely appeared in court to represent blacks in actions against whites. Instead, they focused on work dealing with black churches, fraternal organizations, domestic relations, and criminal matters.[18]

Officials and White Collar Workers in Government Employment

All, or at least some, of the black workers previously discussed, i.e., teachers, physicians, surgeons, nurses, social workers, extension service workers, and so on, worked in the public sector for some government agency. Despite adversities, blacks had more opportunity for employment in the government than in any other profession. When government employment of blacks in the military is factored in, it becomes clear that government work has been an important factor in black economic stability. The largest remaining occupation of blacks in government service in 1930 was the 18,000 blacks working in the postal service. Of this number, 7,000 were clerks, 6,000 were mail carriers, and the remaining group occupied various minor categories. This was approximately triple the number of black workers in 1910.[19]

In other public service work, there were approximately 6,000 black officials and white collar workers in 1930. Of these, less than 2,000 were policemen, sheriffs, and detectives. Over 3,000 were clerks and kindred workers. The government employed the remaining blacks in a variety of categories. This group made up approximately one percent of the total.[20]

Whites removed most blacks from positions in state and local government after Reconstruction. The process of eliminating blacks from positions in the federal government, however, was slower. During the Wilson administration, the number of black postmasters began to decline and continued to fall in the coming years. There were 153 black postmasters in 1910 and, by 1930, only 78. Additionally, the federal government began to utilize new methods to screen out potential black job applicants. One screening device simply required that each applicant supply a photograph, which would often be difficult for a black person to obtain. Nevertheless, the expansion of the federal government during World War I, the rapid increase in the number of black voters in the North, and the friendlier attitude toward the employment of blacks under the New Deal era of President Roosevelt counteracted, somewhat, the effects of these discriminatory policies.[21]

Performing Arts

Historically, whites have given blacks somewhat backhanded praise for artistic ability. Blacks created the jazz, blues, rock and roll, and hip-hop art forms and tend to excel in sports.[22] The assumption during the era of segregation was that the arts were the only field in which blacks could attain noteworthy success. The perception, however, was that the arts required less academic prowess.

Prior to 1915, blacks made up very little of the audience attending shows, and whites played most black characters. Blacks served as assistants in these shows and the later migration of blacks to the North greatly increased the number of blacks in show business.

New York was the center for black employment in the entertainment industry during the earlier period of the 20th century. New York was home to the Apollo Theater and provided more opportunities for blacks to find work in the white-owned downtown theatres. Hollywood employed a few hundred blacks, but they mostly played minor parts and acted as extras. Accordingly, economic opportunities for black screen actors were very limited during the first 40 years of the 20th century.

The Black Underworld

The great restrictions of economic and social opportunities for blacks in ordinary lines of work, the encroachments on their rights and personal integrity, and their general experience of exclusion and isolation contributed to the proliferation of the black underworld of crime. Other factors that contributed to this underground economy were crowded ghettos that were often in proximity to "red light districts" and the lack of wholesome recreation for blacks in urban areas. Accordingly, in most large cities, there was a black underworld economy of petty thieves, gambling, racketeers, prostitutes and pimps, bootleggers, dope addicts, and those organizing and controlling these various crimes and vices.[23]

The pervasiveness of institutional racism, based on the premise that blacks were inferior and whites were superior, dictated that they should not mix socially, politically, or economically, and is likely the real reason why many blacks found such little success in business. The policies of segregation and exclusion perpetuated the existence of a black American culture that is different from, and subordinate to, the dominant perspective.[24] Black Americans in business in the early 1900s were still living under the shadow of *Dred Scott v. Sandford*,[25] which declared that they had no rights that the white man was bound to respect.

Myrdal's Findings Compared with Post-Civil Rights Era Developments

John Sibley Butler, in his work entitled *Myrdal Revisited: The Negro In Business, the Professions, Public Service and Other White Collar Occupations*,[26] noted that Myrdal's work stands as the standard for analysis in race relations despite the massive changes that have taken place since the time Myrdal wrote *An American Dilemma*. Those changes include the end of segregation and a massive civil rights movement that resulted in legislation designed to provide equality for blacks in employment, public accommodations, housing, education, government contracting, and other areas. We will cover the changes wrought by the civil rights movement of the 1950s and 1960s in depth in Chapter 7.

Myrdal's discussion of blacks in business and the professions took place when segregation was in full force. Today, blacks are still underrepresented in the professions, although there have been some nominal improvements in certain categories such as nursing. The percentage of black physicians, as a percentage of the black population, demonstrated essentially no growth as of the 1980 census, and black lawyers, who now constitute approximately 3.9 percent of the profession, remain underrepresented. The participation of blacks in the military, however, arguably represents the greatest change since Myrdal's work. The military has provided an opportunity for structure and economic security for blacks that has probably exceeded developments in the civilian sector.[27]

With regard to black businesses, perhaps the greatest change since Myrdal's research is that black businesses now serve the entire business community and not just the black community. Additionally, black businesses are engaged in manufacturing, technology, and other sectors not readily available to black entrepreneurs prior to the modern civil rights movement.

Butler's analysis indicates that regardless of the historical period, blacks who have adjusted to the harsh realities of racism through entrepreneurship rather than assimilation have demonstrated a stronger emphasis on self-help and the value of education. Black entrepreneurs produce, through their children, the greatest number of black college graduates, professionals, and businessmen. Research also indicates that these values are seen in members of the military and their progeny. Butler suggests that future research should examine the black professional and business class in the tradition of middleman minorities to better understand data patterns from a historical view.[28]

Notable Black Inventors Before 1860 and from 1860–1900

As one might suspect, the law did not permit slaves to secure patents on their inventions before the civil war. And free blacks apparently did not seem to have such rights either. One commentator, however, lists approximately 132 black inventors who obtained patents from the government from 1860–1900. It is also widely known that several of these early black inventors created items that we today take for granted. They made these outstanding contributions despite slavery, overt discrimination, a lack of formal education in the sciences (in most instances), and many other obstacles. Below is a partial list of early black inventors, what they invented, and the date the government granted them patents. A complete listing of all black inventors is beyond the scope of this book.

Table 5-1   Inventions by Black Inventors, Pre-1860 and 1860–1900*

Hyram S. Thomas (the potato chip)	**T. A. Carrington** (cooking range, 1876)
Augustus Jackson (ice cream, 1832, but no patent)	**G. F. Grant** (golf tee, 1891)
	A. Miles (elevator, 1887)
I. R. Johnson (bicycle frame, 1899)	**G. T. Sampson** (clothes drier, 1892)
J. L. Love (pencil sharpener, 1897)	**J. Standard** (refrigerator, 1891)
Thomas W. Stewart (the common mop holder, 1887)	**J. A. Burr** (lawn mower, 1899)
J. H. Dickinson (the player piano, 1899)	**Elijah McCoy** (a device to lubricate machines while running, the lawn sprin-
Benjamin Banneker (the first completely American-made clock, 1761, but no patent)	kler, and many more items, 1872— people would often ask whether an item was the "real McCoy")
A. J. Beard (rotary engine, railroad car coupler—the forerunner to today's automatic coupler, 1897)	**Granville T. Woods** (an improved steam boiler for steam engines, the trolley from which the name trolley
L. Bell (locomotive stack, 1871)	car is derived, and an additional 22 patents for electrical devices, 1884 and
A. B. Blackburn (railway signal, 1888)	later)
C. B. Brooks (street sweepers, 1896)	**Lewis H. Lattimer** (electric light
W. F. Burr (switching device for railway, 1899)	filaments)

*Adapted from John Sibley Butler, *Entrepreneurship and Self-Help among Black Americans: A Reconsideration of Race and Economics* (New York: State University of New York Press, 1991).

Most black people in America during this historical period lacked formal schooling, faced overt discrimination, and encountered many other obstacles that largely excluded them from the fields of science. Consequently, these noteworthy examples of black creativity are somewhat astonishing. Moreover, thousands of inventions made by blacks prior to the Civil War were appropriated by whites who placed their name on the patent applications. Nevertheless, the thousands of verifiable inventions of black men and women from 1860–1900 represent a remarkable achievement in light of the obstacles they had to overcome.

Notes

1. Gunner Myrdal. *An American Dilemma: The Negro Problem and Modern Democracy* (New York: Harper & Brothers, 1944, in 1998 reprinted edition), 307–32.

2. Abram L. Harris. *The Negro As Capitalist* (Chicago: Urban Research Press, Inc., 1992, originally published in 1936 by the American Academy of Political Science), 34–37, 50, 55–58, 66–67, 75–196, and Gunner Myrdal. *An American Dilemma: The Negro Problem and Modern Democracy* (New York: Harper & Brothers, 1944, in 1998 reprinted edition), 314–16.

3. Abram L. Harris. *The Negro As Capitalist* (Chicago: Urban Research Press, Inc., 1992, originally published in 1936 by the American Academy of Political Science), 56.

4. Ibid., 50.

5. Ibid., 55.

6. Ibid., 57.

7. Ibid., 75–76, 176–93.

8. Gunner Myrdal. *An American Dilemma: The Negro Problem and Modern Democracy* (New York: Harper & Brothers, 1944, in 1998 reprinted edition), 315.

9. Ibid., 317.

10. Ibid., 319, tbl.3.

11. Ibid., 321.

12. Ibid.

13. Ibid., 319 tbl.3, 321.

14. Ibid., 323.

15. Ibid., 319 tbl.3, 324.

16. Ibid., 319 tbl.3.

17. Ibid., 319, tbl.3.

18. Ibid., 326.

19. Ibid., 327.

20. Ibid.

21. Ibid., 327–28.

22. *African American Desk Reference* (New York: Stonesong Press and New York Public Library, Philip Koslow ed., 1999), 368–71, 510–44.

23. Ibid., 330, 334.

24. *See generally* Robert L. Hayman & Nancy Levit, "The Constitutional Ghetto," *Wisconsin Law Journal,* 628 (1993).

25. 60 U.S. (19 How.) 393 (1856).

26. John Sibley Butler. *Myrdal Revisited, Race Relations in a Changing World* (New York: Russell Sage Foundation Publications, 1996), Obie Clayton, ed.), 138.

27. Ibid., 160–61.

28. Ibid., 146–60, 164–65.

CHAPTER 6

BLACK THOUGHT LEADERS AND ENTREPRENEURS OF THE LATE 19TH AND EARLY 20TH CENTURIES

Rigid segregation produced a significant ideological split among black scholars. On one side of the fence, beginning in the 1880s, black leaders began urging the black population "to place increasing faith in business and property as a means of escaping poverty and achieving economic independence."[1] Black leaders urged this route as a means of black self-help through racial cooperation with the ultimate goal of economic emancipation rather than protesting segregation and pushing for changes in the laws. Black leaders of this era looked to business enterprise as the basis of black economic advancement. They exhorted the black masses to escape the wage-earning class and to become entrepreneurs in charge of their own fate. From 1898–1930, black enterprises grew in number from approximately 1,900 to 70,000. The driving force in this movement became the Negro Business League, formed in 1900. Booker T. Washington was the organization's first president.[2]

On the other side of the fence were such scholars as Harvard-educated W. E. B. Du Bois, who agreed with the notion of building businesses and economic independence as one of the keys to economic parity. However, these scholars also felt that real change would not occur without protest and actively seeking change in the laws. Let's meet some of these strong voices for change now.

Booker T. Washington

Booker T. Washington was a nine-year-old slave in Virginia when General Robert E. Lee surrendered to General Ulysses S. Grant at Appomattox in 1865. Washington enrolled at Hampton Institute in 1872 at the age of 16. He founded Tuskegee Institute, "which he built from the ground up" in 1881, at the age of 25.

In 1884, Washington, the 28-year-old president of Tuskegee, gave a speech to the National Education Association in Madison, Wisconsin. A year earlier in 1883, the U.S. Supreme Court had struck down the Civil Rights Act of 1875, which prohibited private individuals from discriminating against black persons in providing public accommodations such as theatres, hotels, places of public amusement, and other facilities. Washington told the audience at the NEA that it was unnecessary to press for a new civil rights bill to guarantee blacks civil rights, and such efforts should not be undertaken. Instead, Washington said that:

> . . . brains, property, and character for the Negro will settle the question of civil rights . . . good school teachers and plenty of money to pay them will

The Executive Committee of the National Negro Business League. Founder and President, Booker T. Washington is seated in the back row, fourth from left. From the Emory J. Tolbert Collection

be more potent in settling the race question than many civil rights bills and investigating committees.[3]

Washington's speech, eleven years later, at the opening of the Cotton States and International Exposition on September 18, 1895, is his most influential speech. The speech brought Washington national prominence for his position that blacks accept segregation for guarantees of economic progress. Washington's dazzling speech, a parable with extensive use of metaphors, is best summarized by the following:

> . . . in all things purely social blacks and whites can be as separate as the fingers . . . yet one as the hand in all things essential to mutual progress . . . the agitation of questions of social equality is folly and the economic and social equality must be the result of severe and constant struggle rather than of artificial forcing.[4]

Washington became the official spokesman for the black community for the next twelve years, dining with President Theodore Roosevelt and wielding considerable influence.

Positive Aspects of Booker T. Washington's Approach

Washington's approach assumed that whites would have little hostility to black business endeavors because black people would not be protesting for civil rights. Consequently, Washington believed that white people would be willing to contract with black businesses for certain services in which whites were not active. Washington envisioned a captured black market for black entrepreneurs in those types of occupations. He recognized that segregation made it difficult for blacks to venture out of their community with respect to a wide array of endeavors. However, Washington saw the possibility of black economic stability through business enterprises that would be able to cater to the needs of black Americans, and hopefully to the needs of whites.[5] Washington's ideas laid the foundation for economic nationalism, which predated the ethnic enclave theories of later sociologists. None of these sociologists, however, has recognized Washington's contribution.

Washington's motto, that one need not hunt for a job if one can perform some useful service, stressed the need for blacks to own their own businesses and to become economically self-sufficient. Therefore, Washington emphasized the need for blacks to obtain an industrial education to learn a variety of trades that could form the basis of a profitable business.

Washington's entire approach, however, was predicated on black entrepreneurs serving an integrated clientele.

Rigid Segregation Doomed Washington's Vision for Southern Blacks

The system of complete governmental segregation demolished Washington's goals for black economic stability in the South. The rigid system of segregation established in the South applied exclusively to African Americans; it was not applicable to Mexican Americans, Chinese Americans, Jewish Americans, Native Americans, or anyone else. Government-imposed segregation and the customs of white private businesses took away the opportunity for blacks to compete in a truly open market. The fundamental difference between black businesses and other ethnic businesses is that the government forced blacks to find clients within their own communities. The U.S. Department of Commerce acknowledged that the black business market was separate from the general economic market, which included all other groups.[6]

Unfortunate Aspects of Booker T. Washington's Approach

Washington acquiesced on issues of social equality. He did not believe blacks should focus on protesting for civil rights possessed by other Americans. Critics of Washington suggest that his philosophy paved the way for the Supreme Court's decision in *Plessy v. Ferguson*. They also suggest that Washington's passive philosophy may have been responsible for the increased violence against blacks in the 1890s. Lerone Bennett, Jr., in *Before the Mayflower*, wrote:

> Down went the buckets and they came up filled with brine. Economic discrimination continued. Caste lines hardened. Separate became more separate and less equal, and lynchings reached new and staggering heights. Washington was not responsible for these developments. But his "submissive philosophy," C. Vann Woodward said, "must have appeared to some whites as an invitation to further aggression."[7]

Washington's Vision: The Black Wall Street of the Late 1800s to Early 1900s

The Black Wall Street was originally known as the Negro's Wall Street. It is a term reportedly coined by Booker T. Washington, to describe the segregated black business district of Durham, North

Carolina. As early as 1910, Booker T. Washington and W. E. B. Du Bois both visited Durham and hailed it as a national model for the black middle class. A similar Black Wall Street existed on the south end of Greenwood Avenue in Tulsa, Oklahoma, during the early 1900s.

These two areas—Durham, North Carolina, and Tulsa, Oklahoma—prospered in part because segregation laws in effect at the time did not allow blacks to spend their money in white areas. However, blacks could earn money from selling to whites, in some circumstances in the white parts of town.[8] As mentioned earlier in Chapter 4, some commentators estimate that the dollar circulated 36 to 1000 times, sometimes taking a year for the currency to leave the black community. These entrepreneurial enclaves benefited from those who saved and used their black dollars to do business inside the district.

Durham, North Carolina

Black entrepreneurs had fully developed the central business section of Durham, known as Hayti, by the turn of the century. By 1910, Hayti was taking on the appearance of a well-established business section, and Durham's black entrepreneurs had replaced simple frame buildings with attached brick buildings. Fayetteville Street in Durham was home to numerous black businesses. The St. Joseph's AME Church stood as a landmark for this area of bustling black enterprise. By the late 1940s, more than 150 businesses flourished in Durham.[9] These businesses included traditional service industries such as cafes, movie houses, barber shops, boarding houses, pressing shops, grocery stores, and funeral parlors.

Parrish Street, which people referred to as the Negro Wall Street, was lined with black businesses. It was located away from the central district of Hayti. It was distinctive because of the presence of large, successful businesses. The North Carolina Mutual Insurance Company, one of the largest and most successful black enterprises, stood at the center of Parrish Street. Other businesses of note formed a circle around North Carolina Mutual. These other businesses included the Bankers Fire Insurance Company, the Mutual Building and Loan Association, the Union Insurance and Realty Company, the Dunbar Realty and Insurance Company, the Southern Fidelity Mutual Insurance Company, the Home Modernization and Supply Company, the People's Building and Loan Association, the Royal Knights Savings and Loan Association, T.P. Parham and Associates (a brokerage corporation), and the Mortgage Company of Durham. Additionally, the Mechanics and

Farmers Bank, the most stable and financially sound black bank, was located in Durham.

In Durham, the most successful service and retail businesses were able to maintain a white clientele and/or support from the white community. Well-known examples of this phenomenon include Smith's Fish Market, Rowland and Mitchell Tailor shop, the Durham Textile Mill, Payton A. Smith General Contracting Co., R.B. Fitzgerald's brick manufacturing business, R.E. Clegg's brick manufacturing business, and the Mechanics and Farmers Bank of Durham. The Mechanics and Farmers Bank had a tremendous effect on Durham's black community. Its founders established it in 1907 and it began operations in August 1908. The bank encouraged thrift, the building of homes, and the importance of educational achievement as reasons for borrowing. It had the distinction of being the only black bank in the nation to operate a branch office (which was located in Raleigh). The Mechanics and Farmers Bank was the principal reason why all, if not most, of the black businesses in Durham survived the Great Depression—a feat that the great majority of American small businesses were unable to duplicate.[10]

The most celebrated business in Durham was the North Carolina Mutual Life Insurance Company. The enterprise had its beginnings in October 1898 and began operating in earnest by July 1, 1900. The company was originally called the North Carolina Mutual and Provident Association but changed its name in 1910. By 1939, the company had the distinction of being the largest black insurance company in the world. It had about 1,000 employees serving more than a quarter million policyholders. It was the original landlord of the Mechanics and Farmers Bank and had close financial ties to the bank.[11]

During the 1960s, an urban renewal project brought an expressway through the center of Hayti, the heart of Durham's black business enclave. This project destroyed a major section of the Hayti business district consisting of over 100 black enterprises and 600 homes that had been developing for over 50 years in Durham. However, black entrepreneurs and professionals in Durham are still held together by the Durham Business and Professional Chain, an organization founded 68 years ago. And the two major institutions that were the key to the success of the former years—the North Carolina Mutual Life Insurance Company and the Mechanics and Farmers Bank—continue to thrive. The Mechanics and Farmers Bank ranked 11th in the 2007 Black Enterprise top 25 Commercial Banks and/or Savings and Loan Companies with assets of $222.234 million. As of 2008, the bank's assets had risen to better than

$274 million.[12] North Carolina Mutual Life Insurance Company is one of four major black insurers remaining today.[13]

Tulsa, Oklahoma

Tulsa, Oklahoma, was similar to Durham in many respects. Before the riots struck in 1921, the black community in Tulsa, Oklahoma, was a beacon of economic prosperity. The Greenwood district in Tulsa, also known as "Black Wall Street," encompassed numerous black businesses and residences.

The economic prosperity of the Greenwood district can be attributed to the success of the city of Tulsa as a whole. The discovery of oil in the Tulsa area caused Tulsa's population to swell in the early 20th century. The flock to Tulsa rivaled that of the gold rush in the San Francisco area. The population of Tulsa quadrupled from 18,000 to 72,000 from 1910–1920.[14]

Many black Americans also found the economic boom in Tulsa attractive. Blacks comprised 10 percent of the population of Tulsa in 1910. In 1921, Tulsa's black population was 11,000. Many blacks were looking to escape the harsh realities of the post-war South. Some had migrated to Oklahoma as a result of boosters. The persons referred to as boosters were individuals who went across the country marketing Oklahoma to African Americans.[15]

Several African Americans could trace their roots in Oklahoma to a time before the oil rush at the turn of the century. Some had arrived as slaves of the Native Americans who had gone over the "Trail of Tears." The government allotted 40 to 100 acres of land to most of these African Americans after the 13th Amendment abolished slavery. There were numerous treaties between the U.S. government and Native Americans that required Native Americans to allot land to these newly freed blacks.[16]

Like most places in America at the turn of the century, Oklahoma was beset with racial hatred, tension, and animosity. Despite the racist climate, many African Americans in Tulsa were very prosperous. This prosperity was a result of segregation, which forced the isolated African American economy to build upon itself.

African American businesses congregated in one community. This prosperous business community began at the intersection of Greenwood Avenue and Archer Street. Greenwood Avenue became known as "Black Wall Street." It was not uncommon to have black sellers doing business with black buyers on Black Wall Street. This exercise in "buying black" was a necessity due to segregation. Existing laws did not allow blacks to shop or own businesses in the white communities. Therefore, African Americans began to rely on one another in the Greenwood district. Significantly, however, they were able to sell their products to both the black and white communities. The success of the Greenwood district resulted in the establishment of "rooming houses, restaurants, billiard halls, hotels, smoke shops, shoemakers, barbers, hairdressers, shoe shiners, tailors, contractors, doctors, lawyers, dentists, and other professional and business establishments."[17]

In 1905, blacks established a grocery store as the first business in the area. A real estate magnate, physician, and dentist soon followed. Additionally, in 1905, enterprising blacks opened the first school for African Americans in the Greenwood District. In 1907, two black physicians, a newspaper, three grocers, and several other African American businesses opened in the Greenwood district. In 1914 the first African American theatre in Tulsa opened its doors. By the time of the riots in 1921, the community included two schools, a hospital, two newspapers, two theatres, a public library, 23 churches, and three fraternal lodges. Between 1907 and 1921, the number of grocers and meat markets increased from three to 41; restaurants from one to 30; physicians and surgeons from two to 15; shoemakers and shoe repair persons from two to four. The number of skilled craft persons remained small over that time period. Additionally, service workers such as barbers and hairdressers showed small increases during this time period.[18]

As the city of Tulsa, Oklahoma, developed, black Americans engaged in entrepreneurial endeavors to achieve economic security. The Greenwood District was the hub of the social and business life of the community. As the middle class developed, they constructed homes, churches, and other community centers. However, the politics of race, gender, and economics set the spark that saw all of their dreams vanish in clouds of smoke.

The Tulsa Riot: The End of Black Wall Street

In 1921, the prosperity of the Greenwood district came to an end. The horrific end of Black Wall Street was laid out in *Tulsa Race Riot: A Report by the Oklahoma Commission to Study the Tulsa Race Riot of 1921*.[19] Tensions between African Americans and whites began to increase. Many blacks had returned home from World War I and were starting to assert themselves as Americans on equal footing with whites. Those veterans and other blacks began to disregard the Jim Crow status quo. Also adding to the tension was the increase in white worker layoffs because of declining crude oil prices.

On Monday, May 30, 1921, a white person accused an African American man of attempted assault and attempted rape of a white woman. It is not known whether the attack actually occurred. The authorities arrested the black man the next day in the Greenwood district. The officers held the black suspect at the Tulsa County Courthouse.

As the story hit the newspapers on May 31, 1921, whites began talk of lynching the prisoner. Thereafter, many whites gathered at the court-house after they got off work. Eyewitnesses estimated the crowd to have reached into the hundreds by sunset (7:34 p.m. on May 31, 1921). The "would-be lynch mob" refused to leave when asked to do so by the sheriff.

In the Greenwood district, African Americans were adamant about preventing a lynching. Approximately 25 armed African American men drove to the courthouse to offer help to the sheriff in protecting the pris-oner. The sheriff rebuffed the men's offer, and told them to go home. The black men complied with the sheriff's request. However, many whites were surprised by the effort of the African American men, and went home to get their guns.

By 9:30 p.m., eyewitnesses estimated the crowd outside the courthouse to be at 2000. Around 10:00 p.m., 75 armed African American men went to the courthouse to offer their services. Again, the authorities turned them away.

As the men were leaving for the second time, an African American World War I veteran refused to give his pistol to a white man who insisted that the veteran relinquish his weapon. A struggle over the weapon ensued and the weapon discharged. The African American men began to exchange shots with the white mob. The black men then retreated back to Greenwood because they were outnumbered 20 to 1. This exchange resulted in the death or wounding of as many as a dozen persons, both black and white.

Many whites thought they were witnessing a negro uprising. Some whites began to look to kill any black person on the street. The police department commissioned "Special Deputies," many of whom were part of the would-be lynch mob that would eventually go out and kill black people. Sporadic gunfights took place throughout the night as whites drove into the black district firing shots. Whites also began burning black homes and businesses.

Around 3:00 a.m. a large crowd of whites gathered to announce that they would invade the Greenwood district at daybreak. An estimated 5,000–10,000 whites gathered at the border of Greenwood by dawn. Reports state that an unusual whistle or siren sounded when dawn arrived at 5:08 a.m. At that moment, the mob crossed the railroad tracks separating the black and white areas.

African Americans had only three options: (1) be interned by the police and national guard, (2) flee, or (3) fight. Whites killed many of those who chose to flee as they attempted to escape. The report vividly described the scene:

> As the waves of white rioters descended upon the African American district, a deadly pattern soon emerged. First, the armed whites broke into the black homes and businesses, forcing the occupants out into the street, where they were led away at gunpoint to one of a growing number of internment centers. Anyone who resisted was shot. Moreover, African American men in homes where firearms were discovered met the same fate. Next, the whites looted the homes and businesses, pocketing small items, and hauling away larger items either on foot or by car or truck. Finally, the white rioters then set the homes and other buildings on fire, using torches and oil-soaked rags. House by house, block by block, the wall of flame crept northward, engulfing the city's black neighborhoods.[20]

Government officials declared martial law at 11:29 a.m. The riot had finally run its course. The rioters had burned Greenwood to ashes. They had destroyed almost every home, church, and business. Virtually the entire black community was homeless. Six days after the riot, the city commission passed an ordinance that prevented rebuilding in the Greenwood district. The courts later declared the ordinance unconstitutional. But the ordinance had already done great damage to the black community because many black Tulsans, relying on the validity of the ordinance, had to spend the winter in tents.

In 2001, the Oklahoma legislature codified the findings of the 1921 Tulsa Race Riot Commission. The Commission found that the root causes of the riot were Jim Crow laws, acts of racial violence, and "other actions that had the effect of 'putting African Americans in Oklahoma in their place.'" The Commission further found that there was no "negro-uprising." Also, the Commission found that local officials failed to calm the violence, and in some cases participated in it. The Commission went on to find that the rioters had killed 100–300 persons and destroyed 1256 homes, and every school, church, and business.[21]

W. E. B. Du Bois

William Edward Burghardt Du Bois was born in 1868 and died in 1963. Fisk University awarded Du Bois a degree in 1888. He subsequently graduated with a bachelor's degree from Harvard University in

Dr. W. E. B. Du Bois, Editor of *The Crisis*. From the Emory J. Tolbert Collection

1890 with honors (*cum laude*). In 1895, Du Bois became the first black person to earn a doctorate at Harvard University.

Du Bois was a sociologist by training. He was drawn into the political arena for two major reasons. The first was his antipathy toward racism. The second was his opposition to Booker T. Washington's approach, which encouraged blacks not to protest for social equality and civil rights in the hope that white people would be more inclined to utilize black businesses.[22]

Du Bois urged blacks to protest for civil rights without regard to race. He also encouraged the most intellectually talented blacks to seek a broad liberal arts education that would prepare them to obtain positions of leadership within the American economy. Thus, Du Bois encouraged gifted black students to look beyond Washington's focus on industrial education and labor-intensive industrial occupations. Du Bois was one of the founders of the Niagara Movement and the subsequent NAACP in 1909. He was the editor of the NAACP's journal, *The Crisis*, for the next 25 years.[23]

Du Bois was a prolific writer. He wrote over 4,000 articles and essays, 22 books, five novels, and helped establish four journals. Among his most significant works are *The Philadelphia Negro* (1899), *The Souls of Black Folk* (1903), *John Brown* (1909), *Black Reconstruction* (1935), and *Black Folk, Then and Now* (1939). Du Bois wrote many of his most important works in the early 1900s when prominent white scholars denied the relevance of black people's contributions to American history and civic life. In his epic work, *Black Reconstruction*, Du Bois documented how black people were central figures in the American Civil War and Reconstruction, and why the country turned its back on human rights for black people in the aftermath of Reconstruction. In *The Souls of Black Folks*, Du Bois introduced the concept of a "double-consciousness" among black persons in America and predicted that racism would be the greatest problem in the 20th century.[24]

Also noteworthy among Du Bois' prolific writing is his criminology thesis. Du Bois' thesis noted, among other things, that black crime would decrease as black people moved toward equality; and that a talented tenth, i.e., a group of "exceptional men" of the black race, would be the persons who would lead the black race and save it from its criminal problems.[25]

Du Bois' research indicated that northern black businesses in the services industry, established as early as the 1700s in places like Philadelphia, were being replaced by businesses run by immigrants arriving during the great wave of European immigration. Du Bois noted that the arrival of immigrant groups invaded the black strongholds in these businesses. These black businesses in the North became as vulnerable as those in the South because of the shrinkage of the market to the black community. The development of legal segregation in the South and new racial patterns in the North set the pattern of racial interaction for the next 100 years.[26]

Other Prominent Black Thought Leaders

Richard Allen

Richard Allen was born into slavery in 1760, purchased his freedom while in his twenties, and settled in Pennsylvania. He converted to Methodism and began preaching while serving as a wagon driver during the Revolutionary War. In 1787, Richard Allen (along with Absalom Jones) left the Methodist church after experiencing discrimination and formed the first civil rights organization in America, the Free African Society. In 1787, Richard Allen founded the Bethel Church in Philadelphia, the first African American church in the North.[27]

In 1795, Allen abandoned the Methodist Church for the Episcopal Church and established the African Methodist Episcopal Church (A.M.E.). He articulated a vision of Christianity in which the church took an active role in providing for the needs of the poor and oppressed. In 1830, he helped organize the American Society of Free Persons of Color and became the organization's first president. Allen opposed the idea that black people in America should seek to return to their ancestral land. Instead, he maintained that black people should remain in the United States and fight for justice in a nation for which they had done so much. He died in 1831.[28]

Martin Delany

Martin Delaney was born in 1812 in Virginia and died in 1885. His mother, a free woman, took him from Virginia to Pittsburg to receive a proper education. He became an anti-slavery activist in Pittsburg and co-edited the North Star with Frederick Douglass. He was also an author, lecturer, newspaper editor, trade agent, and government official.

Delaney's 1852 book, titled *The Condition, Elevation, Emigration, and Destiny of Colored People of the United States*, called for black separatism in view of his lost faith in the effectiveness of white abolitionists. He also advocated for resettling American blacks in Central and South America, and in Africa. While in Africa, he obtained permission from African leaders to found a colony in Abeokuta, in present day Nigeria.

In 1863, he returned to the United States and played an important role in recruiting black troops for the Union Army during the Civil War. After the war, Delaney was an important official in the Freedmen's Bureau and later worked in a variety of occupations.[29]

Frederick Douglass

Frederick Douglass was born into slavery in Maryland in 1817. He died in 1885. In 1838, Douglass escaped to New Bedford, Massachusetts, where he worked as a laborer. Some time thereafter, The Massachusetts Anti-Slavery Society became aware of Douglass' oratorical skills and retained his services as a lecturer throughout the North. His 1845 autobiography, *Narrative of the Life of Frederick Douglass, an American Slave*, became a best-seller.

Frederick Douglass. From the Emory J. Tolbert Collection

In 1847, Douglass founded the *North Star,* an anti-slavery newsletter that American blacks largely sustained. In 1855, Douglass published his second autobiography titled *My Bondage and My Freedom.*

Douglass also advocated freedom for women and reform of working conditions in addition to pressing for freedom for blacks. He played a leading role in convincing President Lincoln to recruit blacks into the Union army. Douglass edited a newspaper called the *New National Era* during the Reconstruction era (1867–1877) following the Civil War. He also continued to fight for social justice by urging such measures as voting rights for the recently freed slaves.

In 1872, Douglass moved to Washington, D.C. and held a number of government positions. In 1881, Douglass published the final volume of his memoirs, titled *Life and Times of Frederick Douglass.*[30]

Marcus Garvey

Marcus Garvey was born in Jamaica in 1887 and died in England in 1940. Garvey's economic vision involved development of commercial exchange between African peoples of Africa and the Americas. In 1914,

Garvey founded the Universal Negro Improvement Association (UNIA) with the goal of promoting unity among people of African descent. UNIA "may have been the largest global African political organization in history." UNIA advocated a pan-African, nationalistic, anti-colonialist view. In 1920, at its first convention, UNIA issued a document called the "Declaration of Rights of the Negro Peoples of the World" to protest white oppression of black people. The declaration demanded basic civil rights, political and judicial equality, racial self-determination, and a free Africa under black African government.[31]

In 1916, Garvey brought his message to the United States. He incorporated UNIA in 1918. By 1919, Garvey had established 30 chapters in the United States and 1000 throughout the world. During this time, UNIA had approximately 2 million members throughout the world. Garvey proposed a back-to-Africa movement in which African Americans would be resettled in Liberia. UNIA purchased three ships and created the Black Star Line. Additionally, Garvey intended for the Black Star Line to be the basis for economic development and commercial exchange between African peoples of Africa and the Americas. The Black Star Line collapsed when funds from subscribers vanished. Some cast the blame for the losses on Garvey; however, many believed that his accusers had framed him. The government convicted Garvey of mail fraud in 1925 and imprisoned him for two years.[32]

Garvey returned to Jamaica after his imprisonment as a national hero. He concentrated on projects to benefit poor youths. He moved to England in 1935 and continued to advocate Pan-African ideas until his death in 1940. Important leaders of the African independence movement have relied on the writings of Garvey as the basis of their efforts in achieving independence from European colonial powers. Those leaders include Jomo Kenyatta of Kenya, Kwame Nkrumah of Ghana, and Dr. Nnamdi Azikiwe of Nigeria.[33]

Notable Black Entrepreneurs

It is unfortunate that the stories of preeminent black achievers are unknown to most Americans of any race. Everyone should know the story of the accomplishments of these black entrepreneurs who achieved so much in the face of great adversity. The following are a few examples of black entrepreneurs who emerged during the late 19th and early 20th centuries.

A. G. Gaston: Black Enterprise Magazine's Entrepreneur of the Century

Arthur George Gaston, the grandson of former slaves, was born in rural Alabama in 1892. He began demonstrating entrepreneurial skills in his youth. Neighborhood children were known to pay him in various ways—usually buttons or pins—to ride the swing in his grandparents' yard. Booker T. Washington's exhortations that black persons should strive for economic self-determination had a profound influence on Gaston, who named several of his businesses after Washington.[34]

Mr. Gaston started his business career in 1923, eight years after the death of Booker T. Washington. It was in that year that he established a burial service in Alabama to guarantee blacks in Alabama a decent funeral.[35] In 1932, Gaston launched Booker T. Washington Insurance Company (BTW Insurance). He recognized an opportunity to serve the black community because white insurance companies ignored the needs of blacks during this era in American history. The bitter legacy of slavery, government approved racial segregation, and overt racism was the standard of the day. Booker T. Washington Insurance Co. became the foundation of a fortune of about $130 million and a business empire that included communications, real estate, and insurance.[36]

In 1957, Gaston started Citizens Federal Savings Bank. The bank consistently remained on *Black Enterprise* Magazine's list of top black-owned banks until Atlanta-based Citizen's Trust acquired it in 2002. Black Enterprise Magazine, in 2005, ranked Booker T. Washington Insurance Company, with $56.2 million in assets, among the top five in its annual rankings of the top BE Insurance Companies. Gaston's other enterprises include BTW Business College, Smith & Gaston Funeral Directors, Inc., Vulcan Realty & Investment Co., Inc., and BTW Broadcasting Service.

In 1992—the year of his 100th birthday—*Black Enterprise* named Gaston Entrepreneur of the Century in recognition of his success. He expanded his business holdings through the 1980s. When he died in 1996 at the age of 104, the media reported that Gaston was the wealthiest black man in America. However, his legacy goes beyond the accumulation of riches. "As an activist, he helped to finance Alabama's civil rights movement" although "risking his relationship with white businessmen whose respect he had gained. When blacks in Tuskegee staged an economic boycott in 1957 to obtain voting rights, white banks hassled anyone who possessed unpaid mortgages or business loans. Gaston supported the boycott by vowing to advance mortgage money to protesters."[37]

Gaston was also a man of foresight. He made sure that there would be an orderly succession plan for the ownership of his most valuable business assets. Accordingly, in 1987, he created an employee stock ownership plan and sold all of his BTW Insurance stock worth $34 million to his employees for $3.5 million.[38]

Madame C. J. Walker

Madame C. J. Walker was born Sarah Breedlove, a free woman in Louisiana in 1867 and orphaned at age seven. She was married by the time she was 14 and widowed seven years later, left with a two-year-old child to support and raise on her own. She moved to St. Louis, went to a public night school, and worked as a washerwoman to support herself and her daughter.

The phrase "necessity is the mother of invention" most certainly applied to Breedlove. Because of a scalp condition, she was losing her hair, so she started mixing up her own shampoos and creams to solve the problem. They worked, and as she shared them with friends, they became more and more popular. She eventually began selling them to other black women.

She became Madame C. J. Walker when she married Charles Walker, whom she met after moving to Denver, Colorado. He encouraged her to open a beauty school, and to promote her products more widely. She did just that, and more. She expanded her product line to include cosmetics and invented a hair straightening device much like today's hot comb. She developed the Walker System of beauty and hair care based on her philosophy of "cleanliness and loveliness," and trained other women as Walker agents to promote and sell the products. She also expanded the Walker schools. All of these endeavors not only provided quality products designed for the black woman's needs, but provided thousands of jobs and opportunities for black women all over the country.

Walker was not only one of the first black woman entrepreneurs, she also became the first woman of *any* race to become a millionaire through entrepreneurial efforts. When she died in 1919, she left part of her estate to her daughter, but left the bulk of it to charities and causes she had supported over the years.

Portrait of An Entrepreneur: Maggie Lena Walker

Maggie Lena Walker, in 1903, became the first female to charter a bank and the first female bank president in the United States. The bank survived the great depression and exists to this day, although it has changed its name as a result of a merger. The bank's mission today, according to its Web site, remains the same as Maggie's—to help further the development and prosperity of the black community.[39] Maggie Walker was born Maggie Mitchell in Richmond, Virginia, in 1867 and died in 1934. Maggie's mother had to rear Maggie and her brother alone after her father's untimely death. Elizabeth Mitchell, Maggie's mother, worked as a laundress to support them, and Maggie helped by delivering clean clothes. Maggie attended the Richmond Public School System, taught for three years after graduation, and married Armestead Walker Jr. in 1886.[40]

At age 14, Maggie joined the local council of the Independent Order of St. Luke in Richmond, Virginia. This was a fraternal burial society established in Baltimore in 1867 to administer to the sick and aged, promote humanitarian causes, and encourage individual self-help and integrity. Maggie served in various ways for the order. By 1899, she had ascended to the top leadership position of the order, called the Right Worthy Grand Secretary. She held this position from 1899 until her death in 1934.

Between 1890, when Mrs. Walker first assumed the top leadership position, and 1924, the organization's funds increased from $31.00 to $3.5 million. Mrs. Walker took over leadership of a dying organization, revived it, and helped it flourish through sound policies, good public relations, and tireless work. In 1902, she established a newspaper, the *St. Luke Herald*, to improve communication between the Order and the public.

Mrs. Walker in speeches and written commentaries stressed the need for the black community to pool its money, lend that money to credit-worthy applicants for interest, and reap the collective benefits for the black community. In 1903, she founded the Saint Luke Penny Savings Bank and served as the bank's first president. Thus, Mrs. Walker became the first woman in the United States to charter a bank and to serve as a bank president. By 1920, the bank had financed 645 black-owned homes. Mrs. Walker's management was so effective that the Penny Savings Bank survived the depression. She later served as the chairman of the board of directors when the bank merged with two other Richmond Banks to become The Consolidated Bank and Trust Company. The bank is still in business, the oldest continually African American-operated bank in the country. The bank's Web site, in recognition of its heritage, proudly states that: "Our Mission remains Maggie's; to further develop and prosper the people and communities this Bank was founded to serve for this century and beyond."[41]

This is only the tip of an every-growing iceberg of dedicated individuals determined to succeed in spite of what would seem to be insurmountable odds. As we will see in upcoming chapters, that iceberg of excellence rapidly expanded as a result of the civil rights movement from the 1950s to the 1970s.

Notes

1. Abram L. Harris. *The Negro As Capitalist* (Chicago: Urban Research Press, Inc., 1992, originally published in 1936 by the American Academy of Political Science), 61.

2. Ibid., 66.

3. Lerone Bennett, Jr. *Before The Mayflower* (New York: Penguin Books, 6th Rev.Ed., 1993), 263.

4. Ibid., 265.

5. John Sibley Butler. *Entrepreneurship and Self-Help Among Black Americans: A Reconsideration of Race and Economics: A Reconsideration of Race and Economics* (New York: State University of New York Press, 1991), 64, 66–67.

6. Ibid., 72–73.

7. Lerone Bennett, Jr. *Before The Mayflower* (New York: Penguin Books, 6th Rev.Ed., 1993), 267.

8. John Sibley Butler. *Entrepreneurship and Self-Help Among Black Americans: A Reconsideration of Race and Economics: A Reconsideration of Race and Economics* (New York: State University of New York Press, 1991), 180; *see also* "The Black Wall Street," Wikipedia, http://en.wikipedia.org/wiki/TheBlackWall_Street at p.1, (3-27-07).

9. Thomas Houck, A Newspaper History of Race Relations in Durham, North Carolina: 1910–1940 (Masters' Thesis: Duke University, 1941).

10. John Sibley Butler. *Entrepreneurship and Self-Help Among Black Americans: A Reconsideration of Race and Economics,* (New York: State University Press, 1991), 180–84.

11. Ibid., 182, 184, 188–89.

12. "B.E. 100s: Report on the Nation's Largest Black-Owned Banks," *Black Enterprise* (June 2008): 174.

13. "B.E. 100s Flashback," *Black Enterprise* (June 2007): 176

14. Hannibal B. Johnson, *Black Wall Street—From Riot to Renaissance in Tulsa's Historic Greenwood District* (Austin, TX: Eakin Press, 1998), 1.

15. Ibid., 2, 4–5, 25.

16. Ibid., 2–3.

17. Ibid., 9–10.

18. Ibid., 11, 13–14, 25.

19. Tulsa Race Riot: A Report by the Oklahoma Commission to Study the Tulsa Race Riot of 1921, 1921, 45, 48–49, 57–66, 71–74, 84–89. Available at: http://www.ok-history.mus.ok.us/trrc/freport.htm.

20. Ibid., 74.

21. 24 Okl.St.Ann. § 8000.1, 1(1), 1(3), 1(2), 1(3).

22. John Sibley Butler. *Entrepreneurship and Self-Help Among Black Americans: A Reconsideration of Race and Economics: A Reconsideration of Race and Economics* (New York: State University of New York Press, 1991), 66–67.

23. *African American Desk Reference* (New York: Stonesong Press and New York Public Library, Philip Koslow ed., 1999), 81.

24. Ibid., 339 and and W. E. B. Du Bois, http://en.widipedia.org/wiki/W.E.B._Du_Bois, 2–3, 6.

25. W. E. B. Du Bois, http://en.wikipedia.org/wiki/W.E.B._Du_Bois, 3.

26. John Sibley Butler. *Entrepreneurship and Self-Help Among Black Americans: A Reconsideration of Race and Economics*, (New York: State University of New York Press, 1991), 69–70.

27. *The African American Desk Reference* (New York: Stonesong Press and New York Public Library, Philip Koslow, ed., 1991), 5, 51–52, 368–71.

28. *The African American Desk Reference* (New York: Stonesong Press and New York Public Library, Philip Koslow, ed., 1991), 44, 51–52.

29. Ibid., 53, 62, 63, 268.

30. Ibid., 53.

31. Ibid., 69, 70, 82.

32. Ibid.

33. Ibid., 70.

34. James C. Johnson, "A. G. Gaston: Rough Road To Riches," *Black Enterprise*, (August 2005):26.

35. Black Entrepreneur's Hall of Fame, http://blackentrepreneurshiphalloffame.blogspot.com/, citing Andrew Bernstein, "Black Innovators and Entrepreneurs Under Capitalism" (July 29, 2006): 2. The Black Entrepreneur's Hall of Fame, as of July 30, 2008, can only be accessed through www.blackentrepreneurship.com

36. James C. Johnson, "A. G. Gaston: Rough Road To Riches," *Black Enterprise*, (August 2005), 26.

37. Ibid.

38. Ibid.

39. Consolidated Bank and Trust Co., http://www.consolidatedbank.com/about.html, October 6, 2007

40. *See* Black Entrepreneur's Hall of Fame, http://blackentrepreneurshiphalloffame.blogspot.com/, 111–13 (July 29, 2006); *see also* at 106–08. The Black Entrepreneur's Hall of Fame, as of July 30, 2008, can only be accessed through www.blackentrepreneurship.com. For additional resources, see *African American Desk Reference*, 268.

41. Consolidated Bank and Trust Co., http://www.consloidatedbank.com/about.html, October 6, 2007.

CHAPTER 7

THE CIVIL RIGHTS ERA AND THE END OF AMERICAN APARTHEID: THE 1950S TO THE PRESENT

The modern civil rights movement began after World War II. Blacks who had served in the military and had come home from the battlefield were no longer willing to tolerate discrimination in a country they had fought for and died to defend. The movement began its major phase after the Supreme Court's decision in *Brown v. Board of Education*,[1] which ended the legal apartheid permitted by *Plessy v. Ferguson*.[2] The *Brown* decision rejected the "separate but equal" doctrine of *Plessy* insofar as public education was concerned. Although the *Brown* decision applied only to public schools, the Court extended its rejection of the separate but equal doctrine to many other public facilities and privileges during the following 13 years. Some of the major events of this era include the Montgomery Bus Boycott (1955–1956), formation of the Southern Christian Leadership Conference (1957), the Student Nonviolent Coordinating Committee (1960), the Freedom Rides (1961), the March on Washington (1963), and Freedom Summer (1964).

The *Brown* decision ended the era of legal, state-sanctioned apartheid permitted by the Court's decision in *Plessy*. Although the *Brown* decision ended the era of legal, state-sanctioned apartheid, it did not affect the right of private businesses and individuals to discriminate on the basis of race in employment, the provision of public accommodations, and other aspects of life. These private firms and individuals were able to continue their discriminatory practices without restriction until the July 2, 1965, effective date of the Civil Rights Act of 1964.

During the 1960s, the Supreme Court also gave surprisingly expansive rulings in interpreting several civil rights statutes enacted immediately after the Civil War and during the subsequent Reconstruction era. Prior to these decisions, the legal community assumed that these statutes, §§ 1981 and 1982 of the Civil Rights Act of 1866, and § 1985(3) of the Civil Rights Act of 1871, required "state action" in order to be violated. In several different cases, the Court ruled that private entities and individuals who were not employed by state or local governments could violate these civil rights statutes.[3] Additionally, the Court gave new life to another Reconstruction Era statute, §1983 of the Civil Rights Act of 1871, by overturning a long-standing assumption, based on the *Civil Rights Cases* that you read about in Chapter 4, that the statute only prohibited misconduct resulting from "state action" either officially authorized or so widely tolerated as to amount to a custom or usage under state law. In *Monroe v. Pape*,[4] the Supreme Court held that §1983 could be violated even by the unauthorized conduct of state officials.

Many of the civil rights groups of the modern era also had an economic focus. The major black civil rights organizations that pushed an economic agenda included the National Association for the Advancement of Colored People (NAACP), the National Urban League, the Southern Christian Leadership Conference, the Congress of Racial Equality (CORE), the Nation of Islam, and the Black Panther Party. These organizations recognized that the social and political gains of the 1960s would be incomplete without efforts to achieve economic liberty and equality for all black Americans.

Positive Action from the White House

President Lyndon Johnson issued Executive Order Number 11,246 in 1965. The Executive Order mandated that every nonexempt federal government contract contain provisions that impose dual obligations on contractors and subcontractors not to discriminate against employees or applicants because of race, color, religion, sex, or national origin; and to take affirmative action to ensure that applicants and employees are employed without regard to such factors.

The heart of the order is the requirement that an employer take affirmative action to recruit, hire, and promote women and minorities whenever those groups are "underutilized" in the employer's work force, regardless of whether the employer has discriminated against those individuals in the past. President Johnson delegated responsibility for administration of the order to the Secretary of Labor. The Secretary of Labor, in turn, established the Office of Federal Contract Compliance Programs (OFCCP) within the Department of Labor to enforce and administer the order. The standard contract clause requires that the contractor agree to comply with the provisions of the order and all OFCCP rules, regulations, and orders. The OFCCP may bring administrative enforcement proceedings to impose sanctions, including an order by the Secretary debarring a contractor from future government contracts.

Powerful New Federal Laws

Capitol Hill took significant action as well, passing three laws designed to turn back the devastation to black human rights wrought under Jim Crow and government-imposed segregation. They are the Civil Rights Act of 1964, the 1965 Voting Rights Act, and the Civil Rights Act of 1968.

The Civil Rights Act of 1964

The Civil Rights Act of 1964 is a complex and comprehensive piece of legislation that prohibits, among other things, race discrimination by private persons and entities in the provision of public accommodations, and discrimination on the basis of race, national origin, and religion in federally assisted programs. Title VII of the 1964 Civil Rights Act, as amended, prohibits employment discrimination on the basis of race, color, religion, sex, national origin, and pregnancy.[5]

1965 Voting Rights Act

Congress' efforts to eradicate racial discrimination in the South during the Reconstruction era did not meet with much success. Congress repealed most of these statutory provisions in 1894 instead of reenacting them in modified form to satisfy objections raised in the courts. By then, the former Confederate states had already begun the process of disenfranchising black Americans. The disenfranchisement movement began in the Southern states from 1888–1893.[6]

The Southern states relied on violence, fraud, or hastily enacted voting restrictions to exclude blacks from the vote. These states also enacted residency requirements, poll taxes, literacy tests, property tests, understanding and character clauses, and grandfather clauses as disenfranchisement tools to prevent black Americans from voting. For example, all of the former Confederate states enacted a poll tax by 1904.

Litigation under the Fifteenth Amendment was time-consuming and difficult. Moreover, even when courts ordered states or counties to eliminate a practice found discriminatory, they were able to devise some new scheme to perpetuate racial discrimination in voting. Congressionally enacted civil rights voting legislation passed in 1957, 1960, and 1964 proved ineffective. In January 1965, for example, Selma, Alabama, had allowed only two percent of voting-age blacks to register when Dr. Martin Luther King, Jr. initiated demonstrations in Selma in support of a voter registration drive. The city's vicious response, in which local whites killed two white civil rights activists from Massachusetts and Michigan, was well covered by the media and resulted in national and international shock and denunciation. President Johnson urged new voting legislation in an emotional speech to the nation on March 15, 1965. Five months later, in August 1965, President Johnson signed the Voting Rights Act of 1965 into law.

Congress' intent in enacting the 1965 Civil Rights Act was to eradicate racial discrimination in voting by suspending the practices utilized by Southern states to disenfranchise blacks for a period of five years. This approach made it unnecessary for litigants to challenge such practices on a case-by-case basis. The Supreme Court upheld Congress' power to enact the statute in *South Carolina v. Katzenbach*.[7] The Court relied on Congress' broad remedial powers to combat documented past and prospective violations of the Fifteenth Amendment pursuant to its power to enforce the amendment through appropriate legislation.

Civil Rights Act of 1968

Land is one of the scarce means of production toward the satisfaction of human wants. Ownership of land in capitalistic economies is perhaps the most significant source for building individual and corporate wealth. Accordingly, it was not surprising that the federal government attempted to first outlaw racial discrimination in housing and land ownership almost immediately after the end of the Civil War. To this end, the federal government enacted the Civil Rights Act of 1866, 42 U.S.C. § 1982. That statute provides that all citizens of the United States shall have the same right, in every state and territory, as is enjoyed by white citizens thereof to inherit, purchase, lease, sell, hold, and convey real and personal property.

It was not until the late 1960s, however, that the Supreme Court in *Jones v. Alfred H. Mayer Co.*[8] construed this provision to apply to the discriminatory conduct of private entities and individuals. Prior to that time, most people assumed that only governmental discrimination

against blacks in housing and property matters would constitute a violation of the statute. Although the *Alfred H. Mayer* case was a giant step
forward in vindicating the property rights of black people, the statute, as
construed by the courts, requires that the aggrieved party prove intentional discrimination on the part of the defendant, only covers racial discrimination, and requires that plaintiff bring a lawsuit in court against
the defendant to prevail in his or her case.

Title VIII of the Civil Rights Act of 1968, as amended, generally bans
discrimination on the basis of race, color, religion, national origin, sex,
handicap, or familial status in the sale or rental of housing. The act also
prohibits owners and realtors from engaging in discriminatory preferences among prospective customers, prohibits discrimination in the
financing of housing, prohibits discrimination in the provision of services
and facilities, and prohibits discrimination in advertising concerning
housing. It also provides a simple administrative process for injured
parties to initiate a proceeding against a defendant. And perhaps most
importantly, the plaintiff does not need to prove intentional discrimination against the defendant to make out a prima facie case of discrimination. Instead, a plaintiff need only show that the defendant's conduct has
a discriminatory effect. The Civil Rights Act of 1968, therefore,
expanded the rights of blacks to be free from discrimination in the acquisition and leasing of property. In doing so, the act substantially increased
the opportunity of blacks to economically advance in America's capitalistic economic system.

Government Efforts to Help Black Businesses: Contracting Set-Asides and Other Programs

During the Civil Rights era, several programs were put into place at
both the federal and state levels to boost black businesses in the wake of
the economic caste system legitimized by *Plessy*. Let's take a look at a few
of them.

Minority Contracting Set-Aside Programs

Federal minority contracting programs provide a major point of entry for
socially and economically disadvantaged businesses to enter the American
mainstream. Both federal and state governments created minority business
set-asides to encourage minority business ownership with the principal purpose of overcoming the continuing effects of past discrimination. There are
two basic types of set-asides: pure set-asides, which provide that a certain
percentage of the total number of government contracts be allotted to

minority businesses, and subcontractor goal set-asides, which require that a certain portion of a prime contractor's fee be spent with minority-owned businesses.[9]

In 1968, Congress enacted the Small Business Act, commonly known as the 8(a) program, which requires any prime contractor with a federal construction contract that exceeds $1 million to establish percentage goals for the utilization of both small businesses owned and controlled by socially and economically disadvantaged individuals. The act defined "socially disadvantaged individuals" as "those who have been subjected to racial or ethnic prejudice or cultural bias because of their identity as a member of a group without regard to their individual qualities."[10] The Small Business Act set a goal of awarding to such disadvantaged businesses "not less than [five percent] of the total value of all prime contract and subcontract awards for each fiscal year." The statute states that the five percent minimum applicable to all affected federal programs is a goal rather than a minimum.[11]

The Small Business Act requires federal contracts to state that "[t]he contractor shall presume that socially and economically disadvantaged individuals include Black Americans, Hispanic Americans, Native Americans, Asian Pacific Americans, other minorities, or any other individual found to be disadvantaged" by the Small Business Administration.[12] The Small Business Administration has adopted additional, similar regulations that contain similar presumptions to those of the Small Business Act. The statute's presumption of minority disadvantage is only a rebuttable presumption, however; persons not listed in the enumerated groups have the opportunity to prove that they are entitled to certification as disadvantaged. For example: Such groups as disabled Vietnam veterans, Appalachian white males, and Hasidic Jews may be eligible if they demonstrate they are socially and economically disadvantaged. Disappointed bidders can present evidence to rebut the presumption of disadvantage for particular individuals.

Government set-aside programs have now been in existence for over three decades. President Nixon issued Executive Order Number 11,458 in 1969, to establish the Minority Business Development Agency (MBDA) in the U.S. Department of Commerce to preserve and strengthen minority businesses. President Nixon issued a second Executive Order Number 11,625, to strengthen the MBDA.[13] The MBDA is the only federal agency formed specifically to promote the creation and expansion of minority businesses.

In 1977, Congress enacted the Public Works Employment Act (PWEA), the first federal statutory attempt to utilize expressed racial quotas in the administration of public works contracts. That Act provided that, absent an administrative waiver, at least 10 percent of the federal funds granted for local public works projects must be used by state or local grantees to procure services or supplies from "minority business enterprises." It defined a minority business enterprise (MBE) as a business of which (1) at least 50 percent is owned by minority group members, or (2) in the case of publicly owned corporations, at least 51 percent of the stock is owned by minority group members. The statute defined minority group members as United States citizens "who are Negroes, Spanish speaking, Orientals, Indians, Eskimos, and Aleuts."[14]

In *Fullilove v. Klutznick*[15] the U.S. Supreme Court upheld the use of federal set-asides for minorities contained in the Public Works Employment Act of 1977. Thereafter, set-aside programs proliferated nationwide to include some 36 states and 190 localities by the late 1980s.[16]

Set-asides have had a major impact on the status of minority-owned businesses. For example, by 1986, the federal government reported $4.4 billion in contracts to minority and disadvantaged businesses under the 8(a) program.[17]

Supreme Court Decisions: Positive and Detrimental

The Supreme Court handed down several decisions that had an impact on black enterprise, particularly the set-asides. Some advanced the cause. Others were seen as setbacks.

Fullilove v. Klutznick

In *Fullilove*, the Court had upheld a federal set-aside program against a challenge by white contractors who argued that the statute violated the Constitution's ban on governmentally sponsored race discrimination. The *Fullilove* Court, in upholding the federal set-aside under the Public Works Act of 1977, noted the broad congressional authority under the Commerce Clause to address discrimination against minorities in the federal procurement process. The *Fullilove* Court also pointed to Congress' special powers under §5 of the Fourteenth Amendment to legislatively prohibit state and local discrimination that violates the Fourteenth Amendment's due process and equal protection guarantees. Moreover, a majority of the justices in *Fullilove* expanded the circumstances when governmental bodies could permissibly use programs requiring racial preferences by adopting an intermediate level of judicial review in upholding the Public Works Act of 1977. Chief Justice Burger, also writing for Justice White on the particular issue, seemed to suggest that a congressional enactment establishing racial preferences would be upheld if it:

- was designed to remedy identified discrimination,
- was properly tailored to cure the effects of discrimination with minimal adverse effect on whites, and,
- was limited in time and flexible.

Three other justices, Justices Marshall, Brennan, and Blackmun, would uphold racial preferences that serve "an important and articulated purpose" if the means chosen to implement the preference are "substantially related to achievement" of that purpose. Only Justice Powell, in a concurring opinion, contended that the set-aside provision had to be judged by "the most stringent level of review," strict scrutiny, because the program utilized a racial classification. One dissenting Justice, Justice Stevens, did not believe that the Equal Protection Clause contained an absolute prohibition against any statutory classification based on race but demanded that Congress identify the characteristic that justifies a racial preference. Two dissenting justices, Justices Stewart and Rehnquist, concluded that racial preferences violated the Equal Protection Clause.[18]

In the wake of *Fullilove*, numerous state and lower federal courts interpreted the language of *Fullilove* as authority for state and local governments to also create minority set-aside programs. Consequently, state and local governments patterned set-aside programs after the Public Works Employment Act in an effort to benefit minority enterprises.[19]

Until the *Fullilove* decision, the Court had repeatedly stated that government classifications based on a "suspect" classification, such as race, or which impinge on some "fundamental right" must pass the strictest judicial scrutiny to survive analysis under either the Equal Protection Clause of the Fourteenth Amendment or the Equal Protection component of the Due Process Clause of the Fifth Amendment. In such cases, the Court held that states must show a compelling governmental interest that cannot be achieved through less restrictive means.

The Court used an intermediate level of scrutiny, however, for certain other classifications that required that a state merely establish that a challenged statute was "substantially related" to important governmental objectives. In most instances, however, the Court recognized that states could justify their unequal treatment of persons by simply establishing a rational relationship between the discriminatory state requirement and a legitimate state objective. Thus, the *Fullilove* Court seemed to arguably depart from its earlier precedents by holding that ostensibly benign or remedial race-based affirmative action plans developed by the U.S. Congress should be subjected to an intermediate judicial scrutiny and not the same strict scrutiny as would be applicable to governmental actions that intentionally discriminate against minorities.

City of Richmond v. J. A. Croson

The U.S. Supreme Court's decision in *City of Richmond v. J. A. Croson*[20] represented a dramatic turn of events. In *Croson*, the Supreme Court struck down the city of Richmond, Virginia's, Minority Business Utilization Plan under the Equal Protection Clause of the Fourteenth Amendment. The city's plan required prime contractors of city-funded construction contracts to subcontract at least 30 percent of the contract's dollar amount to minority business enterprises. A business had to be at least 51 percent owned by a minority group to be classified as a Minority Business Enterprise. The city plan's definition of "minority group members" included African Americans, Hispanics, Asians, Indians, Eskimos, and Aleuts. The Richmond city council had no evidence that the city itself had ever discriminated in the award of construction contracts. The city council did have evidence, however, that although Richmond was 50 percent black, the city had only awarded .67 percent of the city's prime contracts to minority business enterprises in the prior five years; and that most of the area's contractors' associations had no minority businesses within their membership. The council also had before it congressional reports containing strong evidence that there had been extensive, nationwide discrimination against African American construction enterprises.[21]

In *Croson*, the Court majority held that ostensibly benign or remedial race-based affirmative action plans developed by state and local governments should be subjected to the same strict scrutiny as are governmental actions that intentionally discriminate against minorities. The Court, in striking down the city's affirmative action plan, noted that the city had not identified itself as engaged in discriminatory behavior, nor had the city shown with specificity that anyone in the Richmond construction industry had discriminated against minority firms. Accordingly, the Court found that the city failed to establish that it had a compelling need to redress past discrimination in its government contract operations and had failed to demonstrate that its plan was narrowly tailored to address its remedial objectives. For example, the city did not show that it had considered race-neutral means (for example, city financing for small firms without regard to the race of their owners) or that it would not increase minority participation adequately. Similarly, the city did not establish that the 30 percent goal was narrowly tailored to any goal because there was no showing that qualified black firms could get 30 percent of the work in the absence of discrimination. Accordingly, the city's 30 percent quota was not a narrowly tailored way of redressing past discrimination even if the city had adequately proven that discrimination.[22]

The Court did not believe, however, that all race-conscious remedial plans would necessarily fail this strict scrutiny test. For example, the Court noted that an inference of discrimination might arise, even in the absence of direct proof, where there is a "significant statistical disparity between the number of qualified minority contractors willing and able to perform a particular service and the number of such contractors actually engaged by the locality or the locality's prime contractors."[23] The Court noted that governmental bodies may create narrowly tailored race-conscious affirmative action plans where there is clear evidence of discrimination by a governmental body, or perhaps private parties. The Court distinguished *Fullilove* on the grounds that Congress possessed special powers to remedy racial discrimination under §5 of the Fourteenth Amendment that state and local legislatures did not possess.[24]

After *Croson,* many jurisdictions utilized disparity studies as the route to justify the continued existence of set-aside plans. These efforts on the part of governmental jurisdictions partially explain why *Croson* did not significantly influence the level of municipal contracting with minority-owned and operated businesses. In 1994, for example, the MBDA reported that minority businesses received $14.6 billion or 8.3 percent of the total value of government contracts through prime and subcontracting procurement.[25]

Metro Broadcasting, Inc. v. FCC

In *Metro Broadcasting, Inc. v. FCC,*[26] the Court upheld, by a five-to-four vote, two federal policies of the Federal Communications Commission (FCC) that favored minority applicants for broadcast licenses. One plan gave a preference to minority-owned broadcasters in the awarding of FCC licenses, and the other plan provided certain tax advantages to marginal licensees who sold their stations to minority-owned broadcasters. The more important policy provided that the FCC would consider minority ownership as one positive factor among several in the application process. The FCC's goal was to enhance broadcast diversity by reducing the industry's 98 percent white ownership. The *Metro Broadcasting* majority applied an intermediate level of judicial review in judging whether race-conscious, but benign, action by Congress violated the Equal Protection rights of non-minorities. The Court, utilizing this standard, upheld the FCC policies as valid even though they were not designed to remedy past governmental discrimination. Accordingly, the FCC (and also Congress, which told the FCC what to do in general terms) only needed to establish that its chosen means were "substantially related" to the achievement of "important" governmental objectives.[27]

Adarand Constructors, Inc. v. Pena

In *Adarand*,[28] the Court overruled *Fullilove* and *Metro Broadcasting* to the extent that the *Adarand* Court held that congressionally authorized race-conscious affirmative action plans must be subject to strict scrutiny review. *Adarand* federalized *Croson* because the federal government must now satisfy the same strict scrutiny standard for race-based affirmative action as state and local governments. Accordingly, the federal government may only use race in a way that is narrowly tailored to achieve some compelling governmental objective. Moreover, the Court's decision was not limited to federal set-asides and contracting.[29]

A brief review of the facts and circumstances in *Adarand* is helpful in understanding the Court's reasoning. Plaintiff Adarand Constructors was a white-owned construction firm that had placed the lowest bid on a subcontract to supply guardrails to a federal highway project in Colorado. The general contractor, however, took a bid from a minority-owned firm that qualified under federal regulations as a disadvantaged business.

The Small Business Act requires that federal prime contracts state that the contractor shall presume that socially and economically disadvantaged individuals include Black Americans, Hispanic Americans, Native Americans, Asian Pacific Americans, and other minorities or any other individual found to be disadvantaged by the Small Business Administration. Small white-owned firms could also be disadvantaged enterprises under the statute, but a firm owned by an African American, Hispanic, or certain other minority groups (as well as a firm owned by a woman), were automatically, though rebuttably, presumed to be disadvantaged. A firm owned by a white male, by contrast, had to prove disadvantage by "clear and convincing evidence." The general contractor's contract did not require that it award the subcontract to a minority disadvantaged business enterprise. However, the contract provided that the general contractor would receive a financial bonus, the lesser of 10 percent of the amount of the subcontract or 1.5 percent of the general contract, if the general contractor chose the minority disadvantaged business enterprise, which it did.[30]

The Court found that the rebuttable presumption in the federal legislation, that racial minorities, but not whites, are presumed to be socially and economically disadvantaged, constituted a suspect racial classification under the Equal Protection component of the Fifth Amendment. The Court, however, did not decide whether the particular set-aside regulations could survive strict scrutiny. Instead, the court remanded the case to the lower courts.[31] Nevertheless, the continuing statistical disparities between whites and blacks in every area of social and economic life reveal the limitations inherent in the Court's decision.

The 8(a) Program and the Future of Set-Asides for Minority Business Enterprises

The U.S. Small Business Administration (SBA), in its Report to Congress on Minority Small Business and Capital Ownership Development for fiscal year 2001, indicated that the 8(a) Business Development Program made significant contributions to the federal, state, and local tax base and created an estimated 181,080 jobs in the nation's economy. The Report noted that, during fiscal year 2001, the 8(a) program assisted small businesses owned and controlled by socially and economically disadvantaged individuals in receiving $6.3 billion in new contract awards to active 8(a) program participants and 8(a) program graduates. Participants can remain in the 8(a) Program for a maximum of nine years. After that time, they "graduate" from the program. Accordingly, the program's benefit to the economy from the $6.3 billion in new contracts awarded to small, disadvantaged businesses and the creation of 181,080 new jobs dwarf the government's $24.5 million in total expenditures in operating the 8(a) Program. [32]

The U.S. government contracted with 8(a) firms for goods and services in 440 different areas of work in 2001. The government awarded the largest dollar amounts in contracts to businesses owned and controlled by socially and economically disadvantaged individuals in the following industries: (1) Commercial and Institutional Building Construction; (2) Facilities Support Services; (3) Engineering Services; (4) Computer System Design Services; (5) Other Computer Related Services; (6) Data Processing Services; (7) Research and Development in the Physical, Engineering, and Life Sciences; (8) All Other Heavy Construction; (9) Custom Computer-Programming Services; and (10) Security Guards and Patrol Services.[33]

There were 6,942 firms participating in the 8(a) program during fiscal year 2001. The ethnic heritage of the owners of these firms during fiscal year 2001 were as follows: "Black American: 2,766 (39.8 percent); Hispanic American: 1,709 (24.6 percent); Asian Pacific American: 868

(12.5 percent); Subcontinent Asian American: 690 (9.9 percent); Native American: 589 (8.5 percent); Native Hawaiian American: 45 (0.07 percent); Caucasian American: 185 (2.7 percent); and Other American: 90 (1.3 percent). Men own 74.5 percent of the firms and women own 25.5 percent of the firms."[34]

Additionally, the SBA, HUD, and other government agencies have a number of programs designed to help small firms and minority firms get their businesses underway or expand their efforts. Let's take a look at a few of them.

The SBA's Small Business Development Centers

The Small Business Administration's (SBA) Small Business Development centers are cooperative efforts involving the private sector, educational institutions, and federal, state, and local government to provide one-stop information, assistance, and guidance to individuals and small businesses through central and easily accessible branch locations.

The SBA's Section 7(a) Loan Guaranty Program

The SBA's section 7(a) loan guaranty program helps small firms secure loans and business financing for business start-ups and expansions. Commercial lenders make and administer small business loans structured to meet SBA's requirements. The SBA, in return, guarantees the loan.

The SBA's Microloan Program

The SBA's Microloan program provides money to nonprofit community-based lenders. These lenders then make very small loans to eligible borrowers for start-ups or growing small businesses. The average loan size is about $11,000.[35]

The SBA's Section 504 Certified Development Company Program

The SBA's section 504 Certified Development Company program is a long-term financing tool that helps start-up firms secure loans for major assets such as land, buildings, machinery, and equipment. Nonprofit certified development companies work with the SBA and private-sector lenders on the financing. The SBA guarantees the junior liens from the certified development companies with an SBA-guaranteed bond.

HUD's Community Development Block Grant Program

The U.S. Housing and Urban Development's (HUD) Community Development Block Grants program provides annual federal funding to cities, urban counties, and states for a wide variety of activities centered on economic opportunity, development, neighborhood revitalization, and housing. At least 70 percent of the funds provided by the program must be used for activities that benefit low- and moderate-income persons. Other activities funded by the program must prevent or eliminate slums or blight, or address community development needs.

The Community Reinvestment Act

The Community Reinvestment Act requires federal regulators to assess how well federally insured financial institutions meet the credit needs of their communities, including low- and moderate-income neighborhoods. This law helps to increase financing opportunities for housing and economic development in core cities and aging suburbs, among others.

The New Markets Tax Credit Program

The New Markets Tax Credit program is an attempt to stimulate investment and economic growth in low-income, high-risk communities. The idea is to direct new business capital to low-income communities. The program seeks to accomplish this by offering a federal tax credit of 39 percent over seven years for qualified equity investments made through community development enterprises (CDEs). The United States Treasury Department's Community Development Financial Institution Fund (CDFI) certifies CDEs. The CDFI allocates the tax credits annually to CDEs through a competitive application process. CDEs, in turn, use capital derived from tax credits to make loans to or investments in businesses and projects in low-income communities.

Other HUD Programs

Other Housing and Urban Development (HUD) programs not previously mentioned include Renewal Communities, Empowerment Zones, and Enterprise Community programs. They use tax incentives and other strategies to encourage business development, job creation, and housing in poor and distressed communities. HUD determines the communities that will participate in the program.

Uneven Distribution of Economic Benefits

The benefits flowing from the civil rights movement have not been evenly distributed in the black community. Blacks with money were able to take advantage of the changes that accompanied the passage of civil rights laws. Stokely Carmichael and Charles V. Hamilton addressed these concerns in their book, *Black Power: the Politics of Liberation.*[36] Integration, according to Carmichael and Hamilton, was based on the notion that to have a decent house or education, black people must move into white neighborhoods and send their children to white schools. The result, they argued, was that a handful of black children got in white schools while the vast majority were left in unimproved all-black schools. They also discussed the class split in the black community that resulted from integration:

> The goals of integrationists are middle-class goals, articulated primarily by a small group of Negroes with middle-class aspirations or status. This kind of integration has meant that a few blacks "make it," leaving the black community, sapping it of leadership potential and know-how . . . those token Negroes—absorbed into a white mass—are of no value to the remaining black masses. They become meaningless showpieces for a conscience-soothed white society.[37]

In the newly integrated America, blacks with credentials were able to take advantage of the newly created opportunities afforded by the Civil Rights Movement. Accordingly, the issue of class has become an undoubtedly important factor in determining life-chances of black Americans in the global economy of the post-industrial services-oriented age. The modern global services-oriented economy has had a negative impact on black workers who largely remain an undereducated industrial labor force. This development has been exacerbated by the practice of U.S. corporations "offshoring" their manufacturing needs to reduce their labor costs.

The Empowerment Zone and the Enterprise Community Program (EZ/EC), however, are showing signs of revitalizing the inner cities and creating jobs for those in the black community who have not benefited significantly from the gains of the civil rights movement. The 1993 legislation creating the EZ/EC Program was designed to promote economic development in less affluent communities. The Department of Housing and Urban Development administers the EZ/EC Program by providing:

> Technical assistance, loans, grants, and tax credits to qualified business organizations. As of 1997, EZ/EC programs were operating in 43 states. In New York City, the upper Manhattan Empowerment Zone, with a total budget of $300 million in loans and grants and $250 million in tax credits, had approved $15.2 million for 12 projects-ranging from a retail and

entertainment complex to a geriatric center that were expected to create 1300 jobs.[38]

Statistics on Black Businesses and the Black Consumer

Historically, black businesses, excluding insurance companies and banks, fell into four main categories by 1930: (1) amusement and recreational enterprises; (2) real estate businesses; (3) retail trade enterprises; and (4) businesses providing personal services. The largest number of successful black enterprises were those providing personal services— restaurants, beauty parlors, barber shops, and funeral parlors. These types of personal service businesses were characterized as "defensive enterprises" because they were the result of racial segregation. Consequently, from 1900–1930, the largest numbers of successful black businesses were in the field of personal service ventures. Blacks during this time period owned no significant commercial or industrial enterprises in "basic industry, natural resources, transportation, and communication. These types of businesses "continued to be owned and controlled by white capitalists."[39]

The size and types of black businesses between the great depression and the decades of the 1950s and 1960s were much like those of the late 1800s to 1930; small service-oriented businesses primarily serving a black clientele. State-enforced segregation was the primary reason black businesses failed to expand into many industries serving the general community. This trend continued through the late 1980s. By 1987, service industries accounted for 49 percent of all black-owned firms and 31 percent of gross revenues. Retail trade comprised the next greatest concentration, comprising 15.6 percent of black firms and 29.8 percent of gross revenues. Automobile dealers and service stations had the highest gross revenues in 1987, totaling nearly $2.2 billion.[40]

From 1898–1930, black businesses grew from 1,900 to 70,000. From 1920–1930, blacks in white collar positions experienced a parallel growth. Black-owned businesses during this time period employed an increasing number of black white collar workers. By 1987, the Census Bureau reported that African Americans owned 424,165 businesses, a 37.6 percent increase from 308,260 in 1982. The number of black-owned firms rose 46 percent from 1987–1992, rising from 421,165 firms to 620,912. On April 18, 2006, the U.S. Census Bureau reported that from 1997–2002, the number of black firms grew to 1.2 million, a 45 percent increase over the preceding five year period, with revenues near $89 Billion.[41]

90–95 percent of Black Businesses Are Sole Proprietorships

An overwhelming number of emerging black businesses that engage in providing some sort of personal service continue to be solely owned by the founder or his successor. In 1987, for example, sole proprietors owned 94.4 percent of all black firms.[42] These figures are consistent with 1982 and 1977 statistics, which indicate that 95 percent and 94.3 percent of black-owned businesses were sole proprietorships in those years.[43] On March 22, 2001, the Census Bureau reported that 90 percent of all black businesses were sole proprietorships in 1997.[44]

3 percent of Black Businesses Are Partnerships

In 1987, 2.7 percent or 11,261 black firms did business as partnerships.[45] That number appears to be holding steady as of the March 22, 2001, Census Bureau Report.

3 to 8 percent of Black Businesses Are Corporations

In 1987, 3 percent of black firms were small, closely held corporations that had elected to be taxed under Subchapter S of the Internal Revenue Code to achieve flow-through taxation similar to the taxation of a general partnership. The Census Bureau's 1997 survey was the first to include so-called C corporations. That data indicated that 5.185 percent of the then 823,500 black businesses were C corporations.[46] Accordingly, the likely number of firms organized as corporations is probably somewhere between 3 percent and 8 percent. No data exists for other types of organizations.

Generally, accountants and tax lawyers recommend that most start-up firms elect a business structure that allows the owners to avoid double taxation. Blacks who can afford an attorney will generally take this route. Let's briefly explain how it works. We will cover them fully in Part II of this book. There are three tax schemes for businesses under federal tax law. Subchapter C describes the traditional corporate income tax. Subchapter K describes the taxation applicable to partnerships and associations taxable as partnerships (other than corporations). Subchapter S is an alternative tax election available to certain closely held corporations that meet its eligibility requirements.[47]

The government subjects the income of "C" Corporations to double taxation. The corporation initially pays income taxes on its net revenues. If the corporation subsequently distributes a portion of the previously taxed income to the shareholders as a dividend, the shareholders must also pay taxes on that income.[48] The government taxes the income of a general partnership only once under Subchapter K.[49] The government also taxes the income of corporations eligible for Subchapter S taxation in a manner that avoids the double taxation on distributions.[50]

Accordingly, there are benefits to black start-up firms under Subchapters K and S that are not available under Subchapter C. However, as we discuss later in Part II, Chapter 15, there are certain "employee" benefits that are available under Subchapter C that are not available under the other subchapters.

Approximately 83 to 89 percent of Black Firms Have No Paid Employees

In 1987, 83.3 percent of black-owned firms had no employees. However, the 16.7 percent of black firms that had employees accounted for 71.5 percent of the gross receipts. There were 189 firms with 100 or more employees at that time.[51] On March 22, 2001, the Census Bureau reported that in 1997, 89 percent of all black firms had no employees. And it noted that the 11 percent that had paid employees of any number accounted for 79 percent of the gross receipts of all black businesses combined.[52]

Rate of Black Entrepreneurship Is Lower Than all Other Ethnic Groups

Blacks make up 12 percent of the U.S. population. However, even though blacks attempt to start businesses at three times the rate of white men and two times that of white women, they only owned three percent of all businesses during the late 1980s and early 1990s.[53] The Census Bureau placed that figure at four percent in 1997 and five percent by 2001.[54] There were 163,000 black-owned businesses in 1969; the number increased to 231,203 by 1977, and by 1982, the number of black-owned businesses had increased to 339,239.[55] The number of black-owned businesses increased, however, by 38 percent from 1982–1987. The number of black-owned firms rose 46 percent from 1987–1992, from 424,165 to 620,912.[56] And between 1997 and 2002, the number of black-owned businesses rose 25 percent over the previous five year reporting period to a total of 1.2 million.[57] Nevertheless, black entrepreneurship remains underdeveloped. In 1995, just 3.7 percent of the 22.87 percent of blacks in the labor force were self-employed, as compared with 9.5 percent of whites.[58]

Gross Revenues of the 1.2 Million Black Businesses in 2002 Near $89 Billion

From 1982–1987, the collective gross revenues of all black businesses increased by 105 percent, from $9.6 billion to $19.8 billion.[59] The collective gross revenues of all black firms rose 63 percent from $19.8 billion to $32.2 billion from 1987–1992.[60] From 1997–2002, the revenues generated by the 1.2 million black-owned businesses rose 25 percent over the previous five year's margin to nearly $89 billion dollars ($88.8 billion), and the number of black firms grew by 45 percent during the same period.[61]

Interestingly, in 1987, only 0.5 percent of black corporations grossed $1 million or more. The corporations grossing over $1 million constituted 37 percent of the gross revenues of all black-owned businesses, although these corporations are miniscule in number at 0.5 percent of the total.[62] By 2002, one percent of the total number of black businesses grossed $1 million or more and constituted 55 percent of the total receipts of all black businesses in 1997.[63]

In 1987, approximately 35 percent of black firms had gross receipts of less than $5,000. The average black business in 1987 had revenue of only $47,000, far below the $192,000 figure for businesses in general.[64] By 1997, the average black business had revenues of $86,500, compared to $410, 000 for all U.S. firms excluding publicly held corporations. The gross revenues of black businesses in 1997 as a percentage of all U.S. non-farm businesses was 0.4 percent of the total of $18.6 trillion.[65]

Black Enterprise Magazine's List of 100s

The combined revenue of the *Black Enterprise Magazine's* 100 largest industrial corporations and the 100 largest auto dealers was $13.19 billion in 1997. This was a 6.49 percent drop from the $14.1 billion figure in 1996 and the first decline since the *Black Enterprise Magazine's* list of 100s combined in 1988. The reason for the decline was the decision of TLC Beatrice International Holdings, Inc., the perennial list leader with $2.2 billion in revenues, to sell all of its subsidiaries that year.[66] By the 1999 listings, TLC Beatrice had decided to liquidate what assets it still retained.[67] By 2002, however, the combined figure for the two groups was $20.979 billion.[68] In 2003, the combined figure was $21.9 billion.[69] In 2006, the figure had increased to $27.570 billion.[70] By 2007, the figure had edged upward to $28.763 billion.[71]

High Percentage of Jobs in Civil Service

It is not surprising that statistics indicate that one-half of black men and two-thirds of black women are civil servants. Historically, blacks have had greater opportunity for employment in the government than in any other sector. Thus, it is clear that government employment has been an important factor in black economic stability. The Office of Personnel Management, in its *Fact Book for 2002*, stated that government employees were 69 percent white, 17 percent black, 7 percent Hispanic, 5 percent Asian, and 2 percent American Indian. These statistics are notable for blacks because they constitute 17 percent of the federal government workforce but only 12 percent of the population.[72] The government astonishingly employs half of all black professionals as opposed to only a quarter of white professionals.[73] Moreover, when government employment of blacks in the military is factored in, the significance of government work to black economic security becomes readily apparent.

Obtaining Business Capital More Difficult for Blacks

The historical inability of blacks to obtain capital is well documented. Of black entrepreneurs, 75 percent state that that they have encountered some discrimination in obtaining bank financing.[74] In 1982, 69 percent of black owners started their businesses without borrowing money.[75] Studies estimate that the gap between the capital available to blacks versus whites favors whites by over $200 million and project the disparity to grow at a rate of $13.8 million a year.[76]

Even with the sweeping changes of the Civil Rights era, black entrepreneurs still faced many challenges. In spite of those challenges, black businesses have continued to grow. In the next chapter, we'll meet some of the thought leaders and inspired entrepreneurs who figured prominently in these times.

Notes

1. 347 U.S. 483 (1954) (*Brown I*).
2. 163 U.S. 537 (1896).
3. *Runyon v. McCrary*, 427 U.S. 160 (1976) (interpreting 42 U.S.C.§ 1981); *Griffin v. Breckenridge*, 403 U.S. 88 (1971) (interpreting 42 U.S.C. § 1985 (3); and *Jones v. Alfred H. Mayer Co.*, 392 U.S. 409 (1968) (interpreting 42 U.S.C. § 1982).
4. 365 U.S. 167, 171–72 (1961).
5. 42 U.S.C. § 2000e (2000).
6. Derrick Bell. *Race, Racism, and American Law* (New York: Aspen Law and Business, 2001), 580.
7. 383 U.S. 301. (1966).
8. 392 U.S. 409 (1968).
9. M. Wilson, "Set-Asides of Local Government Contracts for Minority-Owned Businesses: Constitutional and State Law Issues," *New Mexico Law Review* 17, (1987): 337–59.
10. *Adarand Constructors. v. Pena, 515 U.S.* 200, 206 (1995)
11. Ibid., 206.
12. Ibid., 205 (quoting 15 U.S.C.§ 637(d)(2)(C)(ii)).

13. Mitchell F. Rice, "Government Set-Asides, Minority Business Enterprises, and the Supreme Court," *Public Administrative Review,* (Mar./Apr. 1991): 114.

14. 42 U.S.C. § 6705(f)(2) (1977).

15. 448 U.S. 488 (1980).

16. J. H. Benjamin, "The Supreme Court Decision and the Future of Race-Conscious Remedies," *Government Financial Review* (Apr. 1989): 21.

17. Mitchell F. Rice, "Government Set-Asides, Minority Business Enterprises, and the Supreme Court," *Public Administrative Review,* (Mar./Apr. 1991): 742–57.

18. *Fullilove v. Klutznick,* 473, 477–82, 484–86, 490, 496, 513, 519, 523, 537, 541, 545.

19. Drew S, Days III, "Fullilove," *Yale Law Journal* 96, *(*1987): 453.

20. 488 U.S. 469 (1989).

21. Ibid., 477–84.

22. *City of Richmond v. J.A. Crosson* , 488 U.S at 493–94, 498–506, 509.

23. Ibid., 509.

24. Ibid., 486.

25. Maurice Mongkuo and Mitchell F. Rice, "Did Adarand Kill Minority Set-Asides?" *Public Administrative Review* (Jan/Feb., 1998), 82.

26. 497 U.S. 547 (1990).

27. Ibid., 553, 555–58, 564–66, 579.

28. 515 U.S. 200 (1995).

29. Ibid., 227.

30. Ibid., 205–10.

31. Ibid., 213, 227, 236, 238–39.

32. U.S. Small Business Administration. SBA Office of Business Development Report To Congress On Minority Small Business and Capital Ownership Development for Fiscal Year, (Washington, DC: 2001), 5, 7, 13, 19, 25.

33. Ibid.

34. Ibid., 19.

35. Northeast-Midwest Summary of Notable Federal Business and Economic Development Programs and Initiatives, www.nemw.org/Biz&EconDev _NEMW%20FedCommRevitProgs2006.pdf.

36. Stokely Carmichael and Charles V. Hamilton. *Black Power: the Politics of Liberation* (Vintage, New York, 1967), Reissued 1992, 54.

37. Ibid.

38. *African American Desk Reference* (New York: Stonesong Press and New York Public Library, 1999), 245.

39. Abram Harris. *The Negro As Capitalist,* (Chicago: Urban Press, Inc. 1992, originally published in 1936 by the American Academy of Political Science), 68.

40. *The African American Almanac* (Farmington Hills, MI: Gale Research Inc., 1997), 569.

41. U.S. Census Bureau News, http://www. census.gov/Press-Release/ www/releases/archives/business_ownership/006711 (Released April 18, 2006), 1.

42. John Sibley Butler. *Entrepreneurship and Self-Help Among African Americans, a Reconsideration of Race and Economics* (New York: State University of New York Press, 1991), 296–97.

43. *The African American Almanac* (Farmington Hills, MI: Gale Research Inc., 1997), 568.

44. United States Commerce News, http://www.census.gov/press-release/www/2001/cboi-54.html., 1.

45. John Sibley Butler. *Entrepreneurship and Self-Help Among African Americans, a Reconsideration of Race and Economics* (New York: State University of New York Press, 1991), 297.

46. United States Commerce News, http://www.census.gov/press-release/www/2001/cboi-54.html., 1.

47. Robert W. Hamilton. *The Law Of Corporations in a Nutshell* (New York: West Group, 2000), 28–39.

48. Ibid., 28–29.

49. Ibid., 30.

50. Ibid., 29–30.

51. *The African American Almanac* (Farmington Hills, MI: Gale Research Inc., 1997), 568; John Sibley Butler, *Entrepreneurship and Self-Help Among African Americans, a Reconsideration of Race and Economics* (New York: State University of New York Press, 1991), 297.

52. United States Commerce News, http://www.census.gov/press-release/www/2001/cboi-54.html., 2.

53. Jeanne Saddler, "Black Entrepreneurship: The Next Generation, Young Risk Takers Push the Business Envelope," *Wall Street Journal*, May 12, 1994, sec. B; *see also* "Black Entrepreneurs: Have Capital Will Flourish," *Economist* (Feb. 27, 1993):33 [hereinafter *Have Capital Will Flourish*].

54. United States Commerce News, http://www.census.gov/press-release/www/2001/cboi-54.html., 1., and Revenues for Black-Owned Firm's Near $89 Billion, Number of Businesses Up 45 Percent, U.S. Census Bureau News, http://www. census.gov/Press-Release/www/releases/archives/business_ownership/006711. (Released April 18, 2006), 2.

55. John Sibley Butler. *Entrepreneurship and Self-Help Among African Americans, a Reconsideration of Race and Economics* (New York: State University of New York Press, 1991), 297.

56. *Wall Street Journal Almanac* 1999 (New York: Dow Jones & Co., 1998), 179.

57. Revenues for Black-Owned Firm's Near $89 Billion, Number of Businesses Up 45 Percent, U.S. Census Bureau News, http://www.census.gov/Press-Release/www/releases/archives/business_ownership/006711. (Released April 18, 2006).

58. Abigail Thernstrom and Stephen Thernstrom. *America in Black and White, One Nation Indivisible* (New York: Simon and Schuster, 1997), 188–89.

59. *The African American Almanac* (Farmington Hills, MI: Gale Research Inc., 1997), 568.

60. *Wall Street Journal Almanac* 1999 (New York: Dow Jones & Co., 1998), 179.

61. Revenues for Black-Owned Firm's Near $89 Billion, Number of Businesses Up 45 Percent, U.S. Census Bureau News, http://www. census.gov/Press -Release/www/releases/archives/business_ownership/006711. (Released April 18, 2006), 1.

62. *The African American Almanac* (Farmington Hills, MI: Gale Research Inc., 1997), 568.

63. Revenues for Black-Owned Firm's Near $89 Billion, Number of Businesses Up 45 Percent, U.S. Census Bureau News, http://www .census.gov/Press-Release/www/releases/archives/business_ownership/ 006711. (Released April 18, 2006), 2.

64. *The African American Almanac* (Farmington Hills, MI: Gale Research Inc., 1997), 568.

65. United States Commerce News, http://www.census.gov/press -release/www/2001/cboi-54.html., 1–2.

66. Derek T. Dingle, "B.E. 100's 26th Annual Report On Black Business," *Black Enterprise* (June 1998): 93.

67. Derek T. Dingle, "B.E. 100's Overview," *Black Enterprise* (June 2000): 108.

68. Derek T. Dingle, "B.E. 100's 31st Annual Report on Black Business," *Black Enterprise* (June 2003): 96.

69. Derek T. Dingle, "B.E. 100's Overview, Only the Strong Survive," *Black Enterprise* (June 2004): 102.

70. See "B.E. 100's, Architects of Growth," *Black Enterprise* (June 2007): 88–89.

71. See "B.E. 100's, Bold Leadership for the 21st Century," *Black Enterprise* (June 2008): 98–99.

72. *See* "The Typical Federal Worker," *Washington Post*, Sept. 1, 2003, at A23.

73. Abigail Thernstrom and Stephen Thernstrom. *America in Black and White*, One Nation Indivisible, 188–89.

74. Dorothy J. Gaiter, "Black Entrepreneurship: A Special Report, Short-Term Despair, Long-Term Promise: As Traditional Black-Owned Businesses Lose Ground, Hopes Rest on a New Generation of Entrepreneurs," *Wall Street Journal*, Apr. 13, 1992, sec. R.

75. Butler, *Entrepreneurship*, 309–11.

76. Ibid., 309.

CHAPTER 8

BLACK THOUGHT LEADERS AND ENTREPRENEURS FROM THE CIVIL RIGHTS ERA TO THE PRESENT

The 1960s and early 1970s were times of great upheaval and change. Even those who did not take part in marches or demonstrations or chose not to "wear flowers in their hair" were affected by it. It was a time of questioning—questioning ourselves, our government, and the very fabric of our society. The status quo was no longer acceptable, and had to change. And change it did. In fact, our world might look a lot different now had it not been for the events of those days.

You've already had a look at some of those changes in Chapter 7. Now let's meet some of the people whose voices raised the rallying cry then and now. We'll also meet some of the entrepreneurs of note who emerged from those heady days, and those who have followed and built upon their legacy.

Black Thought Leaders from the Civil Rights Era to the Present

The Civil Rights era produced many great black thinkers and writers. Some wrote of the struggle for black identity within a white society. Others wrote of the social needs for respect and equality in education and basic life services. And some combined the philosophical with the hard economic realities of the times. The following three thought leaders saw the call for social change as inseparable from the call for economic change and pursued both agendas vigorously.

Martin Luther King, Jr.

Many Americans have shaped an incomplete vision of Martin Luther King, Jr. based largely on the almost mystical "I have a dream" portion of the 1963 speech he made during the historic civil rights march on Washington. This view of King ends in victory—the American people join with King, collectively choose the high road, and make great things happen for all people in America.

This view, however, obscures and distorts King's full message. He also spoke in the 1963 address of the magnificent words of the U.S. Constitution and the Declaration of Independence as a promissory note to which every American was an heir. King pointedly noted, however, that America had defaulted on that promissory note as to black people. According to King, America had given black people a "bad check" that had come back marked "insufficient funds."

Although many see that glorious day in 1963 as a pinnacle of sorts, Martin Luther King, Jr. did not "die" in 1963. He continued to pursue a vigorous agenda of social and economic change, often out of the media eye. The theme of his agenda was poverty, economic justice, and the redistribution of wealth. King is regularly on record as decrying not only the South's Jim Crow laws but also the economic condition of black Americans. Indeed, King turned his focus primarily to economic issues after the enactment of the 1965 Voting Rights Act signaled victory in the battle against Jim Crow. King's economic agenda was a more radical challenge to the structure of American society and has yet to be fulfilled in the manner he envisioned. In pursuit of that agenda, he died in Memphis in 1968 leading a strike of sanitation workers.

History should remember Martin Luther King, Jr. as more than the idealistic icon of "I have a dream." King struggled hard for social change. He died trying to put issues such as the reduction of poverty and black economic advancement on top of the agenda. Accordingly, King should be remembered as a thought leader who challenged America on issues that went far beyond those of segregation and Jim Crow laws.

Malcolm X and Elijah Muhammad

Elijah Muhammad was born in 1897 and died in 1975. He was the son of a Georgia sharecropper. He moved to Detroit in 1929 and worked in an automobile plant for several years. In 1931, he adopted Islam and soon became the chief aide of Wallace Fard, the founder of the Black Muslims (now called the Nation of Islam). Wallace Fard disappeared in 1934. Thereafter, Elijah Muhammad and his followers moved to Chicago, where he established a temple and promoted an economic doctrine of black self-help. He stated that his economic self-help doctrine would lead to greater black pride and black solidarity.

The Nation of Islam (NOI), under its guiding principle of "Do for Self," established its own schools, military organization, and a variety of properties and businesses. The NOI achieved its greatest influence during the 1950s and early 1960s when Malcolm X emerged as Elijah Muhammad's chief aide and national spokesman. Malcolm was a towering figure and articulate spokesman, and brought NOI's message to prominence on the national stage. Although they came from different philosophical roots, Malcolm X and Martin Luther King, Jr. were strong allies in the fight for black economic independence. As Malcolm evolved into the "voice of NOI," Elijah Muhammad faded more into the background. Largely because of Malcolm's eloquent discourse on matters of race and economics, NOI's membership grew significantly and reached approximately 500,000 during this period. Malcolm opposed integration as a type of cultural suicide for African Americans and stressed black economic independence, black nationalism, and the concept of "Do for Self."

Jesse Jackson

The Rev. Jesse Jackson founded Operation PUSH (People United to Save Humanity) in 1971 after drifting from the Southern Christian Leadership Conference (SCLC) in the aftermath of the assassination of Dr. Martin Luther King, Jr. Jackson headed the SCLC's Operation Breadbasket program from 1966–1971. During Jackson's tenure as head of Operation Breadbasket, he pushed for greater economic opportunities for African Americans.

Jackson modeled Operation PUSH after Operation Breadbasket. Operation PUSH initially focused on economic issues including support of minority businesses and pressuring white-owned firms to hire a fair proportion of minority employees. PUSH has broadened the scope of its focus over the years to include AIDS, drugs, teenage pregnancy, and violence in the black community.

In 1984, Jackson founded a multiracial political organization called the Rainbow Coalition. The organization reached its highest level of political influence in 1988 when it won nine state primaries and took 7 million votes of 23 million cast. It has not been a major factor in subsequent nationwide campaigns. In 1997, the Rainbow Coalition joined with Operation PUSH to monitor the firing, promotion, and investment policies of Wall Street firms and other wealthy corporations. The name of the new organization is called the Rainbow/PUSH Coalition.[1]

Black Entrepreneurs of the Civil Rights Era to the Present

The ranks of successful black entrepreneurs and businesspeople have grown significantly since the Civil Rights era. Many started with nothing more than a dream under the oppressive cloud of Jim Crow. Others, like sports stars, built upon their name recognition. Let's meet a few of them now.

Publishing Moguls

John H. Johnson: Johnson Publishing—John H. Johnson went from being born into poverty in 1918 in Arkansas to being regarded as one of the most influential black publishers in history. Indeed, his story is compelling.

He was unable to graduate from high school until his family moved from Arkansas to Chicago because his little town had no black high school. He excelled in school in Chicago and graduated with honors. After graduation, he went to work for the black-owned Supreme Life Insurance Company and enrolled in the University of Chicago at the same time.

While working for the insurance company he came up with an idea for a magazine just for black people—news, articles, and the work of black poets and writers. Many people tried to discourage him, saying most blacks simply didn't have the income to waste on magazines, but he was not deterred. In 1942, after he graduated from the university, he published the first edition of *Negro Digest* with loans from friends and family, and advance subscriptions. It was a hit. Three years later, he launched *Ebony*, which has been the top-selling African American magazine since day one. In 1951 came *Jet*, the largest selling African American weekly in the world.

Over the years, Johnson Publishing expanded into book publishing, acquired a large cosmetics company, and produced television programming. Ironically, in later years, Johnson was named chairman and CEO of Supreme Life Insurance, where it all started "way back when."

His savvy and diplomacy led to assignments as a Special Ambassador for the United States at functions in several African nations under presidents Kennedy, Johnson, and Nixon. In 1996, President Bill Clinton awarded him the Presidential Medal of Freedom. Other accolades over the years included the Most Outstanding Black Publisher in History award from the National Newspaper Publishers Association, and the number one spot on *Black Enterprise* magazine's list of top 100 companies for several years. In 2006, the company held the number 6 spot, with over $472 million in sales.[2]

Earl Graves: Black Enterprise Magazine—Born in 1935, Graves grew up in Brooklyn, New York. After graduating from Morgan State University with a B.A. in economics and a two-year stint in the Army, he became an administrative assistant to Senator Robert F. Kennedy until Kennedy's assassination in 1968.

He entered the business world—the publishing world—and put out the first issue of *Black Enterprise* magazine in 1970 as a resource for the African American business community. Today, *Black Enterprise* is considered the "go to" source of the most up-to-date business information for both public and private sector entrepreneurs. In 1995, the 25th anniversary of the magazine, Morgan State renamed its business school in Graves' honor.

He has been honored many times as one of the ten most outstanding black businessmen in the country, received the Spingarn Medal, the NAACP's highest honor for his achievements, and consistently lands in the *Black Enterprise* magazine's list of top 100 businesses. In 2006, the company held 69th place on the list with nearly $60 million in sales.

In 1997, Graves wrote *How to Succeed in Business Without Being White*, which became a business bestseller. It is still considered an excellent resource for aspiring entrepreneurs.

Media and Entertainment Giants

Robert L. Johnson: Black Entertainment Television (BET)—Johnson was born in Mississippi in 1946, the ninth of 10 children, but his family soon moved to Illinois where he grew up. He earned a history degree at the University of Illinois and a Masters in public affairs at Princeton. After graduation, he moved to Washington, D.C., and it was there that the idea for a cable TV company aimed at the African American audience was born.

He worked for the Corporation for Public Broadcasting, the National Urban League, and served as a lobbyist for the cable industry for a number of years before taking the plunge in 1980, founding Black Entertainment Television. The little cable outlet grew from a few hours of weekly programming to a huge network with an audience of more than 70 million households. In 1991, BET became the first black-owned company to gain listing on the New York Stock Exchange. Later, however, in 1998, Johnson took the company private again.

As the audience and programming continued to grow, BET attracted investors from other media companies. In 2001, Viacom bought BET for $3 billion, making Johnson the first black billionaire and the wealthiest black man in the world.[3]

Johnson's next move was to form RLJ Companies with interests in broadcasting, real estate and financial investment, the hotel/restaurant trades, and sports. In 2003 he bought the NBA expansion team, the Charlotte Bobcats, and the Women's NBA team the Sting for $300 million. He continued to focus on strategic partnerships in the entertainment industry (Tele-Communications, Inc. and Time-Warner), the hotel business (Marriott and Hilton), investments (Deutsche Bank), and basketball (Michael Jordon). In 2006, two RLJ companies were listed in *Black Enterprise* magazine's Top 100 with sales approaching $600 million.[4]

Russell Simmons: DefJam Records/Rush Communications—Russell Simmons is widely acknowledged as the man who brought hip-hop into mainstream American consciousness. He and his partner launched DefJam in the mid-1980s and it became the springboard for rap and hip-hop. DefJam is part of the larger Simmons company, Rush Communications, which has branches in clothing (Phat Farm), movies, television, publishing, and marketing. In 1999 Simmons sold his share in the record company to Universal Music Group for $100 million. In 2004, Simmons sold Phat Farm for $140 million. In 2007, *USA Today* named Simmons to its list of Top 25 Most Influential People of the Past 25 Years.

Simmons says although things have changed, and are still changing, race still matters:

> We African Americans have a built-in audience. But that's only because race exists. There's still the negatives of race—prejudice and inequality, for instance. The idea of repairing the past is common sense, but there's a racial factor that keeps people from accepting that. So I think race does matter a great deal, but not as much as it has in the past.[5]

As it does in other areas of life, the racial factor spills over into business as well, but Simmons says often that can be a "plus" for the savvy entrepreneur:

> Hip-hop has transcended race, and the African American cultural experience has become the leading brand-building experience for all Americans.

Decades ago, jazz and blues and rock & roll only became popular when white faces were attached to it. Today the racial tension in this country has lightened so much that now African Americans can carry the torch of African American ideas. Snoop Dogg is on MTV, not only Eminem.[6]

Like many entrepreneurs, Simmons gives back to the community. His Rush Philanthropic organization opens the world of the arts to young people. He is also the Chairman of the Foundation for Ethnic Understanding, which encourages understanding and cooperation among diverse religions and ethnicities.

Damon Dash: Roc-a-Fella Records and RocaWear Clothing—Born and raised in East Harlem, New York, Dash started his career in his teens in the early 1990s hosting parties in the neighborhood. About the same time, he started a music management business and signed his first client—Shawn "Jay-Z" Carter. Money from the party business backed Jay-Z's first album. The "sales department" was Dash's car, but sales grew and in 1995, Dash formed Roc-a-Fella records and worked with Island Def Jam for cutting the discs and distribution. By the late 1990s, Roc-a-Fella was pulling in about $50 million a year.

Next came RocaWear with the built-in "sales machine" of Jay-Z, who wore the clothing in his concerts and music videos. As profits grew, Dash began to expand into films and other areas outside the music industry. He also broadened his appeal from hip-hop fans to a more mainstream audience. One of his independent films—*The Woodsman*, starring Kevin Bacon—won awards at both the Sundance Film Festival and Cannes.

Other areas of expansion include jewelry, a slick magazine, boxing, and a possible cable TV channel in Europe. All this diversity has led some to wonder if Dash may be pushing too far afield from his entrepreneurial roots. His answer:

> It hasn't been done, but with my work ethic, I can have a company in every part of fashion and entertainment.[7]

Sean Combs: Bad Boy Entertainment—Another child of Harlem who eventually soared to great heights, Combs lost his father when he was only a toddler in what was alleged to be a drug gang shooting. His mother moved out of the city to raise her children in Mount Vernon, New York, and set young Sean on a path toward a good education that laid the foundation for his later entrepreneurial efforts. He went to private schools and then on to Howard University where he gravitated toward business and marketing. He also gained a reputation for throwing great parties, so the marriage of business and entertainment was sealed.

After snagging an internship at Uptown Records while he was still in school, he commuted between Washington, D.C. to attend classes at Howard and New York City for his work at Uptown. He moved quickly up through the ranks at Uptown and eventually quit Howard to take a full-time executive position. He signed a number of artists that went on to fame such as Mary J. Blige and Notorious B.I.G. He also put out rap recordings of his own material.

He left Uptown in 1993 to form Bad Boy records, and several of the artists that he had worked with at Uptown went with hm. More artists signed with him and he produced recordings for many more, including Mary J. Blige, L'il Kim, and Mariah Carey.

Like Damon Dash, Combs began to diversify into clothing, films, restaurants, and men's fragrances. One perfume, "I Am King," is dedicated to President Barack Obama, Muhammad Ali, and Dr. Martin Luther King, Jr. On top of all that, he signed a deal to work with Ciroc vodka to develop their brand.

In 2002, he made *Fortune* magazine's list of 40 Richest People Under 40, and was named the top earner in hip-hop. In 2005, he sold his record company to Warner Music Group, and was named one of the Most Influential People of 2005 by *Time* magazine. In 2006, his fortunes topped $346 million, making him one of the richest people in hip-hop. In 2008, he bought the Enyce line of clothing from Liz Claiborne for $20 million.

He is generous with his money and supports organizations such as the Patricia Kirby Foundation, which works with young people with eating disorders. He is committed to furthering education and donated $1 million to Howard University. He also donated several hundred computers to the New York public schools to enhance computer literacy programs.

Fashion and Cosmetics

Joe Dudley: Dudley Products—Dudley Products began in 1967 with Joe and his wife, Eunice mixing up shampoos and cosmetics in their home when they weren't at their full-time day jobs. Over the years, the business grew and today manufactures more than 400 products with revenues in the tens of millions. They also founded Dudley Cosmetology University, offering training in five languages to students from all over the world. They recently expanded the university at two locations in Zimbabwe.

Like many entrepreneurs, Dudley is a philanthropist, investing his money in the education of young black people. His own life stands as an example of what can be done:

I built my company as an example of what you can do with difficulties in life. In first grade I was labeled mentally retarded, and the teachers told my mom and everybody else that I would never get anywhere. Now I want to show young African Americans that they can run a business too.[8]

Many other black companies have been bought up by international cosmetics giants, but Dudley says that's not in the cards for his business:

To me Dudley is a mission for its people. When I was born, 14 of us lived in a shack. I promised God that if he helped me make it, I would spend my life helping other people—not just my family but people in general. We must make a contribution in the world. My people, African Americans, need more help than many others.[9]

Besides, he says that the business means more to him than just making money:

Doing what I'm doing is fun for me. I could sell for money, but why? I have five suits and several nice homes. I don't wear fancy diamonds. I usually drive one car—one Cadillac. But I'm having fun watching young people say, "If Joe Dudley can do it, I can do it better." That's what excites me.[10]

George E. Johnson: Ultra Sheen—Born to sharecropper parents in Mississippi in 1927, Johnson went to work when he was only eight years old shining shoes while he was still in grade school. He did go on to high school, but quit to work full time at a variety of day and night jobs. His break came when he went to work as a production chemist at the black-owned cosmetics firm, S.B. Fuller.

Ten years later, taking with him what he had learned at Fuller, he left the company to found Johnson products, which focused on women's hair care. He developed the Ultra Sheen line of products and within a few years, the company was showing a healthy profit. In 1971, the company was listed on the American Stock Exchange.

In the 1990s, the company was sold to IVAX for $61 million, but Johnson continued to serve as a consultant for the company. He turned his attention to philanthropic efforts through the George E. Johnson Foundation and the George E. Johnson Educational Fund. Recognition for his efforts include the *Ebony* magazine American Black Achievement Award, and the Harvard Club award for public service. He continues to work closely with several civic organizations, including the Chicago Urban League and Jesse Jackson's Operation PUSH.

Daymond John: FUBU clothing—Like many successful entrepreneurs, Daymond John started out as a youngster selling just about anything he thought somebody might buy. After high school, he and some friends set up a little hat-making business in his mother's basement and sold the hats at concerts, craft fairs, and art festivals. They were a hit, so they expanded their basement shop with the help of a mortgage on his mother's house and founded FUBU (For Us, By Us). The hat business expanded to include sports jerseys and caps all bearing the FUBU logo.

FUBU got a highly visible boost from John's friend, rapper LL Cool J, who sported the clothing in concerts, videos, and public appearances. Professional athletes took to it as well, and FUBU began outfitting the Harlem Globetrotters. It wasn't long before FUBU became *the* urban clothing line, and its reach soon extended to general mall sales and internet sites as it gained international appeal.

FUBU clothing inspired and helped finance the launch of FUBU Entertainment music and entertainment promotions. It also helped bankroll the philanthropic FUBU Foundation.

John has been honored many times for his entrepreneurial and philanthropic efforts. Awards include the NAACP's Entrepreneur of the Year, the Congressional Achievement Award for Entrepreneurship, and the Essence Award, among others.

Entrepreneurs of the Sports World

Dave Bing: NBA Hall of Famer, Bing Steel—Dave Bing might be called "The Quiet Man" of basketball. During his 12 seasons of play, he went about the business of the game with determination and tenacity in the face of some daunting physical challenges, yet stayed out of the limelight. In his off-hours and on trips from game to game, he read everything he could about business and finance. He was a man with a plan.

When he retired from the NBA in 1980, he founded Bing Steel in Detroit. Using the same determination he displayed on the court and the vast amount of business knowledge he had gained, he propelled the company to a $61 million enterprise within 10 years. A few years later, he bought out a metal-stamping firm that was bringing in $28 million a year, and added a construction company to his repertoire. By 2006 the

Bing group held the 32nd spot on *Black Enterprise* magazine's top 100 industrial/service companies with sales of more than $135 million.

Vinnie Johnson: the Piston Group—Johnson played for the Detroit Pistons' championship teams in 1989 and 1990 and handed the name on to his auto parts company, founded in 1995. With the help of money from Detroit's Empowerment Zone program, he brought his business head-quarters to a tough neighborhood. His goal was to hire neighborhood locals to provide new opportunities for success where none had existed before. It was rough going at first, with high absenteeism and difficulties getting the right workers for the right jobs. But he persevered, and by 2003, the Piston Group had 500 employees and was bringing in $227 million in sales. Ford and General Motors have been Johnson's main customers, but he has wisely been expanding his base of support overseas, courting Japanese automakers in particular. In 2005, the Initiative for a Competitive Inner City (ICIC) and *Inc.* magazine awarded the Piston Group the Inner City 100 award, recognizing them as one of the fastest growing inner city companies in America.

Earvin "Magic" Johnson: NBA Hall of Famer, Johnson Development Corporation—Known for his on-court prowess and easy, charismatic smile, Johnson has applied that same magic to his business endeavors. Even while he was playing basketball, he had his eye on the future:

> When I was an NBA player, I was always dreaming of business plans. As a black man you have to. Minorities make money, but we don't generate wealth. But a business generates wealth—it is power, it is something that you can pass on to the next generation. That is what is needed in the black community. We can pass on problems—it's about time we passed on wealth. Kids look to ballplayers as idols, but [BET founder] Bob Johnson is my idol. I'm watching his moves.[11]

Today, Johnson Development Corporation is a multi-million dollar enterprise that brings everything from theaters and restaurants to shopping malls to black inner city neighborhoods. He says he doesn't hesitate to play the race card:

> Yes, race matters. I've based my business on it. I wanted to show the business world that you can be successful in minority communities. It was uncharted waters and took some convincing. I would drive companies through places like South Central and say, "I want to bring your business

here," and they would look at me like I was crazy. I knew it would work, though.[12]

You'll find JDC projects in 65 cities and 16 states, with strategic partnerships with the likes of Starbucks, Lowes Cineplex Entertainment, and T.G.I. Fridays. Johnson says he loves steering the course of the company:

For me the best part about being a CEO is creating black vice presidents, black presidents, black general managers, black managers. That is the kind of legacy that matters.[13]

Reggie Fowler: Spiral, Inc—Like many entrepreneurs, Reggie Fowler started out working in his father's business. In this case, it was a high-class restaurant in his hometown of Tucson, Arizona, where young Reggie did everything from washing dishes to sweeping floors. As he grew older, he took over some of the business and accounting duties.

He excelled in school, and as a sixth grader received a Presidential Accommodation from President Nixon. He was as gifted in sports as he was in the classroom, especially baseball and football. He won a football scholarship to the University of Wyoming where he earned a Business Administration degree. After graduation, he went on to professional football and played for three years before hanging up his helmet and turning to graduate school. After earning an MBA at Arizona State University, he was tapped for the Mobil Oil Corporation's Whiz Kids program.

He was a star at Mobil as well, earning Rookie of the Year as the company's top sales person. But his career at Mobil ended when he turned down a promotion that would have taken him out of his beloved Arizona. Instead, he shifted his focus to the private sector, and in the late 1980s founded Spiral, Inc. Over the years, the company has diversified into real estate, aviation, manufacturing, entertainment, and banking. It made the *Black Enterprise* magazine's Top 100 list in 2004 at 11th place. Fowler's most recent coup was becoming the first African American to own a National Football League franchise. He is a limited partner in the group of investors that owns the Minnesota Vikings.

Mannie Jackson: Harlem Globetrotters Owner—Born in a railroad car in Missouri, but raised in Illinois, Mannie Jackson was determined to succeed both academically and on the basketball court from the time he entered grade school. He went on to the University of Illinois, where he became the first black All-American basketball player and the first black captain of the Illinois team. He then played for the Harlem Globetrotters.

He left the team to join the business world, becoming the President and General Manager of Honeywell's Telecommunications division. When he retired from Honeywell, he again turned his sights on basketball, and the Globetrotters in particular. In 1993, he bought the team, which was on the brink of bankruptcy. The move made him the first African American to own a major sports/entertainment organization.

His love for the Globetrotters and his skill at branding helped turn the organization from a losing proposition into a thriving multimillion-dollar enterprise with a fan base at record levels. He did it largely by securing high-profile strategic partners and sponsors, and expanding the number of playing venues worldwide. Among the partners are Burger King, which sponsors the world tour, and Daymond John's FUBU clothing, which produces the team uniforms. Jackson also built a merchandising and licensing arm that brings in over $100 million. Additionally, in keeping with the Globetrotters' moniker of "Ambassadors of Good Will," they have donated more than $10 million to various charitable causes.

Jackson himself has set up family foundations to promote excellence in education, and he is a founding member and president of the Executive Leadership Council, a networking group for black executives. He has been honored over and over again for his efforts to promote youth education, business leadership skills, and for his own entrepreneurial efforts.

Construction and Real Estate Investment Entrepreneurs

Herman J. Russell: H. J. Russell & Company, Construction—Herman Russell began his entrepreneurial career in the late 1930s as a young boy in Atlanta shining shoes and delivering newspapers. By the time he was 12, he was working alongside his father as a plasterer in his father's plastering business. At 16, he bought his first piece of land to build a residential building. In a few years he had saved enough money to pay his way through Tuskegee University. When he graduated, he came home to work with his father again.

At his father's death in 1957, he took over the company and founded the Herman J. Russell Construction Company. He expanded it from just plastering to all types of construction, real estate development, and property management, and by the 1990s it was a multi-million dollar enterprise with over 700 workers. In 2006, with sales of nearly $365 million, the company held 15th place in *Black Enterprise* magazine's top 100 industrial/service companies.[14]

In 1963, Russell became the first black member of the Atlanta Chamber of Commerce. He later went on to become its first black president. Heavily involved in various civic organizations and the civil rights movement, he often worked closely with Dr. Martin Luther King, Jr.

Like many entrepreneurs, he knew that the future of black economic equality lay with black youth. In that spirit, he created the Herman J. Russell Entrepreneurial Scholarship Foundation for Atlanta-area youth.

Victor MacFarlane: MacFarlane Partners—Victor MacFarlane rose from being an impoverished child of a single mother raised in inner-city housing to a multi-billionaire. MacFarlane held the top spot on *Black Enterprise* magazine's 2008 rankings of private equity firms with over $20 billion— more than the other fourteen equity firms on the list combined.[15]

San Francisco-based MacFarlane started his first real estate investment firm in 1987, but his big break came in 1995 when he teamed up with Magic Johnson to revitalize riot-torn LA neighborhoods with $50 million in backing from the California Public Employees Retirement System. Because investment companies had been steering away from urban areas it was a tough sell, but under his guidance an inner-city shopping center got a full facelift and the retirement system made a healthy profit. His career steadily headed upward after that.

Through strategic partnerships, he targeted the East Coast markets of New York, Boston, and Washington, D.C. He started the effort in 2003 by taking a 25 percent share in a $1.7 million development in one of the poorest wards in Washington. Again, he had a tough sell when he went before the city fathers seeking development rights. They wanted to know why a high-roller from San Francisco wanted to invest in a poor neighborhood in D.C. MacFarlane said it made sense for him, as a black man, to put his efforts into a historically African American city:

I didn't grow up with a silver spoon in my mouth. I slept on a couch with my sister in a community that looked like many we go into. . . . I can't sink $10 billion into Detroit.[16]

Next up for MacFarlane—a whole city block in Harlem:

I'm not going to apologize for my success. That's supposed to be what the American dream is all about. But part of giving back is also demonstrating what can be done. If I'm in control of all this capital and won't make a difference, then who will?[17]

Reginald Lewis: TLC Group—Born in 1942 to a working-class family with a strong work ethic in East Baltimore, Reginald Lewis knew from the time he was a little boy that he wanted to be wealthy and he never wavered from that goal. He grew up in pre-civil rights America but that didn't stop him from excelling in school and eventually heading to Harvard for law school. He started his career as a dedicated corporate lawyer until the 1980s, when he left law to form his own investment company, the TLC Group. One of TLC's first purchases was the McCall Pattern Company in 1984 for $22.5 million. Three years later, TLC sold the company for $65 million.

Lewis had clearly made his mark, but he didn't stop there. In that same year, he bought Beatrice International Foods for $985 million, making TLC the largest black-owned business in the U.S. By 1992, he had made *Fortune* magazine's list of the 400 richest Americans, with personal wealth of $400 million. In 1993, at the young age of 50, he died of brain cancer.

Lewis was known as a quiet man, a relentless negotiator who drove a hard but fair bargain, who was also generous with his money. It is said that in the last five years of his life, he gave away "more money than most of us will make in several lifetimes."[18]

Women Entrepreneurs

Valerie Daniels-Carter: V & J Holding Companies, Inc—Valerie Daniels-Carter purchased her first Burger King franchise in Milwaukee, Wisconsin, in 1984. It did so well, and she enjoyed the business so much, that she opened another one a couple of years later, and another after that. Before long, V & J Holding had become the largest black-owned business franchise with over 100 Burger Kings and Pizza Huts in four different states. In 2006, the company ranked 44th on the *Black Enterprise* magazine's top 100 Industrial/Service companies with sales over $97 million. Daniels-Carter says she looks back now and just shakes her head:

> If you would have asked me in 1982, when I first started my application process, whether or not I thought I would have 98 restaurants in 1997, I probably would have said, "Heck, I'm just happy to get one." But it's an evolving industry, and I don't ever say can't, never, or no.[19]

She gives back to her Milwaukee community as well. She spearheaded and helped fund the Daniels-Carter Youth Center, and the Jeffery A. Carter

Sr. Center for Community Empowerment and Reunification. She often works quietly behind the scenes to provide for families in need. She is also a partner with Prison Ministries, helping families of prison inmates.

Juanita Britton: Brooks Brothers Franchiser—The Washington D.C. African American Kwanzaa and Christmas Bazaar was the springboard for Juanita Britton's career. She organized it nearly 20 years ago to showcase and sell arts, crafts, clothing, and other creations by black artisans. Through her savvy promotion and marketing, the event was a huge success and has grown every year since, to the point that she has to turn countless vendors away for lack of space.

It wasn't long before she starting thinking about expanding her marketing efforts, this time the retail trade, specifically the elite men's clothier, Brooks Brothers. She decided she wanted to set up shop in airports outside the security zone so that anyone could come and shop. In fact, they could come to the airport *just* to shop. People told her it was impossible largely because airports are an exclusive and male-dominated market and no other African American had ever secured a franchise with Brooks Brothers. But "impossible" was not part of Britton's vocabulary.

She finally partnered with Paradies Shops, which has the license for Brooks Brothers airport stores. She says she also got some help lobbying the Washington Airport Authority from another African American woman, the only woman on the authority board:

> Airport retail space is completely locked up. She really pushed for minority participation and supported my efforts all the way.[20]

Britton now has two Brooks Brothers shops—one at Ronald Reagan National Airport and the other at Dulles International Airport, and is the first African American to break into the Brooks Brothers network. It's ironic, because there was a time before the civil rights era when blacks were not even allowed to work in the stores. Britton says it has worked out just as she thought it would:

> Now we get men who come to the airport only to shop. They're alone, without the family, so they can take advantage of all the professionals there who know how to help them.[21]

She has since added several more franchises to her repertoire, including three CNBC newsstands/convenience stores and two PGA golf stores. She has also poured herself into her community, setting up the Anacostia

Art Gallery and the Random Acts Foundation, which helps those in need both in the U.S. and in Africa. And she still runs the Kwanzaa Christmas Bazaar, too. No wonder she's won the nickname of "Busy Bee." Britton says it all still seems like a dream come true to her:

> A little girl like me, a partner in nine stores? I still can't believe it. Being able to employ kids in the community, and give back? All I can say is wow. Believe it or not, it's me.[22]

Oprah Winfrey: HARPO Productions, Oxygen Media—Because of her celebrity status and high visibility, as well as her philanthropic efforts, Oprah Winfrey is among the most well-known African Americans in the world. Her early life, however, was at the opposite end of the spectrum. Shuffled from one set of relatives to another, abused and molested as a youngster, she finally ran away from home and ended up on her way to a juvenile detention facility. She escaped that fate at the last minute and was sent to live with her father in Nashville. He "laid down the law" regarding behavior and school performance, and set her on a straight and narrow path that set the stage for her success today. Winfrey says:

> As strict as he was, he had some concerns about me making the best of my life, and would not accept anything less than what he thought was my best.[23]

America got its first glimpse of Winfrey in her portrayal of Sofia in the 1985 movie *The Color Purple*. Her performance earned her both Oscar and Golden Globe nominations. She gained further critical acclaim in Native Son.

Winfrey got her start in broadcasting at 17 in Nashville, first at a local radio station, then becoming a news reporter for a local TV station. She also earned a degree in Speech Communications and Performing Arts at Tennessee State University. Then it was on to an even bigger market in Baltimore where she co-anchored the news on WJZ TV and was co-host of the station's talk show. In the news/talk arena, she found her niche. Before long, she had moved west and taken over the floundering AM Chicago program on WLS-TV and turned it into a hit. In 1985, it became The Oprah Winfrey Show, and a year later the show was at the top of the heap of nationally syndicated talk shows. The following year came the show's first Emmys, the first of many in years to come.

In 1986, Winfrey formed HARPO Productions, Inc. to produce high-quality films and television programming. In 1988, HARPO bought ownership and production rights for the Oprah Winfrey Show from

Capitol Cities/ABC, making her the first black woman in history to own and produce her own talk show. She is also a partner in Oxygen Media, Inc., a cable production company with programming targeting women. Then there's *O* magazine, a slick, informative monthly with Winfrey gracing every cover, and found everywhere from libraries to grocery check-out stands.

Her philanthropic and political profile is almost as high as her entertainment profile. In 1991, she campaigned for a national database of convicted child abusers, even testifying before Congress in support of the National Child Protection Act. President Bill Clinton signed the "Oprah Bill" into law in 1993, creating the national database she had envisioned. Winfrey has been named one of *Time* magazine's 100 Most Influential People of the 20th century, received a Lifetime Achievement Award from the National Academy of Television Arts and Sciences, and the National Book Foundation's 50th anniversary gold medal for her efforts to promote both reading and new authors through her Oprah Book Club. Her most recent effort was the establishment of a school for young women in Africa. In 2003, Winfrey was added to the *Forbes* magazine list of billionaires, making her the first African American woman to become a billionaire.

Cathy Hughes: Radio One—Born and raised in Omaha, Nebraska, Cathy Hughes also got her start in broadcasting there. She rose to prominence quickly and soon found herself in Washington, D. C. teaching at the Howard University School of Communications. In 1973, she became general sales manager at Howard's WHUR-FM, and two years later, became general manager. The station had been scraping by with borderline revenues, but Hughes turned things around quickly. It wasn't long before revenues shot up from about $300,000 a year to over $3 million.

In 1979, she and her husband bought their own station—WOL-AM in D.C.—and that was the beginning of what would become Radio One. It is interesting to note that Hughes, like many would-be black entrepreneurs, had difficulty getting financing and went to 32 banks before finally finding a lender.

Shortly after buying the station, Hughes and her husband split and she bought out his share of the station. Then hard luck hit the now-single mom. The station was trashed by some former employees, and the bills for repairs put her into a financial crush that forced her to give up her home and move, with her son, into the station. Never one to give up, she changed the format of the station from R & B to all-talk format, and revenues began to rise. Her own morning talk show was hugely popular and was the "rainmaker" for the station.

By 1995, her fortunes had turned to the point that she was able to buy WKYS in D.C. for $40 million, and that was just the beginning of the building of the Radio One empire. Today, Radio One owns 70 stations in nine major markets, the largest black-owned radio chain in the U.S. In 2004, she also added TV One, a national cable TV network.

In 2006, Radio One held 11th place on *Black Enterprise* magazine's top 100 industrial/services companies with sales of more than $413 million. It is also the only publicly traded company on the list.

Hughes has some wise words for aspiring entrepreneurs, and her own life bears witness to their truth:

> It is not enough for you to do your very best. You must do what is required of the situation.[24]

Portrait of an Entrepreneur: Michele Hoskins

Michele Foods began over 20 years ago when Michele Hoskins decided to turn an old family syrup recipe handed down through the generations into a business. The driving force behind her idea was the very entrepreneurial desire to create a legacy: "I wanted to leave my daughters a business instead of just a recipe."[25]

Hoskins says her parents' strength and loving guidance when she was growing up gave her the strong foundation to move forward at a time when it wasn't all that easy for any black business person, much less a woman:

> From a young age my parents told me "anything the mind can conceive can be achieved." That's what gave me the ability to start my own company literally with no start-up capital and no business experience. There was no mentor for me as an African American woman entrepreneur. Had I not been naïve as I was, I might not have done this. All I had going for me was my goal.[26]

Like Cathy Hughes and countless others before her, getting the start-up capital was a problem:

> The banking part is still the most difficult aspect for minority entrepreneurs. I invested the capital I made from selling virtually everything I had. I never had any bank loans or investors, only one small line of credit when I started in October 1984. I learned how to live off receivables early on.[27]

However, Hoskins succeeded, and now Michele's Syrups are found in stores nationwide, including Stop & Shop, Super Wal-Mart, Kroger, Super Target, and many others. In 2009 the company finally broke into the highly competitive warehouse market as they were accepted as vendors for Sam's Club and Costco. Michele's Syrups is the first black vendor to be accepted into Costco.

She has been honored many times over for her achievements, has made the rounds of the top news/talk shows, and is a sought-after speaker at business gatherings. She says she most enjoys mentoring young people seeking a career in the food industry. Her biggest pieces of advice to them?

> Invest in yourself. If you don't believe in yourself, no one else will ... I believe that anything can manifest with faith, hard work, and perseverance. So never give up. The dream is something that unfolds to you as you work it. Whatever happens, look at it from a very positive and spiritual way.[28]

This is only a sampling of black entrepreneurs who have coupled the gains of the Civil Rights era with their own creativity and drive. There are many more like them, and their stories and success are an inspiration to any aspiring entrepreneur.

Notes

1. *African American Desk Reference* (New York: Stonesong Press and New York Public Library, Philip Koslow ed., 1999), 67–68.

2. "B.E. 100's: A Blueprint for Growth, Industrial/Services Companies" *Black Enterprise* (June 2007): 109.

3. Derek T. Dingle, "Bob Johnson's Second Act," *Black Enterprise* (June 2007): 200.

4. Ibid.

5. Staff writers, Hip Hop, Inc. National Black Business Trade Association, 2005. http://blackentrepreneurshalloffame.blogspot.com/search?q=russell+simmons (Accessed March 2009).

6. Ibid.

7. Staff writers, Hip Hop, Inc., National Black Business Trade Association, 2005. http://blackentrepreneurshalloffame.blogspot.com/search?q=damon+dash (Accessed March 2009).

8. Staff writers, Joe Dudley, Sr., National Black Business Trade Association, 2005. http://blackentrepreneurshalloffame.blogspot.com/search?q=joe+dudley (Accessed March 2009).

9. Ibid.

10. Ibid.

11. Staff writers, Magic Johnson, National Black business trade association. 2005 http://blackentrepreneurshalloffame.blogspot.com/search?q=magic+johnson (Accessed February 2009).

12. Ibid.

13. Ibid.

14. "B.E. 100's: A Blueprint for Growth, Industrial/Services Companies," *Black Enterprise* (June 2007): 109.

15. "B.E. Investment Banks/Private Equity Firms," *Black Enterprise* (June 2008): 177.

16. David Nakamura, "Spreading Roots Across the Region, Where Others See Blight, Investor Eyes Potential," *Washington Post*, October 4, 2007, sec. B5.

17. Ibid.

18. Staff writers, Reginald Lewis, National Black Business Trade Association, 2005. http://blackentrepreneurshalloffame.blogspot.com/search?q=Reginald +Lewis (Accessed February 2009).

19. Staff writer, Valerie Daniels-Carter, Dominion Power 2005 Honoree, Strong Men & Women—Excellence in Leadership, http://www.dom.com/about/education/strong/2005/carter.jsp (Accessed February 2009).

20. Lucinda Anderson, Franchise Report: Brooks Brothers and Juanita Britton, Special to AOL BlackVoices, 2005. http://www.blackvoices.com/work monmain/smallbiz/brooksb2005 (Accessed March 2009).

21. Ibid.

22. Ibid.

23. Staff writer, Oprah Winfrey, National Black Business Trade Association, 2005. http://blackentrepreneurshalloffame.blogspot.com/search?q=oprah+winfrey (Accessed February 2009).

24. Interview by *The History Makers*, 2004. http://www.thehistorymakers .com/biography/biography.asp?bioindex=857 (Accessed March 2009).

25. Staff writer, Michele Hoskins, National Black Business Trade Association, 2005. http://blackentrepreneurshalloffame.blogspot.com/2005/02/michele -hoskins.html (Accessed February 2009).

26. Ibid.

27. Ibid.

28. Ibid.

CHAPTER 9

A Parting Look at the Foundations of Black Entrepreneurial Excellence

The story of the black quest for economic liberty has been largely lost. The historical exuberance of black Americans for free enterprise is a story of trial, tribulation, and triumph. In the past, the black community has had to rely on its own resources to survive. Black communities, however, because of Jim Crow laws and practices, evolved into viable societies with their own hospitals, banks, restaurants, insurance companies, gas stations, moving companies, and other essential enterprises necessary to maintain the black community's viability. Black newspapers reported on the community's life, black doctors tended the community's sick, and black undertakers buried the community's dead.

Prior to the American Revolution, blacks, determined to succeed in this country, entrenched themselves as workers and entrepreneurs. The total personal wealth of free blacks on the eve of the Civil War has been conservatively estimated at $50 million dollars. Black progress continued throughout the early years of the twentieth century.

Despite the economic and social oppression to which this country subjected slaves, modern research has shown that they created a vibrant family, and religious and cultural tradition that continues to this day. The kind of social dislocation and family instability that plagues today's black ghettos was virtually unknown among the black migrant communities in the North in the early years of the 20th century. In 1925 Harlem, 85 percent of black families were intact and single teenaged mothers were a rarity.[1]

Black Americans now confront a great challenge and an enormous opportunity. The black struggle for equality in American society was born in the dark days of slavery and nurtured with the courage and sacrifice of generations who would not silently accept second-class citizenship. The great challenge facing black America today is the task of taking control of its own future by exerting the necessary leadership and building the necessary institutions to make black social and economic development a reality. Meeting this self-help challenge ultimately depends on black action. It is unwise to suppose that any state or federal government would remain indefinitely committed to the current programs of black revitalization. Nevertheless, such programs are still necessary.

Justice Sandra Day O'Connor, in *Grutter v. Bollinger,*[2] expressed hope that black Americans would achieve parity with whites within 25 years of that decision, which would be June 2028. The American style of capitalism, however, in contrast to European capitalism, deplores government intervention and regulation, and has a high tolerance for inequality. American capitalism, as set forth by conservative economists, views government regulation, no matter how "noble" or "morally perfect," as interfering with the "rights of property owners to pursue their own interests."[3]

Not surprisingly, the United States has a higher economic disparity between rich and poor than any other industrialized nation in the world.[4] This does not bother most Americans because of the belief that the American system will inevitably lead to personal wealth. Indeed, "some 55 percent of Americans under 30 think they will become rich, and by six-to-one believe that poverty is due to personal flaws."[5]

Europeans, on the other hand, have sharp differences with the American view. In contrast, the 15 countries that comprise the European Union believe that civil and social groups should have equal say with commercial interests; favor cultural and linguistic diversity over assimilation; and guarantee all their citizens, as a matter of legal right, access to health care, paid vacations, housing assistance, and continuing education.[6] A European-type approach, though not flawless, seems the more realistic route for America to take if black economic and social parity is to be gained within the next 25 years.

Capitalism, for all its virtues, is not a perfect system and frequently requires government intervention. For quite a few years now markets have been largely unregulated, and while it has had its benefits, it also has drawbacks. Steven Pearlstein, writing in the Washington Post, noted that:

... what Americans have also come to realize is that the same model is less adept at providing other things we value highly—things like safety, fairness, economic security, and environmental sustainability.[7]

He noted that the U.S. health care system is a good example of the downside of privatization:

... it has become one of the least efficient and effective, with extraordinary high costs, mediocre results, and a large and growing pool of working families with little or no insurance and inadequate care.[8]

He points to the 2008 crash of the housing and financial sectors as yet another example:

These bubbles had their roots in deregulated credit markets that were hailed as models of innovation and market-driven efficiency. Now that the bubbles have burst, it is more than a bit ironic that government has had to step in to rescue the markets from their excesses and prevent a meltdown of the financial system.[9]

Accordingly, the government still has an important role to play in providing an economic safety net for workers and innovative programs for prospective entrepreneurs that a free-market economy has not provided, and will not provide.

The economic, social, educational, and political problems of the black poor are enormous. Black America cannot lift itself up by its own bootstraps into great wealth overnight. There is, however, great untapped potential for change at the individual and community level. Blacks are at a turning point in history. The era of the great civil rights marches is over. Although passage of the civil rights legislation of the 1960s aroused hopes that all blacks could finally enter the mainstream of society, this has proven to be more illusion than reality. New policies should be geared toward maximizing independence and economic opportunity. Accordingly, black America must recognize the value of, and expand on, indigenous self-help neighborhood efforts. These efforts should, among other tasks, seek to encourage marriage in the black community. Nevertheless, innovative governmental efforts to improve the education system—to provide greater opportunities for blacks to acquire college and specialized degrees and to assist blacks in employment, business development, and community-based empowerment programs—must be maintained and strengthened for the foreseeable future if black economic, educational, and social parity is to be achieved in the next 25 years.

As Dr. Martin Luther King, Jr. often said, the cause of economic justice is the cause of social justice.[10] The success of various micro-enterprise programs and innovative efforts such as the Prison Entrepreneurship Program buttress the numerous findings that the pursuit of entrepreneurial endeavors plays an important role in bringing prosperity to disadvantaged groups and underdeveloped countries. The Small Business Administration reported in 2007 that entrepreneurial firms contributed over 50 percent of the United States' gross domestic product and created about 78 percent of all new jobs every year for the past 20 years.[11] Additionally, small entrepreneurial firms are responsible for 67 percent of all innovations and 95 percent of radical innovations since World War II.[12]

So now we come to the end of our journey through the history of these extraordinary people who accomplished so much, often in the face of near-impossible odds. Lunsford Lane, Maggie Lena Walker, John H. Johnson, and others like them throughout history all shared the same things—a strong vision, faith in that vision, and the determination to make that vision real. Their lives and their stories are inspirations for us all, especially those setting out on the entrepreneurial path.

Things are very different today than they were in the days of Lunsford Lane, but there are still challenges to be met. You, as an aspiring entrepreneur, have more tools available to you, and more doors open to you than they did, but it is still the power of vision and the determination to forge ahead that will carry you to success. Part II of this book will give you some practical help in bringing your own entrepreneurial efforts to fruition. The rest is up to you!

Notes

1. Glenn C. Loury, "Making it All Happen," in *On the Road to Economic Freedom, An Agenda for Black Progress* (Washington, DC: Regnery Gateway, Robert L. Woodson, ed.. 1987), 118.

2. 539 U.S. 306 (2003).

3. Marcellus Andrews. *The Political Economy of Hope and Fear: Capitalism and the Black Condition in America* (New York: NYU Press, 1999), 151–55.

4. Robert Heilbroner and Lester Thurow. *Economics Explained* (New York: Simon & Schuster, 1998), 193.

5. Peter Engardio, "Nice Dream If You Can Live It," *Business Week*, (Sept. 13, 2004): 22.

6. Ibid.

7. Steven Pearlstein, "Farewell to Free- Market Capitalism: Wave Goodbye to the Invisible Hand," *Washington Post*, August 1, 2008, sec. D1 and 8.

8. Ibid.

9. Ibid., 8.

10. Charles Steele, Jr., "The Color of Credit," *Washington Post*, June 23, 2008, sec. A15.

11. Jeff Cornwall, "Growing Firms in the Entrepreneurial Economy," *Entrepreneurial Mind*, October 25, 2007, http://www.drjeffcoenwall.com (search growing firms).

12. Bruce R. Barringer and R. Duane Ireland. *Entrepreneurship* (Upper Saddle River, NJ: Pearson Prentice Hall, 2006), 15.

PART II

Building Future Excellence: A Primer for Aspiring Entrepreneurs

INTRODUCTION

People become entrepreneurs for a variety of reasons. Some become entrepreneurs to be their own boss, to pursue their own ideas, and to realize financial rewards. Usually, a triggering event prompts an individual to become an entrepreneur. Examples include the loss of a job, receipt of an inheritance (which provides the money to start a business), and lifestyle issues, e.g., the decision to start a business after a young child begins school.

These prospective entrepreneurs usually seek to take advantage of some sort of moneymaking opportunity which has come to their attention. But exactly what is the definition of an opportunity? It is is a situation or set of circumstances that creates a need for a new product, service or business; and it is an attractive, timely idea that can be embodied in a product or service that creates value for its buyers or end users.

The most common definition of entrepreneurship states that entrepreneurship is the process by which individuals pursue opportunities even if they don't have all the funds they need or a full support network in place. Recall Joe Dudley and his wife Eunice mixing up shampoos and cosmetics at home after work at their day jobs or Damon Dash selling records out of his car before he had a distribution contract. Howard University's Entrepreneurship, Leadership, and Innovation Institute defines entrepreneurship and the entrepreneurial mindset as "the process of opportunity discovery, risk evaluation and adding value to situations, projects, activities and organizations." The entrepreneurs you read about in Part I are all living examples of these definitions.

New businesses generally fall into one of three categories. In their book *Entrepreneurship*, Bruce R. Barringer and R. Duane Ireland label them entrepreneurial, salary substitute and lifestyle businesses.[1] Salary substitute businesses include such things as hairstyling salons, law firms, dry cleaners, restaurants, etc. Lifestyle businesses include such things as tour guides, golf pros, etc.

All three types of businesses share the goal of making money. What sets entrepreneurial firms apart from the pack is innovation. They don't simply trade on an existing service or product. They create something new. In his 1934 book, *The Theory of Economic Development*, Harvard University professor Joseph Schumpeter, stated that through a process he referred to as creative destruction, entrepreneurs develop new and better products and technologies that make current products and technologies obsolete.[2]

The facts indicate that small start-up ventures most effectively initiate the process of creative destruction. People often refer to the entrepreneurs who begin such firms as "innovators" or "agents of change." Barringer and Ireland state that:

> Small entrepreneurial firms are responsible for 67 percent of all innovation in the United States, and have been responsible for 95 percent of radical innovations since World War II. Between 1993 and 1996, fast growth young companies created about two-thirds of all new jobs.[3]

Reports from the U.S. Small Business Administration find that entrepreneurial firms are now over 50% of the GDP, and have created about 78% of all new jobs every year for the past twenty years.[4]

You can dream all you want about that house you want to build, but, at some point, you have to get a design down on paper and start hammering nails. That is the focus of the upcoming chapters.

Good Books to Read As You Begin the Quest

- *Entrepreneurship*, Bruce Barringer and R. Duane Ireland
- *The Entrepreneur's Strategy Guide: Ten Keys for Achieving Marketplace Leadership and Operational Excellence*, Tom Cannon
- *How To Succeed in Business without Being White*, Earl Graves

Notes

1. Bruce R. Barringer and Duane Ireland, *Entrepreneurship* (Upper Saddle River, NJ: Pearson Prentice Hall, 2006), 13–14.

2. Paraphrased from Joseph Schumpeter, *The Theory of Economic Development* (Cambridge, MA: Harvard University Press, 1934).

3. Bruce R. Barringer and R. Duane Ireland, *Entrepreneurship* (Upper Saddle River, NJ: Pearson Prentice Hall, 2006), 16.

4. Small Business Administration, Office of Advocacy, *How Important are Small Businesses to the U.S. Economy?* March 2004, Frequently Asked Questions. http://www.sba.gov/advo/stats/sbfaq.pdf (Accessed March 2009).

CHAPTER 10

DEVELOPING YOUR IDEAS

In the early stages of getting your business off the ground, there are several things you will need to do. They will help you bring your idea into a workable form that will help insure its success. You will expand all these components in much greater detail when you write your business plan.

- Develop a concept statement
- Do a feasibility analysis
- Do an industry analysis
- Do a competitor analysis
- Create a business model
- Build a team
- Assess the venture's financial strength

Let's take a look at each.

Concept Statement

The concept statement is the first step. It describes your product or service, the target market you are aiming to reach, the benefits of the product or service, and how you plan to sell or distribute the product.

Feasibility Analysis

Many new businesses fail because the feasibility analysis was weak or not done at all. Feasibility analysis basically shows whether the idea is worth pursuing. It helps you determine whether a business idea is viable and worth the investment of time, money, and effort. The feasibility analysis has three main components.

- Product or service feasibility analysis. This assesses the overall appeal of the product or service you have in mind. Include concept and usability testing in this preliminary analysis. The feasibility study requires that the prospective business owner determine how attractive the market is for the particular product or service he plans to offer to the public. *Primary research* (talking directly to potential customers and industry professionals) and *secondary research* (examining existing data concerning the industry and market) are both effective ways to gauge public interest.
- Organizational feasibility analysis. This analysis looks at management, organization, and resources. Does management have the skills to carry the business forward? Is there a strong, well-planned organizational structure? Are there adequate funds to get the business going comfortably?
- Financial feasibility analysis. Not only must the company have the funds to get going, it must show the promise of being profitable and be attractive to potential investors.

Industry Analysis

Performing an industry analysis will give you and potential investors an idea of the industry's viability as a whole and prospects for growth and expansion in the future. The knowledge you glean from an industry analysis helps you decide whether to enter an industry and if you can carve out a position in the industry that will provide you with a competitive advantage. There is no one-size-fits-all approach to conducting an industry analysis. Your idea or vision will shape the kinds of information you seek, but, in general, you will be looking at an industry's most recent performance and current status and its prospects for the future. Other things you might look at include competition within the industry, the supply chain, and the characteristics of the target market of customers. This kind of information will show you any threats to your new business as well as opportunities, and help you decide if your enterprise will be successful within the industry. Here are some things to consider.

- **Current status of the industry**. Is it young and wide open like the technology industry? Is it established and profitable, but perhaps a bit stale so would benefit from an injection of "new blood" with creative, innovative ideas? Is it declining or maybe even in peril, but offers opportunities for new product strategies or niche marketing?

- **Competition**. How intense is competition within industry sectors? How thick is the competition for the product or service you will offer? Competition is examined more closely in the competitor analysis section.
- **Supply chain**. How are goods and services needed for production moved within the industry? Is there competition among suppliers that could work to your advantage? How reliable is the supply chain, particularly for your product or service?
- **Target market.** Who is the customer base—demographics and buying power? Is that base likely to shift or change in the future?

Competitor Analysis

The competitor analysis looks at the other companies that produce products or services that will be angling for the same or similar markets as yours. Things to cover in your analysis include:

- Direct, indirect, and potential future competitors.
- Are the businesses growing, steady, or declining?
- What can you learn from their operations or advertising?
- What are their strengths and weaknesses?
- How does their product or service differ from yours?
- Is the market strong enough or growing at a rate that will supply enough customers for all players?
- What are your competitors' strategies and objectives?[1]

Where to Get Industry and Competitor Information

- Visit companies within an industry, particularly those that will be your competitors.
- Talk to customers whenever you can.
- Attend speeches and presentations by industry and competitor representatives.
- Attend trade shows, particularly those of your competitors.
- Use general business publications, marketing and advertising publications, local newspapers and business journals, industry and trade association publications, industry research and surveys, and computer databases. Government agencies, such as the Federal Trade Commission, have a wealth of industry information.
- The Internet. Simply said, "Google it."[2]

The Business Model

The business model is a detailed look at the structures and day-to-day functions of the company from top to bottom, inside and out. It helps all players in the operation stay focused on the mission and goals, and can be updated and adjusted depending on economic conditions and customer demand.

The business model looks at both internal and external factors. Internal factors include the following:

- Company structure of divisions and departments, including employee and executive responsibilities and accountability.
- Procedures, processes, and labor needs in manufacture of a product or delivery of a service.
- Expenses and revenue management.
- Operating strategies.

External factors include:

- Target market of customers.
- Marketing and sales strategies based on target market data.
- Pricing strategies based on target market data and current or emerging economic conditions.

Build a Team

Like many of the entrepreneurs you read about in Part I, you may begin your venture virtually alone, or with the help of a few family members or friends. But, as your enterprise grows, you will need to expand your support network. It is, therefore, helpful to know the kinds of people you will need on your team.

The ideal core team is a mix of young, enthusiastic, creative players and seasoned management with a track record that is compatible with your company's goals and philosophy. The most important ingredient for the team is that all members share the vision for the company and are ready to focus their expertise to advance that vision. Other members of the team that may not necessarily be "in house" would include consultants, investment advisors and accountants, bankers, and those people with whom you can network to move the company forward.

Assess Your Venture's Financial Strength

Even if you are just getting started with your idea, it's important to learn to read and prepare financial statements. As your business grows, it becomes even more important that you know every aspect of the financial picture even if you have an army of accountants and financial advisors. It is essential to being a true entrepreneur. You will need to know the following inside and out.

- Income statements—how much money you made and what the expenses were over a period of time; that will show if you're turning a profit or losing money.
- Balance sheets—shows assets against liabilities and reflects the owner's equity (positive or negative) in the business.
- Cash flows—keeps track of ongoing changes in revenues over a certain period of time.

The figures on the financial sheets will let you know if you're meeting your projections and objectives and how you stack up against your competitors in the market.

Financial forecasts are just that—projections of future sales, income, and expenses. Companies that have been doing business for a few years have "real" figures to work with, but when you're just getting started, you have to make estimates based on your market and industry research. All of this information will get plugged into the income statement. Table 10.1

Table 10.1 Sample Year End Income Statement*

Income statement for the year ending December 31, 2008					
	Total	1st Quarter	2nd Quarter	3rd Quarter	4th Quarter
Sales	370,000	70,000	85,000	100,000	115,000
Cost of goods sold	185,000	35,000	42,500	50,000	57,500
Gross margin	185,000	35,000	42,500	50,000	57,000
Operating Expenses					
Selling	90,000	17,500	20,875	24,250	27,375
Administrative	37,000	7,000	8,500	10,000	11,500
Total	127,000	24,500	29,375	34,250	38,875
Net income from Operations	58,000	10,500	13,125	15,750	18,625
Interest expense	450	150	150	150	
Net income before Income taxes	57,550	10,500	12,975	15,600	18,475
Federal income tax (25% average)	14,388	2,625	3,244	3,900	4,619
Net income	43,162	7,875	9,731	11,700	13,856

* U.S. Small Business Administration Publication FM 8, *Budgeting for the Small Business.* Available for free download at http://www.sba.gov.

illustrates a typical end-of-year income statement that reflects all of the firm's income and expenses, including federal, state, and local taxes paid for the year. It gives a clear picture of the financial health of the firm after a year's operation.

Table 10.2 illustrates the monthly income statement that every firm must do to keep a running tab on the financial health of the business. Note that this one does not show expenditures for federal, state, or local taxes, as it was prepared before those taxes were paid. A monthly income statement prepared after quarterly taxes have been paid would reflect those figures.

Once you have completed the sales forecast, you must forecast the costs of sales as well as other items on the firm's income statement. The most common way to do this is to use the percent-of-sales method for expressing each expense item as percentage of sales. You can determine the firm's *costs as a percentage of sales* after determining the *gross margin.* The gross margin is the difference between the cost to produce a good or service and the price for which it sells. Accountants often reflect the gross margin as a percentage of the firm's retained revenues after deducting the direct costs associated with producing that revenue. You can, thereafter, determine from the gross margin percentage figure the cost of producing the product or service as a percentage of the revenues received. Here's an example.

- Subtract the total sales price (for example, $1,544,519) from the cost to produce the items ($341,885) = $1,202,634 and divide the difference ($1,202, 634) by the total amount of sales ($1,202,634 ÷ 1,544,519) = 77.86% gross margin as a percentage of retained revenues (note: you must multiply the result × 100 to get the gross margin as a percentage).
- Thereafter, subtract the gross margin figure (77.86%) from 100.00% = Cost as a percentage of sales = 100% − 77.86% = 22.14%.

Alternatively, you may divide the direct costs to produce a good (e.g., $341, 885) by the total amount of sales (e.g., $1,544, 519) = a cost as a percentage of sales of 22.13537%.

Thereafter, subtract from 100.00% the cost as a percentage of sales (22.13537%) to determine the gross margin which equals 77.86%.

Relationship of the Balance Sheet to the Income Statement

All of the assets on the balance sheet have two sources—outside sources (loans, i.e., *liabilities,* provided by creditors) and inside sources

Table 10.2   Sample Monthly Income Statement*

New Business Monthly Income Statement
(Current Year-To-Date)

	Current Month		Year-To-Date	
	$	%	$	%
Sales				
Beginning Inventory	38,000	100.00	450,000	100.00
Materials purchased	143,000		138,850	
Ending inventory	23,500		286,150	
Cost of goods sold	23,500	92.00	279,000	62.00
Gross profit	14,400	38.00	171,000	38.00
Operating and Fixed Expense				
Wages	7,500	19.74	90,000	20.00
Payroll tax	750	1.97	9,000	2.00
Benefits	400	1.05	5,000	1.11
Accounting and legal	0	0.00	1,000	0.22
Advertising	475	1.25	5,265	1.17
Sales expenses	85	0.22	1,000	0.22
Interest	700	1.84	9,000	2.00
Utilities	275	0.72	3,000	0.67
Telephone	330	0.87	4,000	0.89
Supplies	400	1.05	5,000	1.11
Office supplies	140	0.37	1,570	0.35
Repair and maintenance	100	0.26	1,100	0.24
Freight	50	0.13	450	0.10
Insurance	833	2.19	10,000	2.22
Depreciation	425	1.12	5,100	1.13
Vehicles	200	0.53	2,600	0.58
Rent	0	0.00	0	0.00
Outside services	75	0.20	1,000	0.22
Miscellaneous	165	0.43	2,000	0.44
Total operating and fixed expenses	12,903	33.96	156,085	34.69
Operating profit	1,537	4.04	14,915	3.31

*United States Small Business Administration, Publication EB 7, Financial Management for The Growing Business. In the public domain. Available for free download at http://www.sba.gov.

(assets put into the business by owners, i.e., *equity*). Thus, the total of assets on the balance sheet always equals the total of liabilities and equity on the balance sheet.

The income statement shows the earnings of the business between successive balance sheets. If the business has net income during that period, the equity account called earned surplus (or retained earnings) on the balance sheet would show an increase by the amount of the profit.

In Table 10.3, you can see how this works. On any balance sheet, if one subtracts total assets from total liabilities, it will always show the net

Table 10.3   Sample Balance Sheet*

Assets	
Current Assets	
Cash	$ 2,174
Accounts receivable	28,459
Notes receivable	24,216
Inventory	143,000
Total current assets	$ 197,849
Property, plant and equipment	
Equipment	17,988
Vehicles	8,000
Furniture and fixtures	
Total cost of PPE	25,988
Less accumulated depreciation	18,892
Book value of PPE	7,096
Total assets	$ 204,945
Liabilities and Equity	
Current Liabilities	
Accrued expenses	
Accounts payable	71,000
Current portion of long-term debts	11,802
Total current liabilities	82,802
Long-term debt	64,198
Total liabilities	147,000
Owner's equity	57,945
Total liabilities and equity	$ 204,945

*United States Small Business Administration, Publication EB 7, Financial Management for The Growing Business. In the public domain. Available for free download at http://www.sba.gov.

worth (equity) belonging to the owners. A firm is *insolvent in the bankruptcy sense* if its liabilities exceed its assets. A firm is *insolvent in the equity sense* if it cannot pay its bills as they come due. And corporations, for example, are forbidden by law from declaring a dividend to shareholders if they are insolvent.

Why the Balance Sheet Balances

Every transaction involves making both a **debit (left-side entry to the ledger)** and a corresponding **credit (right-side entry to the ledger)** for the same amount to some account (double entry accounting). This involves debits and credits to the three categories of accounts that appear on the balance sheet—assets, liabilities, and owner's equity.

Sometimes the debit will be made to an account in one main category (e.g., cash in the asset account) and the credit will be made to an account in another main category account (e.g., stated capital in the equity account).

Bookkeepers make these entries in *journals* and post these transactions at some point to the *general ledger*. Accountants create balance sheets from this data. Accordingly, accountants do not make debit and credit entries directly on the balance sheet. Rather, accountants create the balance sheet from these records.

Take a look now at Table 10.4, which illustrates double entry accounting. Note that a debit (left side entry) to an asset account (e.g., cash) represents an increase in that account while a debit in the other accounts (i.e., the liability account and the equity account) represents a decrease in those accounts. Similarly, a credit (right side entry) to an asset account represents a decrease in that account while a credit to a liability account and an equity account represent an increase in these accounts.

Table 10.4 Double Entry Accounting

Main Categories:	Assets		Liabilities		Equity	
Example of Asset Accounts:	+	−	−	+	−	+
1. Cash	* left side (debit)	* right side (credit)	* left side (debit)	* right side (credit)	* left side (debit)	* right side (credit)
2. Inventory	debit increases credit decreases		debit decreases credit increases		debit decreases credit increases	

Double Entry Accounting and the Income Statement

The applicable accounts with respect to the income statement are as follows: revenue, expense, and the cost of goods sold. They are temporary proprietorship accounts that accountants will zero out and reflect as either an increase to shareholders' equity or a decrease to shareholders' equity at the end of the relevant accounting period. And an increase in equity (an accountant would credit equity under double entry accounting conventions) would result in an increase in cash (an accountant would debit cash/assets under double entry accounting). The debits and credits for these accounts are as follows:

- Expenses: debit expenses and credit assets/cash
- Cost of goods sold: debit the cost of goods sold account and credit cash/assets
- Revenues: debit cash/assets and credit revenues

A detailed discussion of bookkeeping is beyond the scope of this book. However, the entrepreneur should generally know at least this much about the process.

Information That Can Be Gleaned from the Income Statement

Some of the information which one my obtain from the income statement are as follows:

- Net profits: revenues less expenses and taxes.
- Cash flow: net profits plus depreciation, depletion, and amortization.
- Operating cash flow: cash flow plus interest expense plus income tax expense.
- Free cash flow: cash flow minus capital expenditures minus dividends.
- Operating margin of profit: operating income divided by net sales. This shows the percentage of each sales dollar that the company retained after expenses. It measures the efficiency of the management operating the business.
- Earnings per share of common stock: net profits ÷ number of shares issued and outstanding.
- PE Ratio (price-earnings ratio): market price of common stock ÷ earnings per share of common stock.

Information Which Can Be Gleaned from the Balance Sheet

Some of the information which one may obtain from the balance sheet are as follows:

- Net working capital: (current assets minus current liabilities)
- Current ratio: (current assets ÷ current liabilities)
- Quick assets: current assets minus inventories
- Net quick assets : current assets less inventory minus current liabilities
- Book value per share: balance sheet value of common stock minus intangible assets ÷ outstanding common shares
- Total capitalization: long-term debt plus the value of all the company's ownership/equity units
- Capitalization ratio for long-term debt: long-term debt divided by total capitalization
- Capitalization ratio for firm's ownership units: total value of the ownership units—i.e., common stock and any preferred stock—divided by total capitalization). Note: a conservative capitalization is one with little or no debt. This is because interest on debt is an obligation of the corporation.

This gives you a snapshot of the kinds of financial data you will need to know and track throughout the life of your enterprise. In the next chapter, we'll look at the organizational and legal form of your business.

Some Good Resources to Help You Shape Your Ideas

- *Simplified Accounting for the Non-Accountant*, Rick S. Hayes and C. Richard Baker.
- U.S. Small Business Publication EB 7, *Financial Management for the Growing Business.* Available for free download at http://www.sba.gov.
- *Before You Quit Your Job: Ten Real Life Lessons Every Entrepreneur Should Know About Building a Multimillion-Dollar Business*, Robert T. Kiyosaki.

Notes

1. http://www.sba.gov/smallbusinessplanner/manage/marketandprice/SERV_COMPANAYLSIS.html Paraphrased. (Accessed April 2009).

2. Adapted from Ibid.

CHAPTER 11

CREATING THE LEGAL FRAMEWORK FOR YOUR BUSINESS

Virtually all black businesses are closely held businesses owned by one or two persons. Only a handful are publicly held enterprises with stock that is traded over a secondary market. Interestingly, in 2001, only six African American–owned companies had shares listed for trading on a secondary market. Moreover, several of those companies appeared to be on the verge of being delisted.[1] And only one company—Radio One, Inc.—appeared to have its ownership units traded on a secondary market as of the June 2008 *Black Enterprise* rankings of America's largest black-owned businesses.

Owners of businesses with more than one owner must be concerned with issues of management control, fair treatment of other owners, and a host of other matters. Anecdotal evidence suggests that African Americans, because of their long exclusion from being able to enter the world of business enterprise on a nondiscriminatory basis, need assistance in understanding the pros and cons of doing business in a particular form of business organization. Even in 2008, many African Americans were the first in their families to graduate from college or to start a business enterprise. Accordingly, this section of the book discusses some of the legal considerations that African Americans and other prospective entrepreneurs should consider in selecting the most appropriate business organization.

Ideal Organizational Features for Start-up Firms

The proposed business structure for enterprises with two or more owners should, ideally, be one that provides its owners with:

1. equal opportunity and the right to take an active role in the management of the business.
2. limited liability.
3. the right to individually take tax deductions for expenses incurred by the business (sometimes referred to as flow-through taxation).
4. the ability to recoup one's equity investment upon leaving the business (usually accomplished via a buy-sell agreement between the owners).
5. the ability to prevent new persons from becoming owners in the business without the consent of all existing owners (equity transfer restrictions on owners).

The general partnership, with the exception of the limited liability feature, provides owners all of these benefits. Traditional corporation law, with the exception of limited liability, provides none of these protections to small closely held businesses. Accordingly, the owners need to have a specific, comprehensive written agreement between them that addresses the expectations of the owners with respect to these matters. Individuals who are considering launching a business enterprise should be particularly careful in addressing these issues.

Importance of Agreements between Owners in Closely Held Businesses

An agreement between owners in closely held businesses should be entered into by owners of closely held businesses regardless of the type of business organization. The agreement between owners in a limited liability company (LLC) is called an operating agreement between "members"; the agreement between owners of a corporation is called a shareholders' agreement; and the agreement between owners of a partnership is called a partnership agreement.
The most essential features in such agreements among the owners are:

1. how an owner gets his/her portion of the net worth of the business upon departing the business (i.e., a buy-sell agreement).
2. restrictions on an owner's ability to transfer his or her ownership units without the consent of the other members.
3. the profit/loss split.
4. the management rights of the owners of the business.
5. other closely related matters (e.g., whether to limit the right of an owner to pledge his/her right to receive his share of the profits as collateral for a personal loan).

The Seven Most Common Forms of Business Organizations

New businesses generally structure themselves into one of seven categories. Each has its advantages and limitations. Let's take a look at each of them.

The Sole Proprietorship

The sole proprietorship has only one owner by definition. The owner does not need to file any articles of organization with any governmental agency in order for a sole proprietorship to exist. The same is true of general partnerships. However, the owners of all the other business organizations discussed in this book (the corporation, the limited liability partnership, the limited partnership, the limited liability limited partnership, and the limited liability company) must file articles of organization with the appropriate state governmental agency to exist.

The statistics indicate that approximately 90–95 percent of all Black enterprises are sole proprietorships. The owner need not file any articles of organization with any governmental agency to exist as a sole proprietorship. This form of business fails to protect the owner from personal liability for the debts of the business. Accordingly, the sole proprietor has unlimited personal liability for all the contractual debts of the business if the business is unable to pay its debts. The sole proprietor is also liable for torts committed by the proprietor's agents in performing work on behalf of the owner/proprietor. Therefore, the sole proprietor should maintain adequate insurance because the proprietor's agents may render the proprietor liable as a principal in contract and tort. African American and all prospective entrepreneurs should be aware of these potential dangers in doing business in the sole proprietorship format. However, the sole proprietorship does provide the owner with all of the other features normally desired by one starting a small start-up business as the sole proprietor has the exclusive right to make all the decisions for the business.

The General Partnership

A general partnership is an association of two or more persons who combine to carry on as co-owners of a business for profit.[2] As stated earlier, the owners do not need to file any organizational documents for a general partnership to exist between themselves. Partnership law states that sharing of profits from the business constitutes prima facie evidence that one is a partner in the business.[3] Other rules for determining whether a partnership exists between two or more persons can also be found in the partnership statutes. The general partnership, like the sole proprietorship, renders its owners unlimitedly, personally liable for the debts of the partnership if the partnership cannot pay its bills. African American entrepreneurs should be aware of the ramifications of joint and several liability in doing business as a general partnership precisely because of the reality that creditors of the business can seize their personal assets if the business fails. Moreover, it makes no difference if a particular partner is innocent of any wrongdoing that may cause the partnership to be liable. If one partner is held liable, all partners are liable under general partnership laws regardless of fault or involvement in the wrongful act.

The general partnership, however, provides the business owners with all the other features normally desired by one who is starting a business enterprise. Unless there is another kind of partnership agreement in place, the general partners are presumed to have equal rights to participate in the management and control of the partnership; they are able to recoup their investment stake in the net worth of the partnership upon withdrawal from the partnership; they have a veto power over anyone becoming a new owner in the business; and they have the right to individually take tax deductions for expenses incurred by the business (i.e., flow-through taxation).[4]

The Corporation

The owners must file articles of incorporation with the appropriate governmental agency in order for a corporation to exist. Under traditional corporation law, the primary benefit that the corporate form of business provides to owners of small start-up businesses is limited liability. The corporation is deficient in every other respect, however. There have been developments in the law, however, which allow owners to achieve all of the features normally desired in a business structure for a small start-up business. Accordingly, prospective entrepreneurs who are considering starting a business enterprise should carefully consider these deficiencies before choosing this business format.

Traditional corporate law does not vest management control in the shareholders directly. Instead, these statutes place control of the corporation in a board of directors and designated officers who are accountable to the board. Directors, however, need not be owners of the corporation.[5] Accordingly, persons with no ownership stake in the business can participate in the control of the corporation. Additionally, tax law does not provide flow-through taxation to the shareholders. Consequently, tax law does not permit shareholders to deduct expenses incurred by the corporation unless the corporation is a small closely held business that applies for and meets the eligibility requirements for flow-through taxation under Subchapter S of the Internal Revenue Code. Additionally, traditional corporation law also makes it potentially difficult for owners to recoup their investment in the business after they withdraw from the business and allows for persons to become owners without the consent of the other owners. Corporations can only be dissolved under traditional statutes if shareholders approve by a vote sometimes as high as two-thirds.

Traditional corporation statutes also assume that each owner can freely transfer his/her stock ownership interest. The traditional corporation law feature of free transferability of one's ownership units (stock) allows an owner to, potentially, transfer all or a portion of his/her ownership interest to complete strangers. When this happens, discord often follows and the business may soon cease to exist as a viable concern. This is because the ability of business owners to successfully operate a business is dependent, to a large extent, on being able to work with people the owners know and trust. Therefore, placing some sort of restrictions on the ability of owners to freely transfer their ownership units to a third party serves an important purpose in small start-up firms.

There are generally three types of restrictions on shareholders' ability to transfer their shares—first refusal restrictions (owner must first offer shares to corporation or other shareholders); first option restrictions (same as first refusal restriction except that owner must offer shares at a predetermined price); and consent restrictions (owner cannot sell his shares without permission of corporation's board of directors or the other shareholders).

Nevertheless, it is possible for a business organized as a corporation to have all the features normally desired in a start-up business. The owners, however, must:

1. incorporate under a close corporation statute.
2. have a detailed shareholders' control agreement, which provides a method of assuring that the owners have an equal right to manage the corporation, relative ease in obtaining their investment in the net worth of the business upon leaving the business, and a veto power over the admission of new owners in the business.
3. apply to the Internal Revenue Service for recognition as a Subchapter S Corporation in order to achieve flow-through taxation.

Small, closely held corporations are distinguished from publicly held corporations chiefly by three characteristics:

1. a small number of stockholders
2. no ready market for the corporate stock to be traded
3. substantial majority stockholder participation in the management and operations of the corporation.[6]

Interestingly, well over 98 percent of all corporations are closely held, with less than 100 shareholders. Approximately 94 percent have only 10 or less shareholders.[7] Thus, the bulk of corporations are essentially incorporated sole proprietorships and partnerships in which the owners work in order to make a living. Usually, the owners need a "business prenuptial" agreement (called a shareholder's control agreement) to govern such matters as:

1. management rights of the owners.
2. ensuring that a shareholder will be able to recoup his investment upon his voluntary or involuntary withdrawal from the business.
3. the mechanics of determining whom will be allowed to become a new shareholder, and a myriad of other matters.

The expectations of shareholders in closely held corporations, which are basically incorporated partnerships in which the shareholders are running a business to make a living, are vastly different than the interests of shareholders in publicly held corporations who view their ownership as a pure investment in a company run by others. Accordingly, state legislatures have attempted to relax traditional corporate statutory norms to give closely held corporations the flexibility and simplicity of partnerships. Under traditional corporate norms, shareholders do not have power to manage the corporation, do not have agency authority to bind the corporation, do not owe other shareholders a fiduciary duty of care and loyalty, but they do have the power to freely transfer their ownership interests to strangers, have relative difficulty in obtaining their portion of the net worth of the business upon withdrawal from the business in the absence of owning a majority or sometimes as high as two-thirds of the outstanding shares of the business.

Thus, legislative and, in some instances, judicial attempts have been made:

1. to make it easier for shareholders in closely held corporations to obtain their stake in the net worth of the business when they voluntarily or involuntarily withdraw from the business.
2. to give shareholders the right to veto the admission of new owners in the business.

3. to pass close corporation statutes giving such businesses the flexibility of general partnerships.

4. to impose partnership-like fiduciary standards on shareholders. Courts, however, have held that controlling shareholders of publicly held corporations also have a fiduciary duty of loyalty to the corporation and its shareholders.[8]

The Limited Liability Partnership

The owners must file articles of organization with the appropriate governmental agency to create a limited liability partnership (LLP). The LLP may be an excellent choice of business format for prospective entrepreneurs starting a small business enterprise, depending on the protections provided by the particular state statute. The LLP is a general partnership in which there is no joint and several liability for partners who did not participate in the matter that gave rise to tort liability. The limited liability partner, under the first LLP statute enacted in Texas, remained liable for the contractual obligations of the firm. That statute was enacted by the Texas legislature in response to claims brought against innocent partners in litigation resulting from the collapse of real estate and energy prices in the late 1980s. More than one-third of all the bank failures occurred in Texas.[9]

Statutes creating limited liability partnerships basically do away with joint and several liability of general partners for wrongdoing/professional malpractice in which they had no involvement. Nevertheless, a partner is not shielded from the consequences of his own wrongdoing or from negligent supervision of others. Other states have passed so-called full shield statutes that extend liability protection to all types of claims. In 1997, Texas broadened its statute to cover contract as well as tort claims. A full broad shield LLP provides limited liability for partners similar to the limited liability available to shareholders in a corporation or to limited partners in a partnership that do not participate in the management of the business.[10]

The Limited Partnership

The owners must file articles of organization with the appropriate governmental agency in order for a limited partnership to exist. A limited partnership must have at least one general partner and at least one limited partner. The limited partnership fails to provide management control for all of the owners because the limited partners cannot take part in control of business without sacrificing limited liability. Legislative changes in the statutes, however, have made it possible for limited partners to engage in some management-related activities without losing limited liability protection.

The limited partnership is also deficient since the general partner remains unlimitedly liable. There are ways, however, for even a general partner to escape liability. The general partner in a limited partnership may accomplish this by incorporating the general partners or forming a limited liability limited partnership. Additionally, it is relatively difficult for a limited partner to withdraw his or her equity interest in the typical limited partnership as limitations on limited partner withdrawal of their equity interests are allowed under the limited partnership statutes and are common in limited partnership agreements. For this reason, prospective entrepreneurs should not choose this business format for doing business unless they are engaged in real estate syndications for construction and management of commercial shopping centers, office projects, and similar real estate ventures. The limited partnership is also an excellent choice of business format for other types of firms that produce substantial depreciation and similar tax write-offs which may be proportionately deducted by the limited partners.

The Limited Liability Limited Partnership

Some jurisdictions have adopted limited liability limited partnership (LLLP) statutes. These statutes limit the liability of general partners in a limited partnership to the extent afforded to general partners under the LLP statute of the particular jurisdiction. The LLP statute limits the joint and several liability of general partners for professional malpractice that would otherwise apply under general partnership statutes, among other things.

As is true with all other business organizations (with the exception of sole proprietorships and general partnerships), the owners must file articles of organization with the appropriate governmental agency in order for a limited liability limited partnership to exist. These organizations still have the other deficiencies listed in the section discussing the limited partnership and the limited liability partnership. The LLLP statute is not in wide use today. The more common practice in limited partnerships is to have only a single corporate general partner that is usually minimally capitalized and has nominal equity interest in the limited partnership. For these reasons, prospective entrepreneurs should not generally choose this form of business in their entrepreneurial endeavors.

The Limited Liability Company

The limited liability company (LLC) is an excellent organizational format for entrepreneurs operating closely held businesses. The LLC is a hybrid between a general partnership and a corporation. However, it is neither a general partnership nor is it a corporation. The owners of a LLC are referred to as its "members." In order to establish a LLC, the organizers must file articles of organization with the appropriate governmental agency. The LLC, when properly structured, provides owners with management control, limited liability, flow-through taxation, ease in recouping the owner's stake in the net worth of the business, and the ability to veto the admission of new owners to the business. The details concerning the agreement between the members of a LLC are set forth in a document referred to as an operating agreement. Accordingly, the LLC affords its owners all of the features normally desired by persons starting a small closely held business. For these reasons, the LLC is probably the best business organization format for most individuals taking the entrepreneurial plunge.

Protecting Corporate Shareholder Rights

Both shareholders in closely held corporations and the owners of partnerships and other small businesses should always enter into agreements that protect their rights to participate in the management of the business and outline a process whereby they can obtain their portion of the net worth of the business upon withdrawal from the business. Aspiring entrepreneurs should enter into these agreements as a matter of course.

Following are some methods of protecting the rights of the corporation's shareholders. Because of the peculiarities of corporations, these methods apply solely to them, with the exception of buy-sell agreements. *Every* business with two or more owners should have a buy-sell agreement in place. Buy-sell agreements and other remedies that apply to all businesses with two or more owners, including corporations, are discussed in upcoming sections of this chapter.

Pooling Agreements—Pooling agreements with respect to shareholder voting are when shareholders agree to agree as to how they will vote their shares.

Voting Trusts—Voting trusts are somewhat like a pooling agreement except the shareholders transfer the legal title to their shares to the trustee who then votes the beneficial owners' shares as per the trust agreement.

Cumulative Voting—The number of votes that shareholders have to vote for directors at an annual meeting is determined by multiplying the number of shares owned by the shareholder by the total number of directors to be elected at the meeting. The shareholder, in normal, straight voting, can only give the number of shares he/she owns to each director to be elected. Thus, if the shareholder owns 10 shares and there are 9 directors to be elected, the shareholder has a total of 90 votes to expend. The shareholder, however, can only give no more and no less than 10 votes to each of the 9 directors to be elected in straight voting. Under cumulative voting, however, the director can bunch his total votes and give all 90 votes to one nominated director, 30 to 3 nominees, 45 to 2 nominees and any other formula for bunching his 90 votes.

Classified Stock and Weighted Voting—Classified stock and weighted voting can be used to regulate voting control in a closely held corporation. For example, the shareholders may agree that the owners of class A stock can have the power to elect three directors while the owners of class B stock are allowed to elect two directors. Another example would be a shareholder arrangement whereby class A voting stock is issued to the owners in equal amounts while class B stock is issued to the owners according to how much capital they have contributed to the business. Accordingly, the owners will have equal voting rights but share profits based on the percentage of money invested in the business.

Control Agreements, which Stipulate the Persons who shall Serve on the Board of Directors—Control agreements may stipulate that the shareholders who are parties to the agreement will vote for each other to be directors and that, in their capacity as directors, they will vote for each other to be executive officers of the corporation. *McQuade v. Stoneham*[11] (upholding the first portion of such an agreement as a pooling agreement but striking down the second portion of the agreement which dictated the way directors must vote for election of officers as against public policy). The New York legislature, in response to *McQuade*, enacted section 620(b) of the New York Corporations Statute, which explicitly allowed shareholders in closely held corporations to enter into agreements encroaching on directors' independence if such a restriction is included in the articles of incorporation of the corporation.

Supermajority Voting Provisions—A supermajority provision can be used to give a minority owner (i.e., a noncontrolling owner) a veto power over policies and decisions that a majority of the owners would otherwise be able to enact over the minority owner's objections.

Buy-Sell Agreements—This enables an owner to recoup his/her investment in the business upon the voluntary and/or involuntary withdrawal of the owner from the business. In his book *The Law of Corporations*, Robert W. Hamilton states:

> A mandatory buy-sell arrangement is often recommended as the best solution in possible deadlock situations, where (usually) two equal shareholders operate the business but fear that there may be disagreements in the future … In the event of significant … disagreement, it seems much neater and cleaner that one shareholder should buy out the other.[12]

Such arrangements also allow a deceased owner's interest to be purchased with life insurance proceeds and, thereby, prevent disruption or possible liquidation of the corporation.

Other Safeguards—Other protections include restrictions on an owner's ability to sell his equity interest to a person not currently an owner in the business or other persons; and preemptive rights (i.e., a type of right of first refusal) in the owners to purchase his current percentage of ownership in any new corporate offering of stock for cash to prevent dilution of the shareholder's percentage of ownership.

Things You Should Know about Business Continuation Agreements

Successful black businesses often disappear if one of the founding owners and/or employees dies, retires, or becomes disabled. An entrepreneur should plan in advance on how he and/or his estate will recover his equity interest in the business under such circumstances. The entrepreneur should also consider various ways of ensuring that the business continues after his/her death, retirement, or disability. This will typically require that the entrepreneur enter into a buy-sell agreement that sets forth a process by which the surviving owners, if any, or a third party purchase the departed owner's portion of the net worth of the business. Additionally, there are ways in which the owner can transfer his voting rights to co-owners or a third party, but give his right to receive his share of the profits from the business to his family members. In any case, the entrepreneur must contact a knowledgeable professional with experience in this area to accomplish these goals. Such professionals would include persons in the legal, financial services, and insurance fields.

There are generally four circumstances that trigger a potential transfer of an owner's interest in a firm under a buy-sell agreement.

1. an owner dies and has previously taken steps to leave his/her portion of the income of the business to family members or to sell his ownership share to others. This may not be an option for owners in firms providing professional services such as the practice of law. In the legal profession, for example, as a general proposition, all owners must be professionally licensed to practice law in order to receive a share of the profits.

2. an owner retires from the business and desires to sell his/her shares to the firm pursuant to a right of first refusal held by the business.

3. an owner retires from the business and desires to sell his shares to the other owners (if any) on a pro rata basis pursuant to a right of first refusal.

4. an owner retires from the business and desires to sell his or her ownership interest to a third party who becomes a new owner (i.e., a substitute owner) in the business after obtaining approval from the other owners

The Use of Life Insurance

Business continuation insurance is often used to finance buy-sell agreements to facilitate the continuance of a small, closely held business upon the death, disability, or retirement of an owner or key employee. These firms typically have the following characteristics:

1. a small number of owners
2. the owners' equity interest (e.g., shares of stock) in the business do not trade on any secondary market
3. the owners usually participate in the management of the business (i.e., they are owner-managed firms).

The ownership interests of the owners in such businesses is illiquid, that is, the interests cannot be readily sold because there is no market in which the ownership units trade. Lack of liquidity also exists because the owners usually enter into agreements that prevent the other owner(s) from selling their interest in the firm without their approval. Compounding these issues of lack of liquidity is the fact that neither the business nor the other owners may have sufficient resources to purchase the interest of a deceased or retiring co-owner. Therefore, life insurance is often used to finance buy-sell agreements.

The most commonly used tools in business markets insurance used to finance buy-sell agreements are permanent life insurance and disability income insurance. This subsection focuses on using life insurance to finance buy-sell agreements. We will also take a look at using disability income insurance to finance buy-sell agreements in the immediately following subsection. Keep in mind that this is only an introductory guide. You must consult with persons knowledgeable about these insurance and disability products to determine their affordability and a host of other matters.

A life insurance contract lists three parties: the owner, the insured, and the beneficiary.

The policy owner is typically the purchaser and payer of the premium. The policy owner, among other things, names the insured and beneficiaries. The policy owner must also pay taxes on any taxable income from the policy during the life of the insured.

The insured is the person covered by the contract, and his or her age and health determines the cost of the contract. A nonperson (aka nonnatural person)—a trust, a corporation, or a limited liability company, and so forth—may own a life insurance policy, but the actual insured must be a "real" (natural) person.

Beneficiaries receive money from the policy when the insured dies. Any entity, be it a natural person or an unnatural "person" like a trust or business, can be a beneficiary.

There are two types of beneficiaries—revocable and irrevocable. A revocable beneficiary can be changed at any time during the life of the insured. An irrevocable beneficiary, however, cannot be changed without the beneficiary's permission.

Pros and Cons of Various Life Insurance Products

Just as there are many different organizational forms a new company might take, there are also several different kinds of life insurance. Some may be appropriate for your purposes. Others may not. Let's take a look at them now.

Whole Life Insurance—is the primary tool in business markets insurance. It is considered permanent life insurance, which means it builds cash value over the life of the policy, much like a long-term savings account. Unlike a savings account, however, the cash value that accrues is tax-deferred. Even though the cash values of the policy belong to the policy owner, they cannot usually be withdrawn like funds in a savings account. If, however, the policy owner surrenders the policy, the cash values, less processing fees, are paid to the policy owner. The policy owner may use the cash value of the policy as collateral for loans from the insurance company, based on the insurance company's guaranteed credit rate. Under a limited pay policy, the owner does not pay premiums for the entire life of the insured, but pays for a specified time period to achieve a certain return. There is a payment schedule for whole life insurance and the policy owner must pay the premiums on time.

Whole life insurance has several features that make it so desirable:

- consistent, unchanging premium payments
- coverage up to age 100
- cash values that build over time
- consistent, unchanging face (payout) amount
- guaranteed death benefits.[13]

Universal Life Insurance—policies, unlike whole life insurance policies, allow more wiggle room in the premium payment schedule. The policy owner can skip or suspend premium payments for a time. Also, the owner may change the death benefit during the life of the policy. When the owner pays a premium, the insurance company places the premium in a reserve fund. The insurance company subtracts the cost of insurance and policy expenses from the reserve fund and pays interest on the balance remaining in the fund. In contrast to whole life, owners can withdraw cash in addition to using the policy for policy loans. However, under most contracts, if the cash value falls below the level set by the insurer, then the insurer has the right to cancel the policy.

Variable Life Insurance—is a type of whole life insurance but differs from whole life in that the insurance company does not credit cash values with a guaranteed amount. Instead, the insurance company places the policy's cash value in variable subaccounts. Subaccounts are separate from the insurer's own assets and are investment/securities accounts that belong to the policyholder. They function much as a mutual fund would. This separation protects the policyholder's assets against any claims that creditors might bring against the insurer. As with whole life insurance, a policyholder may obtain loans against the funds, but many variable policies prohibit actual cash withdrawals. Variable life policies may also offer other investment options such as fixed accounts, which include guaranteed rates for a designated time period. The return on the investment is the obligation of the issuing insurance company, rather than the return coming from dividends on the value of the investments in a subaccount.[14]

Variable Universal Life Insurance—is a hybrid of variable life and universal life insurance. Like universal life, once the policy owner accumulates sufficient cash reserves, the owner may skip or suspend premium payments.[15]

Term Insurance—is used primarily within group benefit plans. It pays a death benefit if the insured dies within the policy period. Otherwise both face value and premiums paid are lost. It only covers the insured for a specified term and builds no cash values. Accordingly, the owners would need to supplement the policy with regular investments in a mutual fund or other investment vehicle to produce a cash fund to support the buy-out of an owner's interest in the event that the owner decided to retire from the business.[16]

Buy-Sell Agreements Which Can Be Funded by Life Insurance

There are essentially five types of buy-sell agreements that utilize life insurance:[17]

1. share redemption buy-sell agreements
2. cross purchase buy-sell agreements
3. no-sell buy-sell agreements
4. wait-and-see buy-sell agreements
5. third-party buy-sell agreements

Each has advantages and disadvantages. As you read through each one, you will find the one most suitable for your business.

Share Redemption Buy-Sell Agreements—Under this arrangement, the business purchases life insurance on each owner. If the owner dies, the business uses the proceeds from the policy to buy the owner's shares from his estate. If the owner retires, the business may use the accumulated cash value from the policy to supply the funds to buy the owner's shares. *The business owns the policy, the insured is the business owner/shareholder, and the beneficiary is the business.* This type of agreement is also known as an entity purchase buy-sell agreement.

Cross Purchase Buy-Sell Agreements—In a cross-purchase buy-sell agreement, each of the owners buys a policy on the life of each of the other owners. This sort of arrangement is best for a business with two or three owners. *The insurance owner would be owner A, the insured would be* *owner B, and the beneficiary would be owner A*Otherwise, each owner would need to purchase so many policies that the plan would not be economically or administratively feasible.

No-Sell Buy-Sell Agreements—A no-sell buy-sell agreement is sometimes used when owners do not want the business sold when one of the owners dies. The business gives each owner one voting share and 99 nonvoting shares. In a cross-purchase by-sell agreement, the owners agree that when one owner dies, the surviving owners will purchase the voting share, and the remaining shares will pass to the owner's heirs. *The owner of the policy is an irrevocable trust set up specifically for the insurance, the insured is the business owner, and the beneficiary is the owner's heirs.*

The primary purpose of such an arrangement is to keep the life insurance policy separate from the estate of the owner/insured. The trust must either purchase the policy or the owners must make a gift of the policy premium to the trust. Businesses that establish this type of buy-sell agreement must adhere to the following rules: the policy must be free from any incidences of ownership by the grantor; the grantor must have gifted the policy to the trust at least three years prior to the insured's death; and the grantor should gift the premium payments to the trust and have the trust purchase the policy.

Wait and See Buy-Sell Agreement—A wait-and-see buy-sell agreement provides more than one method of disposing of an owner's shares. The policy owner can be either the business or another owner in the business. The policy owner purchases a life insurance policy on the life of each owner. If the business is the owner, it can use proceeds from the death benefit to purchase the deceased owner's share of the business outright, loan the money to the remaining owners to buy up the deceased owner's share, or purchase the shares from the deceased owner's estate through a section 303 Redemption. *The owner of the policy can be the business, the insured can be the owner, and beneficiary can be the business. Alternatively, the owner could be owner A, the insured could be owner B, and the beneficiary could be owner A.* The business owners may structure the insurance policy so that:

(a) the business is the owner and the beneficiary, or
(b) the owners purchase policies on the lives of the other owners (as in a cross-purchase agreement) and when the insured dies, can loan the proceeds to the business to buy the deceased owner's shares.

Third Party Buy-Out Agreement—In some cases, a non-owner (third party) will purchase an owner's share when that owner dies. The business owner, in this instance, will enter into a third party buy-out agreement. *The third party takes out a life insurance policy on that owner, becomes the owner and beneficiary of that policy, and uses the proceeds to buy that owner's shares when that owner dies.*

The Use of Disability Income Insurance and Buy-Sell Agreements

A disability income insurance policy pays benefits if an insured becomes disabled. The type of disability income policy that is used with buy-sell agreements is generally called a business buy-out policy.

Insurance companies will only issue a disability income business buy-out policy if the following exists: there must be a formal buy-sell agreement; the insured must not own more than 90 percent of the business; and the insured must be actively working in the business. Business buy-out policies may have waiting periods of one or two years before the insurance company begins payment.

The business may use the income from the policy to purchase the disabled owner's share of the business. Some policies pay a lump sum to the beneficiary after the expiration of the waiting period. Other policies have a benefit payment period of up to five years.

Now that you have some ideas about the best way to structure your business, it's time to look at some issues you'll need to consider as you're shaping your business or getting ready to put together a formal business plan. Chapter 3 will give you a glimpse of what's involved with intellectual property rights, copyrights, patents and trademarks, and a few other things you may find handy.

Recommended Reading on Organizational Structure

- *The Small Business Legal Tool Kit,* Ira Nottonson and Theresa A. Pickner

Notes

1. Jeffrey McKinney, "The Perils of Being Public," *Black Enterprise* (April 2001): 99.

2. UNIF. PARTNERSHIP ACT § 6, 6 U.L.A. 313 (2001)(pt. I); REV. UNIF. PARTNERSHIP ACT § 202(a), 6 U.L.A. 92 (2001).

3. UNIF. PARTNERSHIP ACT § 7(4), 6 U.L.A. 418 (2001)(pt. I); REV. UNIF. PARTNERSHIP ACT § 202(c), 6 U.L.A. 92–93 (2001)(pt. I).

4. *See* UNIF. PARTNERSHIP ACT § 18(g), 6 U.L.A. 101. (2001) (Pt. II); REV. UNIF. PARTNERSHIP ACT § 401. (i), 6 U.L.A. 133 (2001)(pt. I).

5. *See, e.g.*, Delaware General Corporation Law, 8 DEL. CODE ANN. 141(b).

6. *Donahue v. Rodd Electrotype*, 328 N.E.2d 505, 511(Mass. 1975).

7. William Lucius Cary & Melvin Aron Eisenberg. *Cases and Materials on Corporations*, (New York: Foundation Press, 1995), 168. (citing to 1970s data as probably representative of today's percentages).

8. *Kahn v. Lynch Comm. Sys., Inc.*, 638 A.2d 1110, 1113-14 (Del. Sup. Ct. 1994).

9. Robert W. Hamilton. *The Law of Corporations* (New York: West Publishing Group, 2000), 20, 22.

10. Ibid., 23.

11. 189 N.E. 234 (N.Y. 1934).

12. Robert W. Hamilton. *The Law of Corporations* (New York: West Publishing Group, 2000), 295–303.

13. Dana Dratch. *Major Types of Life Insurance: Whole Life*, Bankrate.com, http://www.bankrate.com/brm/news/insur/20020917b.asp (Accessed May 2009).

14. Staff writer, Pacific Life, *Various Types of Life Insurance*, http://www.pacific life.com/Chammel/Educational+Information/Life+Insurance+Concepts/Various +Types_of+Life+Insurance.htm.

15. *Key Business Needs Insurance*, Cape Insurance Education, http://www .capeschool.com/md_ins/md_download_welcome_1.html (August 7, 2008), 21.

16. Ibid., 21–22.

17. Information on buy-sell agreements gleaned, in part, from *Key Business Needs Insurance*, Cape Insurance Education, 27–30. http://www.capeschool .com/md_ins/md_download_welcome_1.html (August 7, 2008), 181–82, 184, and Staff writer, *Buy-Sell Agreement Checklist: Has Your Company Addressed the Critical What Ifs?*, http://morebusiness.com/templates_worksheets/checklists/buysell.brc. (Accessed May 2009).

CHAPTER 12

THINGS YOU SHOULD KNOW ABOUT INTELLECTUAL PROPERTY

As an aspiring entrepreneur, you obviously have an idea or dream that has inspired you to begin your business. This chapter is about that idea or dream—your intellectual property. And it's every bit as important as the physical property of your business—the office equipment, your building, your assets, and so forth—and like them, must be protected. As you are planning and structuring your business, it's important to ensure their safety. It's also important that you do your homework to be sure that your ideas do not tread on those of another person or company.

Intellectual property is any product of the human mind—idea, dream, vision—that ends up having value in the marketplace even though the idea itself is intangible. Examples include new products, logos, unique advertising, even your company name. These are all products of creative thinking and need to be protected. Let's take a look at some of the ways you can do just that.

Patents

An invention must produce a novel, useful, concrete, and nonobvious tangible result to be patentable.[1] In other words, the invention must be able to perform some sort of novel and useful "function." In contrast, copyright law and trademark law do not protect functional matters. The inventor of a product or process can seek a patent on his invention from the U.S. Patent and Trademark Office. Patents generally refer to **utility**

patents (meaning patents on inventions). These patents are good for 20 years from the date of the application. The patent statute also provides for **plant patents** (any new varieties of plants that can be reproduced asexually). These patents are also good for 20 years from the date of the original application.

The patent statute also provides for **design patents** (invention of new, original designs for manufactured products). These patents are good for 14 years from the date the U.S. Patent and Trademark Office (USPTO) grants the patent. The dictionary definition of the word "patent" generally means a "grant of some privilege, property, or authority, made by the government or sovereign of a country to one or more individuals." [2] Thus, government grants of land to homesteaders were sometimes referred to as patents.

The laws of nature, physical phenomena, and abstract ideas, just as mathematics and other abstractions, are not patentable.

The inventor may apply for a patent himself or hire someone licensed to practice before USPTO, such as a patent lawyer or patent agent. The inventor must file a patent application with the USPTO. The USPTO examines the application to determine whether a patent should issue. A patent attorney normally spends several hours searching USPTO's database (which is available online at www.uspto.gov) to study similar patents. An examiner who works in the subject matter area of the invention performs the examination.

Unlike copyright and trademark applications, which owners can easily prepare and file, patent applications are highly technical and almost always require expert assistance. The patent application must contain a precise and extensive written description of the invention. The enablement requirement mandates that the applicant disclose to the public how to make use of the invention, as of the date of application.[3] Additionally, the inventor must disclose his/her best mode for enabling others to engage in the practical use of the invention. The heart of the application is the claims portion, which determines whether the invention is patentable and determines the patentee's exclusive rights. Section 112 of the patent statute requires that patent claims be definite and particularly point out and distinctly claim the subject matter which the applicant claims as his invention.[4]

Utility Patents. The patent statute states that "Whoever invents or discovers any new and useful process, machine, manufacture, or composition of matter, or any new and useful improvement thereof, may obtain a patent therefore, subject to the conditions and requirements of this title."[5] Patent law refers to these categories of inventions as "utility patents." This is because an invention must be "useful" in order to be patented.[6] A *process* could be a method of *making* something (e.g., a method for making a high strength polymer); *using* something (e.g., a method for controlling weeds near rice plants by applying a specific chemical compound); or *doing* something (e.g., administering a mutual fund or creating an anti-gravity illusion).[7] An inventor may invent a process, a product or both (e.g., a new manufacturing process to build a new type of chair). However, many processes do not produce a new product (e.g., a process for purifying water or isolating chemicals may produce cleaner water or purer chemicals that are not new). Other processes may produce a nonpatentable product (e.g., a new process for producing a common chair).[8]

Products include the other three categories listed in 35 U.S.C. § 101 (machines, articles of manufacture, and compositions of matter). The categories are not mutually exclusive. For example, a genetically altered organism is both a manufacture and a composition of matter.[9] Consequently, a patent claim may be an invention as a product and as a process, but it must do so in separate claims.

"The term **machine** includes every mechanical device or combination of mechanical powers and devices to perform some function and produce a certain effect or result."[10] A cell in an organism is a machine: it performs various intracellular processes such as producing hormones.[11] A computer is a machine. Loading a computer program on a general purpose computer can create a new, patentable machine.[12] Thus, software inventions are often covered as both a product and a process, to give patentees broader rights. However, one should note that a patent of a machine does not automatically apply to the processes that the machine carries out. Rather, the machine itself is the subject of the patent. A different machine that carries out the same process does not necessarily infringe the patent.[13]

The term **manufacture** means "the production of articles for use from raw or prepared materials by giving to these materials new forms, qualities, properties, or combinations, whether by hand-labor or by machinery."[14] The article of manufacture is within the patentable subject matter only if the invented elements are functional. Descriptive or aesthetic elements lack the requisite functionality. Accordingly, a writer cannot patent a book with the text of his new novel because the book itself is simply a standard product of a printing press.[15]

A composition of matter includes "all compositions of two or more substances and . . . all composite articles, whether they be the results of chemical union, or of mechanical mixture, or whether they be gases, fluids, powders or solids."[16] Like the other categories, "composition of matter" is very broad. It reaches from human genes to toothpaste.[17]

An inventor may patent a product or process, or an "**improvement thereof.**" Assume that inventor A owns the patent on a rocket launcher and inventor B owns the patent on the improvement. No one could make, use, sell, and offer to sell and import the improved version of the rocket launcher without the permission of both inventors. Such patents are called *blocking patents.* Only if inventors A and B enter into some kind of agreement, such as a cross-license, could either practice the second invention (or license it to others) free of infringement claims. The existence of blocking patents illustrates the technical legal nature of a patent holder's right. The patent holder has the right to *exclude* others from doing things, not necessarily the right to do them himself.[18]

Copyrights

Copyright law protects rights in the expression of ideas in books, articles, music, and other tangible medium. However, the law allows others to make fair use of these works (brief quotations, etc.). The work must be an original, independent creation. Copyright protection applies to original works of authorship as soon as they become any tangible form of expression (e.g., a poem, photograph, recordings of songs, making a sculpture). Therefore, an author owns the copyright in any original work of authorship as soon as he fixes it in some tangible form. Accordingly, copyright does not depend on complying with formalities such as registering the copyright, depositing copies with the Library of Congress, or using copyright notices on copies of the work. The copyright term lasts for the life of the author plus 70 years (or a fixed term of 95 years for contracted works and some other categories of works).

Copyright only covers creative expression. It does not cover the idea itself or the process of expressing it (such as a painting technique), principles of science, theories, and similar things. Accordingly, copyright does not cover how the work might be used (i.e., it does not cover the functional aspects of the work). However, copyright ownership in the expression found in a tangible object is not the same as owning the object. Therefore, a painter may sell a painting he created to a buyer without selling the copyright. Likewise, if the painter had sold the buyer the copyright (protection under copyright law), the sale would not implicitly include the sale of the painting (protection under state property law).

The author of the work initially owns the copyright, although he/she may transfer those rights to others. Those rights include:

- the exclusive rights to reproduce the work.
- produce variations based on the copyrighted expression.
- sell the work to the public
- transfer of ownership, or by rental sale, or lending.
- to publicly perform a work such as a play or display art work to the public.[19]

Additionally, authors of works of visual art are entitled to proper attribution of authorship and to protection of the physical work itself. This latter right is often referred to as *"moral rights."*[20] If the work is created by an employee (a work made for hire), the author is deemed to be the employer.

Copyright vests initially in the author, but he can authorize others to take advantage of these exclusive rights through either a transfer of copyright ownership or a nonexclusive license. The copyright laws provide that an author has an inalienable right to terminate any exclusive or nonexclusive grant of a transfer or license of any or all the rights under a copyright during a 5-year period after 35 years from the date of the grant by the author. There must be written notice to the grantee or successor within certain time limits, and a copy of the notice must be recorded in the United States Copyright office. The right of termination does not apply to works made for hire.[21]

Registration of a copyright requires filling out the appropriate form, paying a modest fee, and depositing a copy of the work. Forms and clear directions are available at the U.S. Copyright Office Web site: www.loc.gov/copyright/. An action for infringement of a copyright in a "United States work" cannot be brought until the copyright holder registers the copyright (or, if the U.S. Copyright Office refuses registration, until the copyright owner files the application, tenders the fee, and meets the deposit requirement). The certificate of registration is prima facie evidence of the validity of the copyright, provided the work is registered no later than five years after the first publication.[22]

Within three months of publication, a copyright owner must deposit two copies or phonorecords with the U.S. Copyright Office, "for use or disposition of the Library of Congress."[23] U.S. Copyright regulations exempt many works from this requirement. There are, technically, two separate deposit requirements. Copyright owners that *register* a work must deposit one copy with the U.S. Copyright Office. Copyright owners of *published* works are required to deposit two copies with the Library of Congress. But a copyright owner is permitted to use the Library of Congress deposit to also fulfill the registration deposit requirement. Copyright owners that neither register nor publish have no deposit requirement to meet.[24]

Trademarks

Trademark law protects words and symbols indicating the source of a product or service. The trademark owner acquires trademark rights by making bona fide use of the mark in commerce. The symbol can be a word, a phrase or a clause (see, e.g., Michael Buffer's "Let's Get Ready To Rumble"), a design, an image, a sound, a color (a color is not inherently distinctive but it may become so if used consistently over time), or even a fragrance. As with copyright law (and unlike patent and trade secrets), trademarks do not protect functional matter. The law deems a feature functional if, among other things, it is essential to the use or purpose of the device.

There is no time limit on the duration of the mark. The owner retains ownership of the mark until he/she abandons use of the mark. Trademark registration offers a number of legal and practical advantages, but it is not necessary to create a trademark through the federal registration process. Trademark law developed as state law. The federal statute does not preempt the field. Rather, state statutes and common law provide similar protections. The owner of registered federal trademarks, service marks, collective marks, and certification marks may renew the registration of these federal marks every 10 years as long as the mark remains in use.

A **trademark** is a symbol used by a person to identify and distinguish his goods from those manufactured or sold by others and to indicate the source of the goods. Goods are any type of product (e.g., Coca-Cola, Nike, Cannon, Tonka).[25]

A **service mark** identifies the source of the services (e.g., eBay and MTV). The same rules apply to both service marks and trademarks.[26] The symbol must be used to identify specific services that the mark owner performs for the benefit of others. A symbol that merely identifies someone engaged in some activity for his own benefit is not a service mark. Some notable examples of service marks are FedEx and Google.

Trade Dress is a particular type of trademark or service mark. It refers to the total image of the product and its overall appearance. It is "the design and appearance of a product, together with the elements making up the overall image that serves to identify the product presented to the consumer."[27] Today, trade dress can be the design of the product itself or the design of the packaging of the product. Trade dress can include "features such as size, shape, color or color combinations, texture, graphics, or even particular sales techniques."[28] Moreover, trade dress is not limited to goods; the product can be services, or a combination of goods and services. In *Two Pesos v. Taco Cabana*,[29] the United States Supreme Court stated that the trade dress for the Taco Cabana restaurant was "the total image of the business. Taco Cabana's trade dress may include the shape and general appearance of the exterior of the restaurant, the identifying sign, the interior kitchen floor plan, the decor, the menu, the equipment used to serve food, the servers' uniforms and other features reflecting on the total image of the restaurant."[30]

The Lanham Act defines a **collective mark** as a trademark or service mark used by the members of a group or organization.[31] The term includes marks indicating membership in a union, an association, or other organization. Examples include such organizations as the Jaycees (association promoting community improvement).[32]

A **certification mark** is a symbol used by a person *other than its owner* "to certify regional or other origin, material, mode of manufacture, quality, accuracy, or other characteristics of such person's goods or services or that the work or labor on the goods or services was performed by members of a union or other organization." A certification mark is not used by the owner of the mark. Rather, persons other than the owner use the mark to certify to potential purchasers that their goods or services meet the standards set by the mark's owner.[33]

Inherently distinctive marks are those whose intrinsic nature serves to identify a particular source. **Arbitrary and fanciful marks** are those that do not describe or suggest any characteristic of the product (e.g., Apple used to describe computers). **Suggestive marks** are those that suggest but do not describe the nature or characteristics of the product.

Several classes of symbols cannot be protected under federal trademark law:

1. those likely to cause confusion with an existing mark.
2. those that involve functional matter that is essential to the use or purpose of a device.
3. deceptive matter.
4. geographically deceptive descriptive marks (e.g., Wisconsin used on cheese from Illinois).
5. marks suggesting a false connection with persons, living or dead, institutions, beliefs, or national symbols.

6. immoral or scandalous matter.
7. disparaging marks (Washington Redskins football team according to Trademark Trial and Appeal Board (TTAB) but later reversed by the federal courts).
8. generic terms that consumers understand to refer to a category of goods and services as opposed to the source of the product (e.g., "ale house," "crab house").
9. government symbols such as the flag and other insignia (although narrowly construed); and
10. use of the names and likenesses of living individuals without their consent.[34]

Nevertheless, some marks that would be otherwise incapable of protection can become protected marks if they acquire a distinctive secondary meaning to the public as the source of a product (e.g., Coca Cola, the surname McDonalds, and primarily geographically descriptive marks).[35]

Trademark searches can be made for free at http://www.uspto.gov. One can do a search of the federal registers and pending applications. Pending trademark applications, unlike patent applications, are not confidential. A number of commercial services offer more comprehensive searches. Such a search covers other likely sources that would disclose use of relevant marks, such as trade publications and databases of trademarks, domain names, and business names. A good trademark search greatly reduces the chances of using a mark that conflicts with an existing mark.

Trademark rights do not depend on federal registration with the USPTO. However registration provides the following advantages. Registration provides:

- nationwide constructive notice of use and ownership of the mark.
- prima facie evidence of the use of the mark.
- a wider array of potential remedies for infringement.
- the validity of marks as "incontestable" after five years of continuous use.

Registered mark owners may use a trademark notice, such as the registered ® symbol, with the mark that serves as a warning to others, although the™ symbol may be used with unregistered marks. Additionally, the mark will show up in trademark searches by others.[36]

The statute permits two types of applications for U.S. marks: **use applications** (for marks already in use) and **intent-to-use applications** (for those setting forth a bona fide intent to use). The statute also provides for two registers, the **principal register** (for marks that meet the requirements for protection) and the **supplemental register** (for marks such as descriptive marks that have not attained secondary meaning but can identify the source of goods and services).[37]

Once the USPTO receives the application and fee, it refers the application to an examining attorney, who determines whether the mark is registrable (or would be registrable on use for intent-to-use applications). If the examining attorney determines the mark is registrable, the USPTO publishes the mark in the *Official Gazette of the Patent and Trademark Office.* Anyone "who believes that he would be damaged by the registration of a mark" may file an opposition in the USPTO within 30 days of publication. Additionally, a party who believes he/she is damaged by the registration may bring a cancellation proceeding. If the proceeding is brought within five years of registration, any grounds for nonregistrability may be alleged. After five years, a cancellation proceeding cannot be based on a claim that the mark is merely descriptive or that the mark is confusingly similar to a prior mark. But cancellation after five years may be based on the grounds that the mark is generic, functional, was abandoned, was registered fraudulently, was "immoral, deceptive, or scandalous," or was disparaging.[38]

Unauthorized use of a trademark in a manner that is likely to confuse consumers about the source of goods or services infringes the trademark. Trademark law also provides causes of action beyond trademark infringement—false designation of origin; false advertising; dilution of famous trademarks; and impermissible registration, use, or trafficking in Internet domain names that are similar to the trademarks of others. The 1999 Anticybersquatting Consumer Protection Act prohibits the deliberate, bad faith, abusive registration of internet domain names in violation of the rights of trademark owners.[39]

Trade Secrets

A trade secret is information that has economic value from the secrecy itself. The information also has value if it cannot be easily figured out by those who might gain from it. Therefore, it is appropriate to apply reasonable security measures to protect it. Typical trade secrets are customer lists, manufacturing processes, computer programs, and blueprints for machines, where such information is kept secret using reasonable security measures. One of the most famous trade secrets is the formula for Coca Cola.

Trade secret law does not grant a set of exclusive rights. Rather, it protects against wrongful access to information. There is no general federal trade secret statute. Rather, trade secret law is generally state law. The Uniform Trade Secret Act (UTSA), which more than 40 states have adopted, is becoming the standard body of trade secret law. Before the UTSA, states generally followed the Restatement of Torts. The drafters of UTSA relied heavily on the Restatement of Torts but included some key differences. Whether courts view trade secret law as tort law or property law may subtly influence its application. Typical trade secret cases involve a business versus a former employee; a business versus the new employer of the former employee; the business versus a former partner or former potential partner; an inventor or author versus a business; a business versus a competitor; a business versus a person who makes information public; and a business versus an agency or court to prevent disclosure to the agency or through discovery by an adversary in court.

Now that you have a better idea about how to protect your ideas and the products or services that spring forth from them, it's time to get down to writing your business plan. You already got some practice at it when you created your business model, so let's move on to Chapter 13 and expand what you've done to get it ready to "take to the bank."

Recommended Resources

- The United States Patent and Trademark Office, http://www.uspto.gov
- United States Copyright Office, http://www.copyright.gov

Notes

1. http://www.cafc.uscourts.gov/opinions/06-1286.pdf (9-27-08) (Accessed May 2009).

2. Stephen M. McJohn. *Intellectual Property* (New York: Aspen Publishers 2003), 105.

3. 35 U.S.C. § 112.

4. Ibid.

5. 35 U.S.C. § 101.

6. Stephen M. McJohn. *Intellectual Property* (New York: Aspen Publishers 2003), 105, n.1, 140–41.

7. Ibid., 106–07.

8. Ibid.

9. *Diamond v. Chakrabarty*, 447 U.S. 303 (1980).

10. *Corning v. Burden*, 56 U.S. 252, 267 (1853).

11. *Amgen v. Chugai Pharmaceutical*, 902 F.2d 1532 1537 (9th Cir. 1990).

12. *In re Alappat*, 33 F.3d 1526 (Fed. Cir. 1994).

13. Ibid.

14. *Diamond v. Chakrabarty*, 447 U.S. 303, 306 (1980).

15. Ibid.

16. *Diamond v. Chakrabarty*, 447 U.S. at 308 (1980).

17. Ibid.

18. Stephen M. McJohn. *Intellectual Property* (New York: Aspen Publishers 2003), 109.

19. 17 U.S.C. § 106.

20. 17 U.S.C. § 106A.

21. 17 U.S.C. § 203.

22. 17 U.S.C. § 411 and 17 U.S.C. § 410 (c),

23. 17 U.S.C. § 407(a).

24. Ibid.

25. 15 U.S.C. § 1127.

26. 15 U.S.C. § 1053.

27. *Chrysler Corp. v. Silva*, 118 F.3d 56, 58 (1st Cir. 1997).

28. *Two Pesos v. Taco Cabana*, 505 U.S. 763, 764 n.1 (1992) (citing case law and the Restatement (Third) of Unfair Competition).

29. 505 U.S. 763 (1992).

30. 505 U.S. at 764 n.1.

31. 15 U.S.C. § 1127.

32. Ibid.

33. Ibid.

34. Stephen M. McJohn. *Intellectual Property* (New York: Aspen Publishers 2003), 223, 231–38.

35. Ibid., 219–23.

36. Ibid., 245–46.

37. Ibid., 246.

38. 15 U.S.C. §1062, 15 U.S.C. §1063 and 15 U.S.C. §1064.

39. *Virtual Works, Inc. v. Volkswagen of America, Inc.*, 238 F.3d 264 (4th Cir. 2001).

CHAPTER 13

BUILDING YOUR BUSINESS PLAN

~ A business plan is where imagination meets discipline. ~[1]

At some point in the life of your enterprise, you will have to write a business plan. Whether you are seeking funding for start-up, or seeking funding for expansion you will need one to "take to the bank," or to present to potential investors. Much of the information in the plan will expand upon what you created in your business model. To help you organize your thoughts, gather the data that you need, and present it in a manner that will give you the greatest chance of success in your quest, this chapter is based on the Syracuse University publication, *The Nuts and Bolts of Business Plans*[2]. It is a product of the Department of Entrepreneurship and Emerging Enterprises at the Whitman School of Management at Syracuse and reproduced here with their gracious permission.

Introduction

A business plan is not a checklist, where you address sections one by one. It is a living, breathing document. You are telling a story, and bringing a venture to life. It is about a company, not a product or an idea. A company has many facets, and these are reflected in the various sections of the plan. Most critically, the sections are **highly interdependent**. They must be internally consistent and "hang together."

As you subsequently make changes to one section, you will find yourself having to go back and make adjustments to a number of other sections.

It is the discipline of the plan that will help you see critical flaws in your idea, in how you plan to price, in your cost requirements, in your operational approach, in your marketing methods and so forth. You will have to continually adapt as you learn more about this business and the industry within which it will operate. Using the plan as a framework, it will help you to 'tweak' or adjust aspects of what you propose to do in ways that make the venture more viable.

A business plan is also an objective and fact-based document. It is not written in first person, so be sure to eliminate all use of 'I,' 'We,' 'Our,' and 'Us.' Use your company name to refer to the business.

A logical approach is to break the overall plan down into **THREE STAGES**.

- First, attack four key sections: the Industry, the Company/Concept/Products, the Market, and Economics (think of this as **stage one**); These sections will lay out the nature of the opportunity and how you are going to capitalize on it;
- Then, go after the Marketing, Design and Development, Operations, and Management Team sections (**stage two**); These sections really get at the nitty-gritty of how you will make things operational;
- Finally, address the Risks and Assumptions, Timetable, Financials and the Offering or Deal (**stage three**). Here you focus on implementation, what can go wrong, how the business will perform, and how much money is needed.

The Plan Is Worthless if You Don't Do the Research

The best plans are almost always the ones where you gather the best information, do the most library and secondary research, do the most field research (talk to prospective competitors, customers and suppliers), and dig as deeply as possible for information. Not only does more information help you to better justify positions, and ensures you have anticipated the real challenges, but it is a rich source of creative inspiration—-when you see some of the more innovative approaches and techniques being employed by others. Most of the answers you seek are hard to find, do not exist in one place, and must be pieced together. The research for a great plan is truly a "scavenger hunt."

We have prepared for you an excellent resource regarding where you can find key facts, figures and insights. Many, but certainly not all, of the specific sources are available electronically. If you limit your search to looking on the web through Google or some other search engine, **you will miss most of the best research that will support your venture**. In addition to the site above that we have prepared for you, it is vital that you go to the library (can do this on-line) and do a search using ABI-Inform (on Syracuse U. website, click Research, then Library, then Databases, then Business and Management, then ABI-Inform. Then enter the key words that relate to your venture.

Librarians can be extremely helpful. You are especially encouraged to seek help from the government publications librarian. **It is also vital that you get out in the field and talk to suppliers, competitors, customers, and potential investors. They will open your eyes to things that you simply had not considered.**

Remember that a business plan is not a term paper, so references should be used sparingly. Nonetheless, they should be used and a 'references' should appear at the back of the plan. Cite references to key numbers or research that support your case. When you conduct interviews, cite the date and place of the interview in your 'references' section.

Outline for Business Plans

Executive Summary

- Opportunity Statement
- Business Concept and Product or Service
- Description of the Target Market
- Competitive Advantage
- Essence of Marketing Approach
- Economics and Breakeven
- Technology and Operational Issues
- The Team
- Financial Highlights
- Financing Needs and How the Team Proposes to Raise the Money

I. **The Industry**

II. **The Company, Concept, and Product(s) and Service(s)**
    A.   The Company and the Concept
    B.   The Product(s) or Services(s)
    C.   Entry and Growth Strategy

III. **Market Research and Analysis**
    A.   Definition of Your Relevant Market and Customer Overview
    B.   Market Size and Trends
    C.   Buyer Demographics and Buyer Behavior
    D.   Market Segmentation and Targeting
    E.   Competition and Competitive Edges
    F.   Estimated Market Share and Sales Figures
    G.   Ongoing Market Evaluation

IV. **Economics of the Business**
    A.   Revenue Sources and Gross and Operating Margins
    B.   Fixed and Variable Costs
    C.   Operating Leverage and its Implications
    D.   Breakeven Chart and Calculation
    E.   Overall Economic Model

F. Start-up Costs

G. Profit Potential and Durability

V. **The Marketing Plan**

    A. Overall Marketing Strategy

    B. Pricing

    C. The Selling Cycle

    D. Sales Tactics

    E. Advertising and Sales Promotions

    F. Publicity

    G. Customer Service

    H. Warranty or Guarantee Policies

    I. Distribution

VI. **Design and Development Plan**

    A. Development Status and Tasks

    B. Difficulties and Risks

    C. Product Improvement and New Products

    D. Projected Development Costs

    E. Proprietary Issues (patents, licenses, copyrights, brand names)

VII. **Operations Plan**

    A. Operating Model and Cycle (front stage and back stage)

    B. Geographic Location and Physical Location Requirements

    C. Facilities and Improvements

    D. Equipment Requirements

    E. Capacity Levels and Inventory Management

    F. Operations Strategy and Plans

    G. Legal Issues Affecting Operations

VIII. **Management Team**

    A. Organization Structure

    B. Key Management Personnel and Responsibilities

    C. Management Compensation and Ownership

    D. Other Current Investors

    E. Employment and Other Agreements, Stock Option and Bonus Plans

    F. Board of Directors

    G. Other Shareholders, Rights, and Restrictions

    H. Supporting Professional Advisors and Services

IX. **Overall Schedule**

X. **Critical Risks, Problems and Assumptions**

XI. **Financial Plan**

    A. Pro Forma Income Statements

    B. Pro Forma Balance Sheets

    C. Pro Forma Cash Flow Analysis

Suggested Length for the Sections of Your Business Plan

Below are some general guidelines for the length of the key sections of your business plan after you have done final editing and streamlining:

Table of Contents (1 page)

Executive Summary (2-3 pages)

Industry Description (2-3 pages)

Company, Concept and Products/Services (2-3 pages)

Market Analysis (3-5 pages)

Economics of the Business (2 pages)

Marketing and Communications Strategy (2-3 pages)

Design and Development (2-3 pages)

Operations Plans (2-4 pages)

Management Team (1-2 pages)

Risk and Assumptions (1-2 pages)

Timeline (1-2 pages)

Financial Projections and Highlights (1-2 pages)
   (note: financial statements will be in appendices)

Offering (1 page)

Appendices (no more than 15 pages)

*Please note: As a general rule, plans are much longer with the **first draft**, and then through revisions are edited down to a content-rich but streamlined **final version**. Page length is determined by the audience for the plan.*

Formatting and Use of Tables and Figures

It is generally expected that you will use one inch margins on all sides, and a 12 font. Anything less than an 11 font is not acceptable. Spacing is up to you, but plans a typically either double- spaced or 1.5 spaced. You should cite key references in the text using the following notation in parenthesis at the end of the sentence from which the citation is taken: (author, year). Thus you will put (Jones, 2005) if Jones is the author. If there is no author, you will put the source and the date, as in: (U.S. Department of Commerce, 2004). If a direct quote, cite the page number, as in (Jones, 2005, p. 45). There then should be a complete set of references at the end of the plan.

One of the worst things you can do is to submit a plan that consists of page after page of unbroken text. You should use headings, sub-heading, and sub-sub-heading to break up the text. Just as critically, you should use tables and figures (exhibits) to break up the text, to illustrate key points, and to bring the plan to life. It is often possible to significantly shorten the text in a given section by using a couple of tables and figures. A picture or diagram can tell a vivid story. Be sure every table and figure is numbered, titled, and referred to in the text.

A Breakdown of the Major Sections of Your Business Plan

The Executive Summary (2-3 pages max)

Although this is the first section of the plan, the Executive Summary is the last section to be written. The Executive Summary concisely summarizes the essence of the business and the key decisions made by the entrepreneur. It is not merely an abbreviated business plan. The reader should be able to get a clear picture so that she/he doesn't have to read more, but at the same time be enticed to want to read more.

Many people fail to consider adequately their markets, their customers and a business model that will enable them to achieve success. Instead they often get wrapped up in an interesting technology or product, which is not the same thing as an attractive business. The questions below will help you focus on the aspects of your executive summary that are relevant to the business plan. These are some initial considerations that first time readers (venture capitalists, banks, business plan judges, etc.) look at before going on to evaluate the members of the team and the soundness of any financial projections. Make sure that you executive summary provides answers to these questions in addition to giving the reader an overview of the highlights from your business plan for the new venture.

Opportunity Statement:
- What is the nature of the opportunity or problem?
- Why is the opportunity now? What is the size of the opportunity?

Business Concept and Product or Service:
- How would you describe the business to a potential investor, team member, or customer if you had only a short elevator ride to share together? Make sure you have a succinct and powerful way to express your business concept.
- What is unique about this venture?

- Develop a brief concept statement for the product or service that can be shown to potential customers.
- How will the product be used? What are some unique features? What existing problem(s) will you solve with your service or product offering? What are the primary benefits to customers? How does your solution improve or replace current offerings?

Competitive Advantage:
- What special knowledge or technology do you possess and how will you protect it?
- What are the barriers to entry?
- Who will the competitors be?
- How will your service or product compare to those of your competitors in terms of usefulness, cost, styling, ergonomics, time-to-market, strategic alliances, technological innovations, compatibility with related product, etc?

Description of the Target Market:
- Briefly define your relevant market.
- What is the current size and expected growth of your target market?
- What segments will you be targeting?
- Who will your first customer(s) be?
- What proof can you offer that your target customers will value your product or service?

Essence of Marketing Approach
- What do you need to do very well in order to win this market?
- Indicate the key marketing methods used to accomplish sales
- Summarize your pricing position relative to the rest of the industry
- Summary the distribution channel approach

Technology and Operational Issues:
- What technology will you employ?
- Where are you in terms of R&D on the products/services?
- Will production be handled by you or outsourced?
- What is unique about your approach to production or operations?

The Team:
- Who are you and why can you do this?
- Briefly summarize your team's qualifications.

Economics:

- What are the firm's margins and volumes?
- Is the cost structure more fixed or variable?
- Make clear the model for making money.

Financial Highlights:

- When will breakeven be achieved?
- What is the level of potential sales of your product or service?
- What level of profits do you expect to achieve?

Financial Need:

- How much money are you requesting?
- From what sources are you looking for money and in exchange for what (e.g., how much equity)?
- What the rate of return investors will receive?

Section I: The Industry

The "industry" refers to the larger landscape, as in the "computer hardware wholesale industry" or the "card and gift industry" or the "architectural services industry." The focus here is on what is happening in, and the relative attractiveness of, the industry as a whole. You are looking at the entire industry in the U.S. or globally. As such, this section does not involve any description of your company or your local market. This section of your plan needs to include the following information:

- Summarize the industry in which the proposed business will operate. Give the relevant SIC/NAICS for the industry. How is the industry constructed/segmented?
- Discuss briefly industry size (in dollars) and annual growth rate (%); Where is the industry in its life cycle – emerging, early growth, rapid growth, early maturity, maturity, decline?
- Discuss the structure of the industry at present. How concentrated or fragmented is the industry? How many players are there, and how many are large versus small? Who are the largest and most important players in the industry? Outline Porter's 5 forces and draw conclusions. Provide a diagram of the value added chain to illustrate the key players in the industry.
- Highlight key trends in the industry. These can be found in the trade literature. Are costs going down or up? What about prices? Discuss any new products or developments, the rate of new product development, new markets and customers, new selling approaches, new pricing methods, new requirements or regulations, new entrants and exits, new technologies, and any other national or economic trends and factors that could affect the venture's business positively or negatively.

- Determine the key success factors for the industry and draw conclusions. What are the winners able to do consistently that the losers or also-rans to not do?
- Find standard financial ratios for the industry and summarize key ones.

Section II: The Company, Concept, and Product(s) or Service(s)

Now the focus turns to your own venture. First outline the nature of the entity you plan to create and where you are in that process, then capture the essence of your business concept and explain that concept, then detail the products and services you anticipate selling, and then talk about your entry approach and your vision for growth over the next five years.

A. The Company and the Concept

- What form will the company take (e.g., partnership, S-corporation, LLC, etc.), where will it be based, and when will it commence operations?
- *Briefly* summarize the company history, how the concept was discovered, as well as the current status of the company. Spell out the mission and main objectives of the company:
- Describe specifically the concept of the business (i.e. your **unique value proposition** . . . the core benefits you will provide to a user, the need or pain you will address)

B. The Product(s) or Service(s)

- Describe in some detail each product or service you will be selling (what it is and isn't – describe the product fully and provide pictures or a brochure in the appendix if you can). Begin to sell your idea here by generating some excitement about your product or service.
- Discuss the application (what it does) of the product or service and describe the primary end use as well as any significant secondary applications (who will use it and why).
- Provide a picture (a diagram) of the intended depth and breadth of your product/service mix and which products will likely generate the lion's share of the revenue. Emphasize any unique features of the product or service and how these will create or add significant value; also, highlight any differences between what is currently on the market and what you will offer that will account for your market penetration. Be sure to describe how value will be added and the payback period to the customer. More specifically, discuss how many months it will take for the customer to cover the initial purchase price of the product or service as a result of its time, cost or productivity improvements. Describe the competitive strengths and how it differentiates you from competitors.
- Include a description of any possible drawbacks (including obsolescence or ease of someone else copying the product or service).

- Discuss any head start you might have that would enable you to achieve a favored or entrenched position in the industry e.g. proprietary rights (patents, copyrights, trade secrets or non-compete agreements. Describe the key factors that dictate the success of your product/service. Describe any features of the product or service that give it an "unfair" advantage over the competition e.g. proprietary knowledge or skills.
- Discuss any opportunities for the expansion of the product line or the development of related products or services. Emphasize opportunities and explain how you will take advantage of them.

C. Entry and Growth Strategy
- How will you initially enter the market?
- Share your vision for where the firm will be in five years.
- Summarize how quickly you intend to grow during the first five years and your plans for growth beyond your initial product or service.
- Discuss how you will create barriers to entry in terms of others copying your success.

Section III: Market Research and Analysis (aka "The Market")

This section of the business plan is one of the most difficult to prepare, yet it is arguably the most important. Other sections of the business plan depend on the market research and analysis presented here. Because of the importance of market analysis and the critical dependence of other parts of the plan on the information, you are advised to prepare this section of the business plan with great attention to detail. Take enough time to do this section thoroughly and to check alternative sources of market data.

This section should convince the reader or investor that **you truly know your customers**. It should convince the reader that your product or service a) will have a substantial market in a growing industry; and b) can achieve sales in the face of competition. For example, the predicted sales levels directly influence such factors as the size of the manufacturing operation, the marketing plan, and the amount of debt and equity capital you will require. Yet most entrepreneurs seem to have great difficulty preparing and presenting market research and analyses that show that their ventures' sales estimates are sound and attainable. Consult industry publications, articles in trade magazines and trade associations to understand how the industry defines, identifies and segments its customers. Then apply yourself creatively by integrating the information in a unique way.

A. Definition of Your Relevant Market and Customer Overview
- Provide a very specific definition of your relevant market. Where will your specific customers come from? What are the parameters that you are using to define the relevant market?

- Discuss who the customers for the product(s) or service(s) are or will be.
- Provide general demographics for the customers base in your defined market (note: below you will get into segmentation of this market and descriptors of segments).
- Make it clear if you must serve more than one market (e.g., a website that must sell both to advertisers and to users of the site). Include separate discussions of the issues below for each market.

B. Market Size and Trends:

- For your defined market, estimate market size and potential in dollars and units. You will need to "invent a methodology" for making these estimates based on the kinds of data you are able to fine.
- Note the key assumptions that your projections are based upon.
- Estimate the size of the primary and selective demand gaps.
- Describe also the potential annual growth rate for at least three years of the total market for your product(s) or service(s) for each major customer group, region, or country, as appropriate.
- Discuss the major factors affecting market growth (e.g., industry trends, socioeconomic trends, government policy, and population shifts) and review previous trends in the market. Any differences between past and projected annual growth rates need to be explained.

C. Buyer Behavior:

Here you want to get into who buys, when, why, where, what and how.

- Who is the actual purchase decision-maker? Does anyone else get involved in the buying decision-process?
- How long is the customer's buying process (from where they have never heard of your product through when they make a purchase).
- What are the key stages or steps in the customer's buying process and what happens in each stage that might have marketing implications?
- Show who and where the major purchasers for the product(s) or service(s) are in each market segment. Include regional and foreign countries, as appropriate.
- Indicate whether this is a high, medium or low involvement purchase and draw implications.
- Indicate whether customers are easily reached and receptive.
- Describe customers' purchasing processes, including the bases on which they make purchase decisions (e.g., price, quality, timing, delivery, training, service, personal contacts, or political pressures) and why they might change current purchasing decisions.
- Discuss interviews you have had with users of this product or service category.

- List any orders, contracts, or letters of commitment that you have in hand. These are far and away the most powerful data you can provide. List also any potential customers who have expressed an interest in the product(s) or service(s) and indicate why. Also explain what you will do to overcome negative customer reaction. Indicate how quickly you believe your product or service will be accepted in the market.
- List and describe your five potentially largest customers. What percentage of your sales do they represent?
- In what way are customers dissatisfied with current offerings in the market place or what emerging customer groups are being ignored?

D. Market Segmentation and Targeting

- Discuss how your defined market can be broken down into specific market segments. Be creative and insightful in describing the existing segments.
- Note that potential customers need to be classified by relatively homogeneous groups having common identifiable characteristics (they must be homogeneous in terms of needs or buying behavior). What characteristics define your target customers (demographics, psychographics, benefits sought, information sources utilized, product usage rate, etc.).
- Include a table summarizing the various segments.
- Which segments represent the greatest sales potential?
- Indicate which segments you will be prioritizing.

E. Competition and Competitive Edges

- Identify potential/actual direct and indirect competitors. DO NOT INDICATE THAT THERE IS NO COMPETITION. Make a realistic assessment of their strengths and weaknesses. Discuss the 3 or 4 key competitors and why customers buy from them, and determine why customers might leave them.
- Assess the substitute and/or alternative products/ services and list the companies that supply them, both domestic and foreign, as appropriate.
- Discuss the current advantages and disadvantages of competitor products and the extent to which they are not meeting customer needs.
- Compare competing and substitute products or services on the basis of market share, sales, distribution methods, economies of scale, and production. Review the financial position, resources, costs, and profitability of the competition and their profit trends.
- Compare also important attributes such as quality, price, performance, delivery, timing, service, warranties, and pertinent features of your product/service with those of competitors.
- Compare the fundamental value that is added or created by your product or service, in terms of economic benefits to the customer and to your competitors.
- Indicate any knowledge of competitors' actions, or lack of action, that could lead you to new or improved products and an advantageous position. Why

aren't they doing what you will be doing? Discuss whether competitors are simply sluggish or non-responsive or are asleep at the wheel.

- Indicate who are the service, pricing, performance, cost, and quality leaders. Discuss why any companies have entered or dropped out of the market in recent years.
- From what you know about competitors' operations, explain why they are vulnerable and why you can capture a share of their business. What makes you think it will be possible to compete with them.

F. Estimated Market Share and Sales:

- Summarize what it is about your product(s) or service(s) that will make it saleable in the face of current and potential competition. Mention, especially, the fundamental value added or created by the product(s) or service(s).
- Discuss which customers could be major purchasers in future years and why.
- Based on your assessment of the advantages for your product or service, the market size and trends, customer, the competition and their products, and the trends of sales in prior years, estimate the share of the market and the sales in units and dollars that you will acquire in each of the next three years. Remember to show assumptions used in your calculations. DO NOT INDICATE THAT IT IS A $100 MILLION MARKET AND THAT YOU ONLY HAVE TO CAPTURE EIGHT TENTHS OF ONE PERCENT TO BREAK EVEN——AS THAT MAY SEEM EASILY ACHIEVABLE TO YOU BUT IT IS NOT!
- Show how the growth of the company sales in units and its estimated market share are related to the growth of its industry and customers and the strengths and weaknesses of competitors. Remember, the assumptions used to estimate market share and sales need to be clearly stated.

G. Ongoing Market Evaluation:

- Explain how you will continue to evaluate your target markets so as to assess customer needs and service and to guide product-improvement programs and new-product programs, plan for expansions of your production facility, and guide product/service pricing. Explain how you make the necessary strategic changes in your plan.

Section IV: The Economics of the Business

The economic and financial characteristics, including the apparent magnitude and durability of margins and profits generated, need to support the fundamental attractiveness of the opportunity. The underlying operating costs and each conversion cycle of the business, the value chain, and so forth, need to make sense in terms of the opportunity and strategies planned.

A. Revenue Sources and Gross and Operating Margins:

- Summarize the major revenue sources (products and services) of the business and proportionately where you expect to make your money.
- Describe the size of the gross margins (i.e., selling price less cost of goods sold or variable costs) and the for each of the product(s) and/or service(s) you are selling .. Where you have multiple products or product lines, calculate the contribution margin for each product line and then determine the weighted average contribution margins by weighting the individual contribution margins based on the percentage of total sales expected to come from that product line. Include results of your overall contribution analysis.

B. Fixed and Variable Costs:

- Provide a detailed summary of fixed and variable costs, in dollars and as a percentages of total costs, for the product or service you offer and the volume of purchases and sales upon which these are based. For analysis purposes, classify semi-variable costs as either fixed or variable.
- Show relevant industry benchmarks for costs.

C. Operating Leverage and its Implications

- Characterize whether your cost structure is predominantly fixed or variable and then indicate the implications. For example, if you have a high fixed cost structure, you have high operating leverage which means it takes longer to reach breakeven, but once there, much more of your revenue flows straight to the bottom line. High operating leverage (high fixed costs) suggests a riskier venture, at least initially.

D. Overall Economic Model

- Look at operating leverage especially as it relates to margins and volume to argue the viability of your business.
- Put the pieces above together. Indicate how you will make money in terms of the combination of margins, volumes, operating leverage and revenue source flexibility.

Breakeven Chart and Calculation

- Make clear what your unit of analysis is for the purpose of calculating breakeven.
- Calculate breakeven and prepare a chart that shows when breakeven will be reached and any stepwise changes in breakeven that may occur. Present a chart for the break-even point in the appendix.
- Discuss the breakeven shown for your venture and whether it will be easy or difficult to attain breakeven, including a discussion of the size of break-even sales volume relative to projected total sales, the size of gross margins and price sensitivity, and how the break-even point might be lowered in case the venture falls short of sales projections.

F. Profit Potential and Durability:

- Describe the magnitude and expected durability of the profit stream the business will generate (before and after taxes) and reference appropriate industry benchmarks, other competitive intelligence, or your own relevant experience.
- Address the issue of how solid or vulnerable the profit stream appears to be. Provide reasons why your profit stream is solid or vulnerable, such as barriers to entry you can create, your technological and market lead time, and so on.

Section V: The Marketing Plan

The **Marketing Plan** describes how your projected sales will actually be attained. How will you make sales actually happen? A great idea is meaningless if you cannot find customers. Thus, this section builds on the **Market Section**, where you defined your market and outlined your targeted segments and their buyer behavior. The marketing plan needs to provide detail on the overall marketing strategy that will exploit the opportunity and your competitive advantages. Include a discussion of sales and service policies, pricing, distribution, promotion and advertising strategies, and sales projections. The marketing plan needs to describe what is to be done, how it will be done, when it will be done, and who will do it.

A. Overall Marketing Strategy:

- Describe the specific marketing philosophy and strategy of the company, given the value chain and channels of distribution in the market niche(s) you are pursuing. Include, for example, a discussion of the kinds of customer groups that have already placed orders, have expressed an interest, or will be targeted for either initial intensive selling efforts. Explain how you will try to position your products or services in the marketplace and in the minds of particular target audiences.
- How will you differentiate your product/service from your competitors?
- Make it clear how your marketing strategy reflects the characteristics of the primary market segments you will be targeting.
- Indicate whether the product(s) or service(s) will initially be introduced internationally, nationally, regionally, or locally; explain why, and indicate any plans for extending sales at a later date.
- From an overall standpoint, make it clear whether marketing efforts will center on personal selling, media advertising, or what (you will get into specifics below).

B. Pricing:

- Discuss pricing strategy, including the prices to be charged for your product and service, and compare your pricing policy with those of your major competitors, including a brief discussion of payback (in months) to *the customer*.

- Explain how the price you set will enable you (1) to get the product or service accepted, (2) to maintain an increase in your market share in the face of competition, and (3) to produce profits.
- Justify your pricing strategy and differences between your prices and those for competitive or substitute products or services in terms of economic payback to the customer and value added through newness, quality, warranty, timing performance, service, cost savings, efficiency, and the like.
- If your product is to be priced lower than those of the competition, explain how you will do this and maintain profitability (e.g., through greater value added vial effectiveness in manufacturing and distribution, lower labor costs, lower material costs, lower overhead, or other component of cost).
- Discuss pricing structure, or how your prices will differ by aspect of the product or service, by customer group, and by time and form of payment (e.g., the discount structure).
- Discuss the use of special price offers, rebates, coupons, and so forth. This can be done under price or under sales promotion.

C. The Selling Cycle

- In the MARKET section you described the customer's buying process. Now, map out a selling cycle or process that reflects that buying process. How do you plan to move a customer from never having heard of you to being a loyal user?
- Make it vividly clear how your overall use of personal selling, advertising, and publicity will reflect a blend of tools that moves your target customer through their buying process.

D. Sales Tactics

- Describe the methods (e.g., own sales force, sales representatives, ready-made manufacturers' sales organizations, direct mail, or distributors) that will be used to make sales and distribute the product or service. Also include both the initial plans and longer-range plans for a sales force. Include a discussion of any special requirements (e.g., refrigeration).
- Describe how distributors or sales representatives, if they are used, will be selected when they will start to represent you, the areas they will cover and the build-up (a head count) of dealers and representatives by month, and the expected sales to be made by each.
- If a direct sales force is to be used, indicate how it will be structured and at what rate (a head count) it will be built up; indicate if it is to replace a dealer or representative organization and, if so, when and how. How will you recruit, train and compensate the sales force?
- Show the sales expected per salesperson per year and what commission, incentive, and/or salary they are slated to receive, and compare these figures to the average for your industry.

- Present a selling schedule and a sales budget that includes all marketing promotion and service costs.
- Discuss any seasonal trends that underlie the cash conversion cycle in the industry and what can be done to promote sales out of season.

E. Advertising and Sales Promotions:

- Describe the media approaches the company will use to bring its product or service to the attention of prospective purchasers. How will you inform your target market about the availability of your product/service and continue to communicate the benefits you are offering to that market
- If direct mail, magazine, newspaper, or other media, telemarketing, or catalog sales are to be used, indicate the specific channels or vehicles, costs (per 1,000), and expected response rates and yield (as percentage) from the various media, and so on, used. Discuss how these will be built up.
- For original equipment manufacturers and for manufacturers of industrial products, indicate the plans for trade show participation, trade magazine advertisements, direct mailings, the preparation of product sheets and promotional literature, and use of advertising agencies.
- For consumer products, indicate what kind of advertising and promotional campaign is planned to introduce the product. Specify types of media to be employed and what kinds of sales aids will be provided to dealers, what trade shows, and so forth, are required.
- Present a schedule and approximate costs of promotion and advertising (direct mail, telemarketing, catalogs, etc.), and discuss how these costs will be incurred. Determine the total marketing budget required.
- Note any viral or buzz marketing efforts you plan to employ.

F. Publicity

- What methods will you use to get free publicity for your business?
- What sort of guerrilla publicity tactics will you employ?
- How might you create news?

G. Customer Service *(can be covered here or in the OPERATIONS section)*

- How will customer service be defined and measured?
- What system will you have in place to manage customer service and ensure service levels are consistent?

H. Warranty or Guarantee Policies:

- If your company will offer a product that will require service, warranties, or training, indicate the importance of these to the customers' purchasing decisions and discuss your method of handling service problems.
- Describe the type and terms of any warranties to be offered, whether company service people, agencies, dealers and distributors will handle service, or simply return to the factory.

- Indicate the proposed charge for service calls and whether service will be a profitable or loss operation.
- Compare your service, warranty, and customer training practices to those of principal competitors.

I. Distribution:

- Describe the methods of distribution you will employ. Why is this best/better?
- Discuss the value chain and the resulting margins to be given to retailers, distributors, wholesalers, and salespeople and any special policies regarding discounts, exclusive distribution rights, and so on, given to distributors or sales representatives and compare these to those given by your competition.
- What distribution channel(s) will be important to your business? How will you gain access to these channels? Note any special issues that need to be resolved, or present potential vulnerabilities.
- Explain any methods to be employed to obtain distributor cooperation and support.
- If international sales are involved, note how these sales will be handled, including distribution, shipping, insurance, credit, and collections.

Section VI: Design and Development Plan

This is a very important section for those teams developing a non-existent product, doing research and development, having technical obstacles to overcome, or seeking patent or copyright protection. However, if you are in a business where research and development is not a major issue (e.g., retailing, many consumer services), then you can leave this section out and just address and technologies you plan to employ in the OPERATIONS section.

The nature and extent of any design and development work, and the time and money required before the product or service is marketable, need to be considered in detail. (Note that design and development costs are often underestimated.) Design and development might be the engineering work necessary to convert a laboratory prototype to a finished product; the design of special tooling; the work of an industrial designer to make a product more attractive and saleable; or the identification and organization of employees, equipment, and special techniques, such as the equipment, new computer software, and skills required for computerized credit checking, to implement a service business.

A. Development Status and Tasks:

- Define the present state of development of the product or service and how much time and money will be required to fully develop, test, and introduce the product or service. If appropriate provide a drawing, or a summary of the functional specifications and photographs of the product, if available.

- Explain what remains to be done to make the product fully useable and ready for sale.
- Describe briefly the competence or expertise that your company has or will require to complete this development.
- List any customers or end users who are participating in the development, design, and/or testing of the product or service. Indicate results to date or when results are expected.
- How do you intend to ramp-up your business? Give a roadmap of how you are going to get from where you are now to where you want to be in the future.

B. Difficulties and Risks:

- Identify any major anticipated design and development challenges and approaches to their solution.
- Discuss the possible effect on the cost of design and development, on the time to market introduction, and so forth, of such problems.

C. Product Improvement and New Products:

- In addition to describing the development of the initial products, discuss any ongoing design and development work that is planned to keep product(s) or service(s) competitive and to develop new related product(s) or service(s) that can be sold to the same group of customers. Discuss customers who have participated in these efforts and their reactions, and include any evidence that you may have.

D. Costs:

- Present and discuss the design and development budget, including costs of labor, materials, consulting fees, and so on.
- Discuss the impact on cash flow projections of underestimating this budget, including the impact of a 15 to 30 percent contingency.

E. Proprietary Issues (THIS IS WHERE YOU DISCUSS INTELLECTUAL PROPERTY):

- Describe any patent, trademark, copyright, or intellectual property rights you own or are seeking.
- Do you have any trade secrets?
- Describe any contractual rights or agreements that give you exclusive or proprietary rights.
- Discuss the impact of any unresolved issues or existing or possible actions pending, such as disputed rights of ownership, regulated to proprietary rights on timing and on any competitive edge you have assumed.

Section VII: Operations Plan

The operations section outlines how you will run your business and deliver value to your customers. Operations is defined as the processes that deliver your products/services to a customer or user and can include the production process for delivering your service to a given customer, manufacturing process if you are a manufacturer, transportation, logistics, travel, printing, consulting, and after-sales service. It also includes such factors as plant location, the type of facilities needed, space requirements, internal processes, capital equipment requirements, and labor force (both full- and part-time) requirements.

For a *manufacturing business*, the manufacturing and operations plan needs to include policies on inventory control, purchasing, production control, and which parts of the product will be purchased and which operations will be performed by your workforce (called make-or-buy decisions).

A *service business* may require particular attention to location (proximity to customers is generally a must), the service delivery system, minimizing overhead, and obtaining competitive productivity from a labor force. In all likelihood 80% of your expenses will be for operations, 80% of your employees will be involved in operations and

80% of your time will be spent worrying about operating problems. You will probably have to make trade-offs with your operations —it is impossible to have the lowest costs, highest quality, best on-time delivery and most flexibility in your industry all at the same time. This is where you have to make trade-off decisions that fit your other plans.

A. Operating Model and Cycle:

* Outline the operations process for your business. Identify the inputs, operations (key steps or stages) and outputs (present a flow diagram). This is a day in the life of actually producing your product or creating and delivering your service—walk us through the mechanics of doing so.

* Distinguish your model for managing 'front stage' versus 'back stage' operations.

* Where are you likely to have bottlenecks in your service delivery or manufacturing process and how will these be anticipated and addressed.

* Describe the lead/lag times that characterize the fundamental operating cycle in your business.

* Explain how any seasonal production loads will be handled without severe dislocation (e.g., by building to inventory using part-time help in peak periods).

* What quality consistency issues exist and how will quality consistency be ensured? What controls exist, for instance, to ensure every burger is cooked exactly the same?

B. Geographic Location:

* Describe the planned geographic location of the business. Include any location analysis, site selection etc. that you have done.

- Discuss any advantages or disadvantages of the site location in terms of such factors as labor (including labor available, whether workers are unionized, and wage rate), closeness to customer and/or suppliers, access to transportation, state and local taxes and laws (including zoning regulations), access to utilities, and so forth.

C. Facilities, Equipment and Improvements:

- Describe the facilities, including plant and office space, storage and land areas, special tooling, machinery, and other equipment needed to conduct business. Discuss any economies to scale.
- Provide a schematic diagram of the layout of your facility.
- Describe how and when the necessary facilities to start production will be acquired.
- Discuss whether equipment and space will be leased or acquired (new or used) and indicate costs and timing of such actions and how much of the proposed financing will be devoted to plant/equipment.
- Discuss how and when, in the next three years, office/ retail site/ plant space and equipment will be expanded to the capacities required by future sales projections and any plans to improve or add to existing space or move the facility; indicate the timing and cost of such acquisitions.

D. Operations Strategy and Plans:

- Describe the management of the manufacturing processes involved in production of your product(s) – what will you do in-house and what will you purchase (i.e. make versus buy decision) or outsource? Or Describe the service delivery processes involved in providing your service(s) and any aspects of the service that are outsourced or provided by others.
- Justify your proposed make-or-buy policy in terms of inventory financing, available labor skills, and other non-technical questions, as well as production, cost, and capability issues.
- Discuss who potential subcontractors and suppliers are likely to be and any information about, or any surveys that have been made of, these subcontractors and suppliers. Discuss relationships with them.
- Discuss your capacity and present a plan for operations that shows cost/volume information at various sales or production levels with breakdowns of applicable material, labor, purchased components, and overhead, and that shows the inventory required at these various sales levels.
- Describe your approach to quality control, production control, inventory control, and explain what quality control and inspection procedures the company will use to minimize service problems and associated customer dissatisfaction. How will you win in the market place on cost, quality, timeliness or flexibility?

E. Legal Issues Affecting Operations:

- Describe any particular legal issues affecting your operations. As examples, in a food service operation, certain permits and venting are required; in a production operation with outsourced production, there are legal issues governing the outsourcing agreement; when selling through a manufacturers rep or a retail channel there are legal issues affecting the distribution agreement; when setting up a franchise system there are legal issues tied to the franchising agreement; when selling something on a university campus there are legal constraints in operating on the campus; when operating in certain countries there may be some legal or regulatory issues that require attention, and so forth. Note that legal issues affecting intellectual property are handled in the 'Design and Development' section.

Section VIII: Management Team

This section of the business plan includes a description of the functions that will need to be filled, a description of the key management personnel and their primary duties, an outline of the organizational structure for the venture, a description of the board of directors and key advisors, a description of the ownership position of any other investors, and so forth. You need to present indications of commitment, such as the willingness of team members to initially accept modest salaries, and of the existence of the proper balance of technical, managerial, and business skills and experience in doing what is proposed.

A. Organization:

- Present the key management roles and responsibilities in the company.
- Discuss the individuals who will fill each position.
- If it is not possible to fill each executive role with a full-time person without adding excessive overhead, indicate how these functions will be performed (e.g., using part-time specialists or consultants to perform some functions), who will perform them, and when they will be replaced by a full-time staff member.
- If any key individuals will not be on board at the start, indicate when they will join the company.
- Discuss any current or past situations where key management people have worked together that could indicate how their skills complement each other and result in an effective management team.

B. Key Management Personnel:

- For each key person, describe career highlights, particularly relevant know-how, skills, and track record of accomplishments that demonstrate his or her ability to perform the assigned role. Include in your description sales and profitability achievements (budget size, numbers of subordinates, new product introductions, etc.) and other prior entrepreneurial or general management results.
- Describe the exact duties and responsibilities of each of the key members of the management team.

- Complete resumes for each key management member need to be included here or as an exhibit and need to stress relevant training, experience, any concrete accomplishments, such as profit and sales improvement, labor management success, manufacturing or technical achievements, and meeting of budgets & schedules.

C. Management Compensation and Ownership:

- State the salary to be paid, the stock ownership planned, and the amount of their equity investment (if any) of each key member of the management team.

D. Other Current Investors:

- Describe here any other investors in your venture, the number and percentage of outstanding shares they own, when they were acquired, and at what price.

E. Employment and Other Agreements, Stock Options and Bonus Plans:

- Describe any existing or contemplated employment or other agreements with key members.
- Indicate any restrictions on stock and vesting that affect ownership and disposition of stock.
- Summarize any incentive stock option or other stock ownership plans planned or in effect for key people and employees.

F. Board of Directors:

- Discuss the company's philosophy about the size and composition of the board.
- Identify any proposed board members and include a one or two sentence statement of the member's background that shows what he or she can bring to the company.

G. Other Shareholders, Rights, and Restrictions:

- Indicate any other shareholders in your company and any rights and restrictions or obligations, such as notes or guarantees, associated with these. (If they have all been accounted for above, simply note that there are no others.)

H. Supporting Professional Advisors and Services:

- Indicate the names and affiliations of the legal, accounting, advertising, consulting, and banking advisors selected for your venture and the services each will provide.

Section IX: Overall Schedule

A graphical schedule that shows the timing and interrelationship of the major events necessary to launch the venture and realize its objectives is an essential part of a business plan. The underlying cash conversion and operating cycle of the business will provide key inputs for the schedule. In addition to being a planning aid by showing deadlines critical to a venture's success, a well-presented schedule can be extremely valuable in convincing potential investors that the management team is able to plan for venture growth in a way that recognizes obstacles and minimizes investor risk. Since the time necessary to do things tends to be underestimated in most business plans, it is important to demonstrate that you have correctly estimated these amounts in determining the schedule. Create your schedule as follows:

Step 1:   Prepare a month-by-month schedule that shows the timing of such activities as product development, market planning, sales programs, production, and operations, and that includes sufficient detail to show the timing of the primary tasks required to accomplish an activity.

Step 1:   Show on the schedule the deadlines or milestones critical to the venture's success, such as:
- Incorporation of the venture.
- Completion of design and development.
- Completion of prototypes.
- Rental of facilities.
- Obtaining of sales representatives.
- Obtaining product display at trade shows.
- Hiring of key managers.
- Obtaining critical financing.
- Initiating marketing activities and in what order.
- Signing up of distributors and dealers.
- Ordering of materials in production quantities.
- Starting of production or operation.
- Receipt of first orders.
- Delivery on first sale.
- Receiving the first payment on accounts receivable.

Step 3:   Show on the schedule the "ramp up" of the number of management personnel, the number of production and operations personnel, and plant or equipment and their relation to the development of the business.

Step 4:   Discuss in a general way the activities most likely to cause a schedule slippage, what steps will be taken to correct such slippages, and the impact of schedule slippages of the venture's operation, especially its potential viability and capital needs.

Note: You want to be fairly detailed for the first six months to a year, and then just hit key developments or benchmarks for years two and three. A three-year schedule is adequate.

Section X: Critical Risks, Problems, and Assumptions

The development of a business has risks and problems, and the business plan invariably contains some implicit assumptions about these issues. You need to include a description of the risks and the consequences of adverse outcomes relating to your industry, your company and its personnel, your product's market appeal, and the timing and financing of your startup. Be sure to discuss assumptions concerning sales projections, customer orders, and so forth. If the venture has anything that could be considered a fatal flaw, discuss why you do not see it as a problem or how you intend to overcome it. The discovery of any unstated negative factors by potential investors can undermine the credibility of the venture and endanger its financing. Be aware that most investors will read the section describing the management team first and then this section. It is therefore recommended that you not omit this section. If you do, the reader will most likely come to one or more of the following conclusions:

1. You think he or she is incredibly naïve or stupid, or both.
2. You hope to pull the wool over his or her eyes.
3. You do not have enough objectivity to recognize and deal with assumptions and problems.

Identifying and discussing the risks in your venture demonstrate your skills as a manager and increase credibility of you and your venture with a venture capital investor or a private investor. Taking the initiative on the identification and discussion of risks helps you to demonstrate to the investor that you have thought about them and can handle them. Risks then tend not to loom as large black clouds in the investor's thinking about your venture.

1. Discuss assumptions implicit in your plan. Examples of key assumptions might include:
   - Revenue forecasts (price, volumes, discounts, margins).
   - Development expenses (number of people, key salaries, sub-contracts)
   - Average cost of a unit.
   - COGS (material, etc.).
   - Working capital (accounts receivable, inventory, payables)
   - Capital expenditures (major items).
   - Ability to obtain key distribution channel.
   - Getting a patent licenses or permit.
   - Rate of growth in sales.

- Obtaining a particular site or facility that is key to the business.
- Hiring of key staff members with experience in a critical area.
- Approval of critical financing.
- Overcoming key obstacles in product design.

2. Identify and discuss any major problems and other risks, such as:
   - Running out of cash before orders are secured.
   - Competitor risks e.g. you are pre-empted in the market by a competitor
   - Technological risks i.e. cannot make the product work
   - Potential price-cutting by competitors.
   - Any potential unfavorable industry-wide trends.
   - Design or manufacturing costs in excess of estimates.
   - Sales projections not achieved.
   - Difficulties or long lead times encountered in the procurement of parts or raw materials.
   - Difficulties encountered in obtaining needed bank credit.
   - Larger-than-expected innovation and development costs.
   - Running out of cash after orders pour in.

3. Indicate what assumptions or potential problems and risks are most critical to the success of the venture, and describe your plans for minimizing the impact of unfavorable developments in each case. What is the worst-case scenario and how will you respond? Focus on risks that are important and critical to your business, not the ordinary operating risks faced by any business.

Section XI: Financial Plan

Documents To Be Developed For This Section (Put In Appendix)

   i. Pro forma income statements (3-5 years, done monthly for at least the first 1-2 years)
   ii. Pro forma balance sheets (3-5 years)
   iii. Pro forma cash flow analysis (3-5 years, done monthly for at least the first 1-2 years)

This section lays out exactly what you are requesting from investors; it is number-oriented. Give the investors the columns and rows that they want to see. The more you give them, the more difficult it will be for them to challenge the assumptions that you have made to produce those numbers.

The financial plan is basic to the evaluation of an investment opportunity and needs to represent your best estimates of financial requirements. The purpose of the financial plan is to indicate the venture's potential and to present a timetable for financial viability. It also can serve as an operating plan for financial management using financial benchmarks. In preparing the financial plan, you need to look creatively at your venture and consider alternative ways of launching or financing it.

As part of the financial plan, financial exhibits need to be prepared. To estimate cash flow needs, use cash-based, rather than an accrual-based, accounting (i.e., use a real-time cash flow analysis of expected receipts and disbursements). This analysis needs to cover three years (or five depending on your type of business). Included also are pro forma income statements and balance sheets; and a break-even chart.

On the appropriate exhibits, or in an attachment, assumptions behind such items as sales levels and growth, collections and payables periods, inventory requirements, cash balances, cost of goods, and so forth, need to be specified. Your analysis of the operating and cash conversion cycle in the business will enable you to identify these critical assumptions.

Pro forma income statements are the plan-for-profit part of financial management and can indicate the potential financial feasibility of a new venture. Usually the level of profits, particularly during the start-up years of a venture, will not be sufficient to finance operating asset needs, and since actual cash inflows do not always match the actual cash outflows on a short-term basis, a cash flow forecast that will indicate these conditions and enable management to plan cash needs is recommended. Further, pro forma balance sheets are used to detail the assets required to support the projected level of operations and through liabilities, to show how these assets are to be financed. The projected balance sheets can indicate if debt-to-equity ratios, working capital, current ratios, inventory turnover and the like are within the acceptable limits required to justify future financing that are projected for the venture.

Finally, a break-even chart showing the level of sales and production that will cover all costs, including those costs that vary with production level and those that do not, is very useful:

A. Pro Forma Income Statements:

- Using sales forecasts and the accompanying operating costs, prepare pro forma
- income statements for at least the first three years. Be sure these numbers are consistent with what is being proposed in all the earlier sections of the plan (marketing, operations, management team, etc.)
- Fully discuss assumptions (e.g., the amount allowed for bad debts and discounts, or any assumptions made with respect to sales expenses or general and administrative costs being a fixed percentage of costs or sales) made in preparing the pro forma income statement and document them.
- Draw on Section X of the business plan and highlight any major risks, such as the effect of a 20% reduction in sales from those projected or the adverse impact of having to climb a learning curve on the level of productivity over time, that could prevent the venture's sales and profit goals from being attained, plus the sensitivity of profits to these risks.

B. Pro Forma Balance Sheets:

- Prepare pro forma balance sheets semi-annually in the first year and at the end of each of the first three years.

C. Pro Forma Cash Flow Analysis:

- Project cash flows monthly for the first year of operation and quarterly for at least the next two years, detailing the amount and timing of expected cash inflows and outflows; determine the need for and timing of additional financing and indicate peak requirements for working capital; and indicate how needed additional financing is to be obtained, such as through equity financing, bank loans, or short-term lines of credit from banks, on what terms, and how it is to be repaid. Remember they are based on cash, not accrual, accounting. Explain how much money you will need. For debt funding, what will you use as collateral? How will the money be used-for working capital, R&D, marketing, capital acquisitions? This dictates the level of risk of the investment. Investors generally feel that expenditures for R&D and marketing are riskier than are expenditures for capital acquisitions.
- Discuss assumptions, such as those made on the timing of collection of receivables, trade discounts given, terms of payments to vendors, planned salary and wage increases, anticipated increases in any operating expenses, seasonality characteristics of the business as they affect inventory requirements, inventory turnovers per year, capital equipment purchases, and so forth. Again, these are real time (i.e., cash), not accrual.
- Discuss cash flow sensitivity to a variety of assumptions about business factors (e.g., possible changes in such crucial assumptions as an increase in the receivable collection period or a sales level lower than that forecasted).

D. Months to Breakeven and to Positive Cash Flow:

- Given the above strategy and assumptions, show when the venture will attain a positive cash flow. Show if and when you will run out of cash. Note where the detailed assumptions can be found. Note any significant step-wise changes in cash flow that will occur as you grow and add capacity
- Given your entry strategy, marketing plan, and proposed financing, how long it will take to reach a unit breakeven sales level. How many months to breakeven? Briefly describe your break-even estimates. In other words, how many units (or dollars' worth) of the product (or how many hours of the service) must be sold to cover your costs?

E. Cost Control:

- Describe how you will obtain information about report costs and how often, who will be responsible for the control of various cost elements, and how you will take action on budget overruns. Explain any unusual items not identified in the financial statement.

F. Highlights of the Financial Statements:

- Highlight the important conclusions, such as what is the maximum amount of cash required is and when it will be required, the amount of debt and equity needed, how fast any debts can be repaid, etc., start up costs, etc.
- To help validate your financials compare critical financial ratios from your plan with those of your industry. Explain and justify significant differences.

Section XII: Proposed Company Offering

The purpose of this section of the plan is to indicate the amount of any money that is being sought, the nature and amount of the securities offered to the investor, a brief description of the uses that will be made of the capital revised, and a summary of how the investor is expected to achieve its targeted rate of return.

It is important to realize the terms for financing your company that you propose here are only the first step in the negotiation process with those interested in investing, and it is very possible that your financing will involve different kinds of securities than originally proposed.

A. Desired Financing:

- Review the monthly real-time cash flow projections and your estimate of how much money is required over the next three years to carry out the development and/or expansion of your business as described.
- Determine the amount and timing of cash infusions required to prevent cash balances from going negative. Add a cash safety cushion (~25% as a good "guesstimate") to the anticipated cash needs to protect against unexpected expenses or delayed income.
- Determine the type of funding that will suit your business: debt/equity or non-traditional financing. Indicate how this capital requirement will be obtained — from whom and how much will be obtained via term loans or lines of credit.

B. Offering (this is the deal structure – your pitch for money):

If you have decided to seek equity capital, then you need to describe the type of security being offered (e.g., common stock, convertible debentures, debt with warrants, debt plus stock), the unit price, and the total amount of securities to be sold in this offering. If securities are not just common stock, indicate by type, interest, maturity, and conversion conditions.

Show the percentage of the company that the investor in this offering will hold after it is completed or after exercise of any stock conversion or purchase rights in the case of convertible debentures or warrants i.e. what share of your company does the investor get for a specified investment.

Securities sold through a private placement and that are therefore exempt from SEC registration should include the following statement in this part of the plan: "The shares being sold pursuant to this offering are restricted securities and may not be resold readily. The prospective investor should recognize that such securities might be restricted as to resale for indefinite period of time. Each purchaser will be required to execute a Non-Distribution Agreement satisfactory in form to corporate counsel."

If you are seeking a loan, then you need to indicate to the potential lender how the loan will be repaid and what the interest rate is. What is the collateral for the loan?

C. Capitalization:

- Present in tabular form the current and proposed (post-offering) number of outstanding shares of common stock. Indicate any shares offered by key management people and show the number of shares that they will hold after completion of the proposed financing.
- Indicate how many shares of your company's common stock will remain authorize debut un-issued after the offering and how many of these will be reserved for stock options for future key employees.
- Identify any other terms that you are willing to negotiate as part of the deal e.g. right of first refusal, seat on board, voting rights, and other rights and preferences.

D. Use of Funds:

Investors like to know how their money is going to be spent. Provide a brief description of how the capital raised will be used. Summarize as specifically as possible what amount will be used for such things as product design and development, capital equipment, marketing, and general working capital needs.

E. Investors' Return (Exit Strategy).

- What is the value of your company? How did you calculate this value?
- Indicate how your valuation and proposed ownership shares will result in the desired rate of return for the investors you have targeted. What will be the likely harvest or exit mechanism (IPO, outright sale, merger, MBO, operate and grow, etc.)?
- What is the exit strategy for the investors and founders?

Covering Your Bases: Forty Issues To Die For

As the Nuts and Bolts booklet makes clear, there is much that goes into a great business plan. Below is a checklist of things you might want to ensure appear somewhere in your plan. While this is not a comprehensive list, it covers the primary issues.

1. Define the industry and characterize it in terms of size and the life cycle and draw implications. If it has an SIC or NAICS industry code, indicate so.
2. Develop a diagram of the value-added chain and the approximate number of firms at each level, and indicate the proportion that are large firms or chains.

3. Evaluate the attractiveness of the industry in terms of Porter's 5-factor model.

4. Identify at least three ways that companies are differentiating themselves in this industry.

5. Specify other leading trends in the industry (e.g., in costs, prices, marketing approaches, new products or services, use of technology, etc.) and identify the three most critical success factors in this industry.

6. Summarize key industry financial norms for companies in this industry.

7. Identify the principal components of the business concept. Be sure you are defining the concept in terms of customer value and customer benefits. Apply the five key criteria for a good business concept.

8. What is the need that the business exists to satisfy? How well satisfied is that need already? How high are the customer's switching costs from whatever they are currently using or doing?

9. What is the set of forces creating the opportunity? What is the likely window of opportunity?

10. How is the market defined? What is the size of the market opportunity in dollars, units or both? Distinguish current market size from market potential and estimate the size of the primary and selective demand gaps. What is the growth rate of the market?

11. How are you segmenting the market? Are the key segments homogenous, sizeable, reachable, and responsive? Provide descriptors of the customers who make up the key segments. Which segments will you be targeting (provide a prioritization)? Who will be your early adopters? Are their segments with different price elasticities?

12. Develop a simple model of customer buying behavior for this product or service. How long is the buying process? Who is the decision-maker? Why do they buy? It is a high or low involvement purchase? How loyal are customers to existing vendors/products?

13. What are the key factors affecting sales in the market? Will there be patterns to the company's sales. Is seasonality an issue? Is the business cyclical? Do interest rates have an impact?

14. Who are the direct competitors? Identify the strengths and weaknesses of each. How is each differentiating itself? Who are the indirect competitors? As a group, how much of a threat are they and why?

15. Be sure that you have developed a price list. Do prices adequately reflect: a) overall marketing strategy, b) costs, c) competition, d) customer demand, and e) legal issues?

16. Explain whether the company will be set up as a sole proprietorship, a partnership, an S corporation, a C corporation, or a limited liability company.

17. Describe the economics of the business. What is your average price, average cost per unit and average margin? How much of your cost structure is fixed versus variable? How much operating leverage do you have, and what are the implications of this? Calculate your contribution margin and

breakeven levels in dollars and units. Make it clear where you will be making your money (for instance, in a bar, how much of profit will come from drinks versus food, in a copier business how much will come from selling machines versus selling service?)

18. Have you formulated measurable objectives? Are you certain you've established objectives in all the appropriate performance areas?

19. How will you ensure that the company has a strong market-orientation?

20. What will be the principal or core competencies of the company? Is strategy built around these competencies.

21. Separate from the business concept, define the company's product mix. Assess the company's principal offering to customers in terms of the core, tangible and augmented product. Be sure to include such product-related issues as hours, facility layout, parking, etc.

22. How will the company's products be positioned?

23. If it is a service business, develop a diagram of the visible and non-visible aspects of the service delivery system.

24. How will operations be organized? If it is a manufacturing or assembly operation, what is the overall layout. Provide a schematic as well as a diagram of the workflow. If it's a service business, again describe the operational layout, and then how the service will be delivered.

25. Are any product policies needed (warrantees, returns policies)? If so, what will they be.

26. What is the company's unique selling proposition?

27. Have you developed an integrated communications mix that matches the customer's buying process. Summarize the company's complete mix of customer communications, including personal selling, advertising, sales promotion and publicity. Explain how they will be coordinated and managed as a mix.

28. What will the distribution channel look like? How much market coverage will this give you? What key approaches will be used to achieve cooperation among channel members?

29. How is customer service to be defined, measured and managed? What are the key components of customer service? Construct a comprehensive list of the points of customer contact involving any personnel, paperwork or facilities of the company.

30. What is the current stage of product development? Is a prototype completed? What further R&D work is needed and by when will it be completed? What's the ongoing plan for R&D?

31. Provide a detailed cash flow statement for each of the first 3-5 years of operation. Provide pro forma income statements and balance sheets for the first three years.

32. Have you identified all of the resources (human, financial, channels, customer base, information) the company will require to start up and achieve success over the first 3 years?

33. Identify the major direct competitors and assess the strengths, weaknesses, strategy and source of differentiation relied upon by each of them.

34. How will the firm's logistical arrangements work (inventory policies, physically getting products to customers, warehousing/storage)? What is the intended order cycle time?

35. Who will be the key members of the management team? Provide a resume of each of these individuals in an appendix. Briefly describe the role of each in the firm and how it fits their background and experience. Also, will there be a board of directors or advisors?

36. What are your staffing needs beyond the management team? What kind of people are you looking for and what is your plan for getting them?

37. Identify the major technology, legal/regulatory, economic and social developments that are likely to impact on this business in the next two years, and indicate the likely impact.

38. How much money are you asking for, from which sources, how will investors earn their return, and when? Will funding come in stages?

39. Identify the five major downside risks or things that could go wrong, and indicate your contingencies for dealing with each of them.

40. Is there internal consistency in your plan? For example, can one see the logical fit and consistency between you target market, the product/service you are selling, your marketing approach, and the budget you have put together.

At the bottom of each page of the booklet are the words:

DREAM>BELIEVE>PURSUE.

These are at the heart of the entrepreneurial mindset. Make them a part of your own.

Recommended Resource:

- Sample completed business plans – http://www.sba.gov

Notes

1. *The Nuts and Bolts of Business Plans,* Department of Entrepreneurship and Emerging Enterprises, Whitman School of Management, Syracuse University, Syracuse, New York, 2008, p. 2. Used with permission.

2. *The Nuts and Bolts of Business Plans,* Department of Entrepreneurship and Emerging Enterprises, Whitman School of Management, Courtesy Syracuse University, Syracuse, New York, 2008. All rights reserved; used with permission.

CHAPTER 14

RAISING CAPITAL FOR YOUR BUSINESS

Not every new entrepreneur has an abundance of cash, or a legion of venture capital investors, "angel" investors, or big start-up loans from banks. As you learned in Part I, nearly all of the most successful black entrepreneurs started with next to nothing or worked day jobs while building their businesses. Here are a few more brief examples of mega-companies that began with very little.

- Apple Computer: Steve Jobs and Steve Wozniak sold a VW van and a programmable calculator for $1350 and in 1976 built the first Apple I in Job's garage.
- Dominos Pizza: Tom Monaghan bought a small pizzeria with his brother for $900.00 in 1960 and expanded by locating stores near campuses or army bases, and delivering within half an hour. We all know where that went.
- Black and Decker Corporation: Started in 1910 with $1200 and has grown into a $6 billion tool manufacturer.
- Dell Computers: Michael Dell started selling computers from his college dorm room in 1983. When his sales increased, he dropped out of school. In 2008, Dell's sales were nearly $60 billion.

All of these entrepreneurs rose to success through "bootstrapping"—the art of doing more with less. For black entrepreneurs, it was a routine matter. Bootstrapping techniques should be studied and utilized by African American entrepreneurs and other disadvantaged groups who may be starting their business enterprises with minimal resources. Even though many things have changed over the years, African Americans have always found it more difficult to obtain capital to start, maintain, and grow their business enterprises largely due to discrimination and social realities. Challenges in the area of financing still remain today, so this chapter will not only cover funding sources for all aspiring entrepreneurs, but will also focus on sources for blacks and other minority groups.

The author, based on over 30 years of interaction as a lawyer involved in the black community, has concluded that a substantial lack of knowledge exists, even among educated blacks, about techniques for raising capital for new businesses. This should not be a surprise, however, given the primary role of African Americans as laborers or employees working for others, whether employed by the government or private industry. Accordingly, the author has included this portion of the book as both a public service and a convenient information source concerning basic aspects of corporate law and finance.

Sources of Capital

The sources of capital fall into two main categories—debt financing (borrowed funds obtained from third parties which must be repaid) and equity financing (internally generated funds obtained from investors who become owners in the company which do not have to be repaid by the company).

Debt Financing

Sources for debt financing include commercial banks, commercial finance companies, state and local government lending programs, trade credit and consortiums, and company issued debt instruments. Some commercial banks are more willing to provide start-up capital to small businesses if the loans they provide are guaranteed by the Small Business Administration. Accordingly, African Americans considering starting a business enterprise should become familiar with this process that is discussed later in this chapter. Additionally, one could use leasing companies instead of debt financing to obtain the necessary equipment to operate the business.

Equity Financing

Sources of equity funding include private investors, institutional venture-capital firms, merging with and acquiring or being acquired by another well-funded company, venture capitalists, and overseas investors.

The ultimate form of equity financing to promote the growth of a business is the initial public offering (IPO).

Underwritten Initial Public Offerings (IPOs)—When successful closely held businesses go public, the corporation directly sells, usually through an investment banker, a certain amount of its authorized but not yet issued shares to investors in the primary market who have expressed a willingness to purchase shares directly from the corporation. In a primary market transaction, the corporation (or other business) sells its securities to raise money for the corporation directly to the subscribing purchaser. The Securities Act of 1933 regulates the process of going public. The 1933 Securities Act applies whenever entrepreneurs wish to raise money for their business by selling investments in the business to anyone who will listen to the organization's sales pitch. The Act is applicable whenever the value of the investment depends on the performance of the business and the entrepreneur causes the investor to expect profits solely from the efforts of the entrepreneur or a third party. In such instances, the investment meets the definition for a "security" under the Act.[1] Entrepreneurs register the securities being offered by filing a disclosure satement, called a prospectus, with the Securities Exchange Commission in the absence of an exemption.

The market value of the original owners' stock is sometimes billions of dollars after the corporation completes a textbook initial public offering of a company with a solid track record of earnings prior to the offering. This occurs when the stock acquires a market value in subsequent secondary trading of the stock. The original owners or entrepreneurs cause the corporation to issue millions of shares to themselves for a pittance when the corporation is still closely held. When the corporation goes public, these shares now have a market value that creates instant billionaires in some instances. A classic example is how things came down when Steve Jobs first went public with Pixar. After the first day of secondary trading in Pixar stock, subsequent to the company's initial public offering, the stock of the "tiny company from Richmond, California with 150 employees and sales of less than $5 million had a market value of about $1.5 billion. And with 80 percent of the company stock still in his portfolio, the 40-year old Jobs entered the select fraternity of billionaires."[2]

When corporations go public, the government subjects them to intense federal regulation under the 1934 Securities and Exchange Act if they fall in either class of publicly held corporations as set forth under the Act's statutory provisions and rules. The process of going public can be very expensive. Small offerings are those that attempt to raise about

$10 million, while average offerings attempt to raise in the neighborhood of $30 million, and large offerings begin at approximately $50 million. The issuer must register the securities with the SEC, in the absence of an exemption, and must also register the securities in each state in which the issuer intends to sell the securities (i.e., comply with state blue sky regulations). Andrew J. Sherman, in his excellent book entitled *Raising Capital*, lists the following as typical expenses associated with the going public process: [3]

- Underwriter's compensation (about 7% of the anticipated gross proceeds)
- Legal fees (anywhere from $100 thousand to over $600 thousand depending on the size of the offering)
- Accounting fees (anywhere from $50 thousand to over $200 thousand depending on the size of the offering)
- The road show (presentations by corporate executives to potential investors that describe the corporation and its operations)
- Printing and engraving costs ($50 thousand to $250 thousand to print all the necessary documents and to engrave stock certificates)

A business seeking to raise capital through this route will incur these expenses even if the IPO is not completed. As you can see, these expenses can hit nearly $1 million on smaller offerings, over $1 million on average size offerings, and well over $2 million on large offerings

Accordingly, many organizations seeking to raise funds through an initial public offering attempt to qualify for an exemption from the registration requirements. The most common exemptions include the private offering exemption. To qualify under the private offering exemption, it is necessary that the business sell its securities only to: (1) persons who have sufficient knowledge and experience in financial matters who are capable of evaluating the risks and merits of the investment; (2) persons who have access to the type of information normally provided in a 1933 Act prospectus; (3) persons who agree not to resell or distribute the securities; and (4) persons who have not been approached by the company through any form of public solicitation or general advertising. In other words, the business may not sell the securities through any form of public solicitation or general advertising.[4] Other exemptions include the Regulation D exemptions under SEC Rules 504, 505, and 506, so called SCOR offerings, the Regulation A exemption, and the intrastate offering exemption. The Rule 504 exemption allows a business to offer and sell not more than $1 million of its securities during any 12-month period. Rule 505 permits a business to sell up to $5 million of its securities within a 12-month period to an unlimited number of accredited investors and up to 35 nonaccredited investors. Rule 506 is similar to Rule 505 but has no dollar limit. SCOR allows a small company to raise up to $1 million over a 12-month period. A SCOR offering is meant to be simpler and less expensive, and is used in conjunction with Rule 504 of Regulation D. A company engaged in an offering that is up to $1 million may market the offering using television, radio, and print ads.[5] To qualify for the intrastate exemption, the business must (1) be incorporated in the state where it is making the offering; (2) carry out a significant amount of its business in that state; and (3) make offers and sales only to residents of that state. The exemption is intended to facilitate the local financing of local business operations.[6]

Direct Public Offerings of Stock (DPOs)—One of the alternatives to an underwritten public offering is a direct public offering of stock (DPO) under either Regulation A or pursuant to Rule 504 of Regulation D via a SCOR offering. However, the most a business can raise in a Regulation A offering is $5,000,000 and, in a Rule 504 offering, $1,000,000.

DPOs are also known as exempt offerings because they are not subject to the same extensive registration requirements, level of expenses, and restrictions as an underwritten IPO. The corporation issuing the stock does all the work that would normally be done by an underwriting and selling syndicate, as is done with an IPO. Direct Public Offerings are not new, but have become more popular since the SEC simplified registrations for small companies.

Probably the biggest boost in popularity of DPOs has been the Internet. It makes it easy for companies to post information and their prospectus online, and for potential investors to easily access that information. The first company to use the Internet for its DPO was Spring Street Brewery in 1995. They not only paved the way for other companies, but their experience pointed up the need for "Internet underwriters" that would serve as a combination of investment banks, brokerage firms, and exchange forums to handle many of the details of setting up the DPO and handling transactions.[7]

DPOs have upsides and downsides. On the one hand, they are great ways for small companies to connect with investors who aren't afraid to take a risk. On the other hand, a DPO may not be appropriate for every small business, nor is putting one together a simples process. The most successful DPOs have been companies that already have a strong customer base, brand recognition, and that have utilized an online underwriter to increase awareness of the offering. Another advantage of a DPO is the reduction in expenses associated with an IPO using an investment banker. Additionally, DPOs help companies target small investors who are more interested in the company's unfolding success over the long term.[8]

However, because the shares are classified as "unregistered shares," stock sold through a DPO can be difficult or impossible to trade because the government places restrictions on any attempt to resell unregistered securities. Additionally, the most one can raise for his business in a Regulation A offering is $5,000,000 and, in a Rule 504 offering, $1,000,000. Finally, in contrast to an underwritten IPO, there is no investment bank to screen companies. This may result in companies that inadvertently (or deliberately) make false and/or misleading statements to investors.[9]

Private Offerings to Accredited Investors as an Alternative—Another alternative a business seeking to raise capital might wish to consider would be to make a private offering solely to accredited investors. This would, probably, be the least costly route to take. To qualify for the private offering exemption, the corporation can only sell its securities to:

1. investors with enough experience in financial matters to evaluate the risks/merits of the investment.
2. investors familiar with and who can access information normally provided in a 1933 Act prospectus.
3. investors who agree to hold the securities for long-term investment and not resell them.
4. investors who have not been approached by the company either directly or indirectly through any form of public solicitation or general advertising.[10]

Securities issued by religious and other charitable organizations are "exempted securities" and do not fall under the 1933 Securities Act. However, nonprofit organizations selling such investments would still be called to task for any misleading or fraudulent statements related to the offering even though they may be exempt from the registration requirements of the Act.[11]

Rule 501 defines the terms used in Regulation D for small (limited) offerings not totaling more than $5 million. It defines "accredited investor" to include:

1. any bank, insurance company, investment company, or employee benefit plan.
2. any business development company.

3. any charitable or educational institution with assets of more than $5 million.

4. any director, executive officer, or general partner of the issuer of securities being offered.

5. any person with a net worth of more than $1 million.

6. any person with an annual income of more than $200,000 (or together with his or her spouse, more than $300,000).

7. any trust with more than $5 million in assets that is managed by a "sophisticated person."

8. any entity in which all of the equity owners are accredited investors. [12]

Under Securities Act Rule 506, an issuer is not limited in the number of securities sold or the number of accredited buyers. It can also sell to up to 35 nonaccredited buyers. Rule 506 also has no limit on the amount the company can raise from investors. Before the sale, however, the issuer must be reasonably sure that nonaccredited buyers or their representatives have enough business and financial savvy to evaluate all aspects of the investment. If there are any nonaccredited purchasers, the information prescribed by Rule 502 must be furnished to them. The exemption is available to all issuers.[13]

Offerings complying with the terms of Securities Act Rule 506 are exempted from all state registration and disclosure requirements. Accordingly, the issuer need not register the securities with every state where the securities might be sold.

Initial Public Offerings via the Internet—Many companies seeking to raise more than the $5 million cap in a DPO pursuant to Regulation A, but are not large enough to use the services of a high-visibility underwriter, find that an initial public offering (IPO) via the Internet is ideal for their purposes. The company posts its prospectus online, and corresponds with potential investors by e-mail. Buyers then place their orders through the online underwriter. Companies going this route generally do not offer, through online sales, all the stock that is available.

Internet IPOs Using the Dutch Auction—The Dutch auction uses bids to get the best market price, generally the lowest price that the company is willing to sell its shares. The U.S. government uses a similar process to sell U.S. Treasury securities. The highest bidders all pay the amount of the lowest winning bid.

This is how it works. Investors bid on the number of shares they are interested in at a given price. The company sets out a price range, but bidders can bid over or under those amounts. The online auctioneer may also lower the starting price to attract more bidders, never going below the company's bottom-line price. Once the auction closes, numbers are crunched, top bidders get the shares all at the same price, and all shares offered are sold over the Internet. Underwriting costs range from 3 percent to 5 percent.

Internet IPOs may be a viable alternative for many small businesses. Certainly, the advantage of being able to post all the information online saves huge amounts of money. Internet IPOs are also more attractive to businesses seeking to raise small to medium amounts of money rather than the multi-million dollar offerings of larger companies. On the down side, Internet IPOs may not attract the upper echelon investors that a traditional stock offering would attract unless the company already has a fairly high profile in the marketplace.

Early Stage Financing

Early stage financing can come from the entrepreneurs' own resources, angel investors, university and private business incubators, economic development agencies and community development corporations, customer financing, and vendor financing.

Other sources of early stage financing include private placements of a company's equity securities, commercial lenders, leasing, and commercial lenders participating in the Small Business Administration's (SBA) section 7(a) Loan Guaranty Program (see Appendix I), Microloan Program (see Appendix II), and the Certified Development Company (504 Loan) Program (see Appendix III).

Growth Financing

Growth financing normally comes from venture capitalists. Venture capitalists generally invest a minimum of $1 million in a single company whereas angel investors generally invest between $25,000 to $150,000 in a single company. African Americans who own businesses that need additional capital to realize their growth potential should be aware of the role of venture capitalists in this process. There are literally hundreds of venture capitalists willing to offer risk capital to small, growing companies. In his book, *Raising Capital*, Andrew Sherman identifies the four primary types of venture capitalists:

- public and private international venture capitalist firms
- small business investment companies (SBICs)
- minority enterprise small business investment companies (MESBICs)
- corporate venture capital divisions.[14]

The start-up company, as consideration for the venture capitalist's investment, will normally issue to the venture capital firm either preferred stock, convertible debentures, or debt securities with warrants. Venture capitalists do not often buy common stock from a business in its formative stages as it fails to afford them any special rights, preferences, or fixed return on their investment. The venture capitalist's focus will be on how the entrepreneur intends to return the venture capitalist's original investment and return on capital within a four-to-six-year period. Accordingly, the venture capitalist is also interested in the exit strategy in which it recoups its investment and achieves a healthy return on its investment. The exit strategies normally utilized by venture capitalists to recoup their investment and obtain a respectable return on their investment include an IPO of the growing company's stock, sale of the company to an interested bidder, and the company's redemption of the venture capitalist's stock at a price reflecting the enhanced value of the company. They might also consider a company restructuring, license agreements for the brand and/or intellectual property, handing off the investment to another interested party, or selling the company off altogether.

Alternatives to Traditional Financing

Entrepreneurs may also seek, as alternatives to traditional financing, to develop their businesses through franchising, joint ventures, co-branding, licensing, and acquisition of other companies through mergers, and other types of acquisitions. The prospective entrepreneur should, at a minimum, be aware of how these alternatives can potentially increase the earnings of their business enterprises.

Recommended Reading
- *Raising Capital*, Andrew J. Sherman

Notes

1. *Reves v. Ernst & Young*, 294 U.S. 56 (1990); SEC v. W.J. Howey Co., 328 U.S. 293 (1966).

2. Steven Pearlstein, "Pixar Stock Offering a Hit for Steve Jobs," *Washington Post*, Nov. 30, 1995, at B11.

3. Andrew J. Sherman. *Raising Capital* (Washington, DC: Kiplinger Washington Editors, 2000), 190–92.

4. Securities and Exchange Commission, *Q & A: Small Business and the SEC Concerning the Private Offering Exemption,* (1993).

5. Andrew J. Sherman. *Raising Capital* (Washington, DC: Kiplinger Washington Editors, 2000), 101, 210-11, and Melvin Aron Eisenberg. *Corporations and Other Business Organizations: Cases and Materials* (New York: Foundation Press/West Publishing Group, 2000), 927–28.

6. Securities and Exchange Commission. *Q & A: Small Business and the SEC, the Intrastate Offering Exemption* (1993).

7. Andrew J. Sherman. *Raising Capital* (Washington, DC: Kiplinger Washington Editors, 2000), 209–10.

8. Ibid.

9. Ibid., 211–12.

10. Securities and Exchange Commission. Q & A: *Small Business and the SEC Concerning the Private Offering Exemption* (1993), 14–15.

11. David L. Ratner and Thomas Lee Hazen. *Securities Regulation* (New York: Thomson/West Publishing Company, 2005), 64.

12. Rule 501, 17 CFR § 230.501.

13. David L. Ratner and Thomas Lee Hazen. *Securities Regulation* (New York: Thomson/West Publishing Company, 2005), 67.

14. Andrew J. Sherman. *Raising Capital* (Washington, DC: Kiplinger Washington Editors, 2000), 160–62.

CHAPTER 15

TAX MATTERS FOR BUSINESS OWNERS

There are some wonderful opportunities available to entrepreneurs to maximize their wealth by taking advantage of a variety of tax saving opportunities. Many persons who are considering establishing a business may not have been aware of or considered some of the following tax saving programs that the government makes available to business owners. Stated simply, owning a business is great. With proper planning, the tax code allows a business owner the opportunity to convert otherwise nondeductible expenses into tax deductible items—a cruise, a party, a luxurious car, 50 percent of meals, extra deductions for a retirement plan set up by the owner's business, and so much more! These are some examples of ways you can lower your taxes as an employer if you follow the guidelines. However, you should note that *the tax code is constantly changing*. Therefore, the prospective entrepreneur *must consult with a tax professional to determine the current status and availability of any of the items the book discusses* in this subsection.

Employees of corporations enjoy certain tax-free fringe benefits under the tax laws. Section 132 of the Internal Revenue Code (IRC) allows business owners the ability to participate in most "employee" fringe benefits on a tax-free basis, particularly if they organize the business as a C corporation. And now, even S corporation shareholder/employees who own more than 2 percent of the company can participate in most benefits. IRS Notice 2008-1 allows an S corporation that has shareholders who own more than 2 percent of the corporation's stock, to deduct health insurance premiums that the corporation pays or reimburses on their behalf. The law requires that the S corporation's payments be included in these employees' incomes. In return, these employees can take an "above-the-line" deduction for these amounts. The new law treats payments by an employer as if the employer had established the individual's plan. However, the tax laws may require that the S corporation include the cost of the benefits in income as wages in order for the corporation to take the tax deduction.[1]

What Are Subchapter C, S, and K Business Organizations Under the Tax Laws?

There are three tax schemes for businesses under federal tax law. Subchapter C describes the traditional corporate income tax. Subchapter K describes the taxation applicable to partnerships and associations taxable as partnerships other than corporations. Subchapter S is an alternative tax election available to certainly closely held corporations that meet its eligibility requirements.[2]

The government subjects the income of "C" Corporations to double taxation. The corporation initially pays income taxes on its net revenues. If the corporation subsequently distributes a portion of the previously taxed income to the shareholders as a dividend, the shareholders must also pay taxes on that income. The government taxes the income of a general partnership only once under Subchapter K. The owners pay the taxes and, more importantly, take the deductions under Subchapter K. Tax experts refer to this as flow-through taxation. The government taxes the income of closely held corporations eligible for the Subchapter S taxation in a manner which avoids the double taxation on distributions similar to the approach taken under Subchapter K.[3]

Accordingly, there are benefits to start-up firms under Subchapters K and S that are not available under Subchapter C. However, there are several tax benefits available to C corporations that are not available to Subchapter K and S organizations, as we shall see.

The owners of self-employed business organizations (i.e., a sole proprietor, partners in a general partnership or an owner of a LLC taxed as a general partnership or a sole proprietorship), are often limited in their ability to take business deductions that the owners of corporations enjoy, such as health insurance expenses and other "employee" fringe benefits (e.g., vacation, sick time, medical plans, group term life insurance up to $50,000, dependent care assistance up to $5,000, education assistance up to $5,250, adoption assistance, various reimbursement plans for things like child care, and more). However, implementing tax strategies such as employing the owner's spouse will permit these business owners to participate in these benefits on a tax-free basis. The employed spouse must, however, be a legitimate employee and all formal requirements must be met.[4]

The business type becomes important if the company can afford to provide other kinds of benefits as well. Let's take a look at some of them.

Retirement Plans

All kinds of business can offer tax-favored retirement plans for owners and employees. Moreover, there are numerous other deductible items available to business owners regardless of the form of the business which we shall address in this chapter.

Health Coverage

Although self-employed businesses cannot take a "business expense deduction" for health coverage for self-employed persons, those who buy coverage in their personal names can deduct the premiums from gross income (above the line) on Form 1040. An "above the line" deduction refers to nonitemized deductions taken as an adjustment to gross income on Form 1040.[5] However, the deduction cannot exceed the net earnings from the business which established the medical insurance plan. Moreover, IRS Notice 2008-1 now allows an S corporation's more than 2 percent shareholders-employees to deduct health insurance premiums that the corporation pays or reimburses on their behalf. The law requires that the S corporation's payments be included in these employees' incomes. In return, these employees can take an "above-the-line" deduction for these amounts on Form 1040 in computing adjusted gross income. The new law treats payments by an employer as if the employer had established the individual employee's plan. However, the government will not allow the more than 2 percent employee to take the deduction during a month in which the taxpayer is able to participate in a subsidized health plan of the employer.

With regard to general partners, the partnership deducts health insurance for their partners as guaranteed payments as the owners cannot receive this benefit on a tax-free basis. The partnership reports the medical insurance it provides to owners on the owners' Schedule K-1. The partners must, thereafter, report this amount as income.[6]

Social Security and Medicare Taxes

Working shareholders and officers of S corporations *must* receive wages with appropriate withholdings for Social Security and Medicare taxes.[7] The Internal Revenue Service (IRS) has begun to crack down on owners of S corporations who do not pay themselves a reasonable wage. This means that the S corporation owners/employees must pay—through withholdings—the 7.65 percent combined Social Security and Medicare tax (i.e., 6.20% Social Security tax up to certain income limits and the 1.45% Medicare tax on the owner/employee's income to the maximum extent of his/her income). Additionally, the S corporation must also pay/match the 7.65 percent withheld from the S corporation owner/officer's wages as the S corporation must match each working employee's contribution. Once the S corporation pays the shareholder-employee a reasonable wage, the shareholder-employee, however, can pass through profits to their personal returns on form K-1 that the government taxes as ordinary income. However, the government does not take FICA (Social Security) and Medicare taxes from this amount, that is, the amounts designated as pass-through profits.[8]

In contrast, self-employed owners, as that term is defined by the IRS (sole proprietors, partners, and those "otherwise in business for themselves"), are subject to a self-employment tax of 15.3 percent of their business profits from Schedule C or Schedule 1065-K-1.[9] Self-employed individuals would include a sole proprietor, partners in a general partnership, or an owner of an LLC taxed as a general partnership or a sole proprietorship as previously noted.

The self-employment tax is equal to an employer's and an employee's portion of the Social Security and Medicare taxes that employers and employees pay on the employee's compensation when received as an employee. The self-employment tax is a Social Security and Medicare tax primarily for individuals who work for themselves as sole proprietors or partners in a partnership. Business owners subject to the tax can deduct half (50%) in figuring their adjusted gross income. However, this deduction only affects their income taxes. It does not affect their net earnings from self-employment or the self-employment tax due.[10]

The Federal Unemployment Tax

Only businesses that have employees must report and pay the federal unemployment tax (FUTA). The FUTA tax is not withheld from the employee's pay. Additionally, sole proprietorships and partnerships don't pay the FUTA tax on the owner's compensation. The tax rate is based on 6.2 percent of an employee's wages up to $7,000. The tax laws give employers a credit of up to 5.4 percent for participating in state unemployment programs. The credit reduces the FUTA rate significantly for most employers.[11]

Employer Identification Number

Self-employed individuals need to obtain an EIN (employer identification number) if they have employees and/or file pension or excise tax returns. Otherwise, their Social Security number acts as the employer ID.[12] One may obtain an EIN online at www.irs.gov/businneses/small/article/0,,=102767,00.html or by filing Form SS-4, (Application for Employer Identification Number) with the IRS service center in the area in which the business owner is based. Application by mail takes several weeks. An SS-4 can be obtained from the IRS website at **www.irs.gov** or by calling a special business phone number (1-800-829-4993) or the special Tele-TIN phone number. The instructions to Form SS-4 list the number for the appropriate IRS service center. If one calls for a number, the IRS assigns it immediately, after which the business owner must send or fax a signed SS-4 within 24 hours.[13]

Selected Examples of Interesting Tax Benefits

There are some other tax breaks that may benefit a small, closely held, or start-up business, as well as a growing enterprise. Here are a few of them.

Hiring Family Members

As a business owner, there are tax benefits to hiring family members, especially those under eighteen under some circumstances. Wages paid to one's children are fully deductible to the business. Allowances are not. The business owner can give his children more money than he gives them now—but the business owner's children must earn it! All of it will be deductible to the owner. If the owner is a sole proprietorship or a partner in a partnership, the wages he pays his children who are under 18 are not subject to Social Security, Medicare, or federal unemployment taxes. Most states also waive payroll taxes—but not all, so the business owner must be sure to check with his state's payroll tax authority. The Web site www.taxadmin.org/fta/link/forms.html has more information.

If the business owner had hired a nonchild employee, he would be paying half the Social Security/Medicare, all the federal and state unemployment taxes, workers' compensation insurance, holidays, sick days, and, possibly, benefits. Those additional expenses could add more than $1000 to the owner's business overhead. In paying his child, the business owner is converting money he would have given to his child anyway into a tax deduction. Even when the owner spends twice as much on his child as before, the government pays for nearly half the money the owner gives the child due to the savings from the deduction.[14]

SEP-IRA Profit Sharing Retirement Plan

Other potentially tax beneficial devices available to owners include retirement plans, especially a defined contribution profit-sharing plan set up as a SEP-IRA. This is true whether the owner is self-employed, as defined by the IRS—that is, the owner is either a sole proprietor or a partner—or whether the owner is a small business organized in some other format. Virtually any business owner can set up an SEP-IRA profit-sharing retirement plan. It's very easy to set up. Indeed, most investment professionals can assist the owner in setting up one of these plans for the owner with no great difficulty.

Additionally, the law does not require that the employer make any minimum contribution to a SEP-IRA retirement plan. Furthermore, the owner can change how much he wishes to contribute based on the income that the business generates. Accordingly, in a poor year, the owner can put in little or nothing. The owner, however, must give his employees, if any, the same benefits he gives himself as an employer. Accordingly, if the owner contributes 10 percent of his earnings, then the owner must contribute 10 percent for his employees. The employer's contributions to an employee's account is excluded from the employee's current income.

In 2008, a business owner could fund 25 percent of the firm's profits or wages from the owner's business, up to $46,000 per eligible employee, in an SEP-IRA. The business owner may set up and fund SEP-IRA's until the due date of the tax return, including extensions. The owner should note that, if he or she were covered by a retirement plan—qualified pension, profit sharing, 401(k), annuity, Keogh, SEP-IRA, SIMPLE IRA, and so forth—at work or through self-employment, the owner's IRA deduction for his/her non-work-related "traditional" IRA may be reduced or eliminated. But owners can still make contributions to a stand-alone non-work-related "traditional" IRA even if the owner cannot deduct them. In any case, the government will not tax the income earned on non-work-related, nondeductible "traditional" IRA contributions to the owner until paid to the owner (i.e., the earnings and growth will be tax-deferred).[15]

Small business owners should also note that, for the self-employed business owner (i.e., a sole proprietor, partners in a general partnership or an owner of an LLC taxed as a general partnership or a sole proprietorship), the SEP-IRA formula is not based solely on earnings as it is with employees, but rather on the business' *net income* (e.g., the figure on the bottom line of Schedule C) minus the amount the self-employed person contributes to the plan, minus half the money paid by the self-employed person(s) in self-employment tax. Accordingly, the maximum amount that self-employed persons can actually contribute is 20 percent of net adjusted self-employment income.

A firm organized as an S or C corporation can make a maximum contribution of 25 percent of an owner's W-2 salary up to the SEP-IRA contribution limit. SEP-IRA contributions are generally 100 percent tax deductible as a business expense.

Health Savings Accounts

Health Savings Accounts (HSA) are individual plans for any person but may be of particular interest to self-employed entrepreneurs (i.e., a sole proprietor, partners in a general partnership, or an owner of an LLC taxed as a general partnership or a sole proprietorship), although anyone can establish a Health Savings Account. This would seem to be especially the case when the self-employed entrepreneur is also the sole breadwinner for his or her family. Therefore, entrepreneurs should be aware of all potential programs that may be of potential benefit to him or her in the event of sickness, disability, or death.

A Health Savings Account operates somewhat like an Individual Retirement Account (IRA). Money that a business owner deposits in an HSA is deductible in the current year. The business owner can draw out money to pay medical expenses tax-free or leave it invested for years until needed to cover medical expenses. Alternatively, the owner can draw it all out and pay taxes on it like he would on a regular tax-deferred IRA. The entrepreneur cuts his/her medical insurance costs because the deductible must be at least $1,100 for an individual plan and $2,200 for a family plan. Medical expenses also drop because there is no copay.[16]

Contributions made by both individuals and family members are deductible for the account beneficiary—even if he or she does not itemize. Employer contributions are made on a pretax basis and are not taxable to the employee. This can result in significant savings. The average cost to insure a family cost $10,888 and $4,024 for an individual in 2005.[17] Therefore, self-employed, sole breadwinners (and others) should consider these plans.

Employers can offer HSAs through a cafeteria plan. Employer contributions to cafeteria plans must be made available on a nondiscriminatory basis (i.e., on behalf of all "participating employees"). Additionally, newer plans such as health reimbursement arrangements (HRA) and IRC section 105 (b) medical reimbursement plans (MERP) offer employers the ability to reimburse employees for their cost of medical expenses, including many expenses not otherwise deductible (e.g., nonprescription drugs). Current law allows self-employed persons to participate directly if they hire a spouse and are covered under their spouse's plan. The law also requires that greater than 2 percent shareholder-employees of S corporations include the cost of the benefit in their income.

There is further discussion of cafeteria plans after the discussion of Section 105(b) Medical Reimbursement Plans.

Section 105 (b) Medical Reimbursement Plans

The most common type of medical reimbursement plan under Section 105 is the self-funded plan. In this case, the company does not pay for traditional health insurance, but funds coverage itself. So, if an employee has a medical expense, it is reimbursed directly by the company. Some companies adopt self-funded plans alongside traditional plans to cover things not covered by the traditional plan. Section 105 plans can be tucked neatly into section 125 plans as Medical Flexible Spending Accounts.

Both companies and employees can enjoy several advantages from these section 105 plans. They include the following:

- The company can take the reimbursements as tax deductions.
- The company can custom design the planning, choosing parameters for reimbursement, eligibility requirements, etc.
- Employees do not have to declare reimbursement payments as income unless they have claimed the original expense as a deduction.

Section 105 plans also work well for sole proprietors who can employ a spouse who is active in the business. The law considers an employed spouse as any other employee with the employer/business owner offering medical benefits as part of the employee's compensation package. Consequently, the law allows the owner to be covered under a spousal family plan.

A partner in a partnership will operate similarly to a sole proprietorship so long as the spouse is a bona fide employee of the partnership. However, a partnership between a husband and a wife will not qualify for the plan as partners are considered self-employed for purposes of Section 105(b) plans.

S corporations can now qualify for Section 105 plans. However, shareholders owning more than 2 percent of the S corporation's stock must report the cost of the benefit as wages. But the IRS allows these employees to take an "above-the-line" deduction as an adjustment to gross income on Form 1040. Therefore, the new law treats payments by an employer as if the employer had established the individual employee's plan.[18]

With C corporations, it is not necessary for spousal employment to occur, unlike sole proprietorships or partnerships. The C corporation may provide and deduct benefits for the owner-employee.[19]

Section 125 Plans

Section 125 plans offer small employers who may not be able to afford such plans an excellent opportunity to allow employees to fund their own plans with *before-tax dollars*. Moreover, employee pretax contributions are exempt from federal tax withholding, Social Security, and federal unemployment taxes.

A business owner may establish a Section 125 plan under one of three possible programs. The first two types are called *premium only plans* and *flexible spending account plans*. Under such programs, the employee pays for insurance premiums with *before tax dollars*. The employee benefits because *the employee's taxable income is decreased*, which means that *the 7.65 percent FICA taxes are decreased*. The employer benefits because *the employer pays less FICA taxes* (the 7.65% matching FICA tax which the employer must pay) because of the decrease in taxable income reported by the employee. The items that employers may include in a Section 125 plan encompass payment of certain child and dependent care expenses, and premiums for health, dental, vision, disability, and life insurance.

A third type of plan is referred to as a *flexible benefits plan*—aka a cafeteria plan. We shall now separately discuss each of the three types of Section 125 plans.

A premium only plan may be suitable for an employer who wants to offer employees health, disability, and life insurance coverage, but cannot afford to pay all or part of the premiums for the employee. Under such a program, the premiums are less expensive to the employee than they would be if the employee were to purchase the insurance with after-tax dollars.

A flexible spending account plan allows employees to determine how much they will spend for medical expenses and dependent care not paid for by insurance. Employees determine how much they will spend for these expenses during the year. The employer deducts an amount from each paycheck based on this amount. As expenses are incurred during the year, the employee submits proof of the expenses and a claim form and is reimbursed for the expenses. Any money left over at the end of plan year is forfeited.

The flexible benefits plan, known as the cafeteria plan, is normally funded by the employer. Cafeteria plans give employees the option of picking from various benefits within the plan. The employee may elect to take some benefits for an additional premium or opt out of other benefits in the basic package and receive a credit. Thus, for example, an employee may be covered under his/her spouse's medical coverage. If that employee participates in a flexible benefits plan, the employee could opt out of the medical coverage and either receive additional cash at each paycheck or use the credit to pay for additional life insurance or disability coverage. The benefits that the employee receives are with before tax dollars.

Section 529 College Education Plans

This is a real sleeper! Section 529 College Education plans are set up by individuals as opposed to businesses. However, these plans may be of special interest to individuals who are also entrepreneurs. The annual contribution limits are set by the plans of the various states. And limits for most state plans are over $200,000. However, the government will require that any individual who makes a contribution over the annual gift tax exclusion of $12,000 (i.e., the current amount of money the owner may give a person as a gift without paying a gift tax on it) file an annual gift tax return.

Section 529 Plans are unique because, although an individual is gifting a fortune to his child, relative, or friend, he or she *still retains control of this asset*. At any time the individual chooses, he may pull it back into his own estate and keep the money. Or, if the beneficiary doesn't use up all the money, he or she may either transfer it to another student—or take it back.

The money may be spent on tuition, fees, books, supplies, room, and board—as long as the school is on the approved list. If the person who sets up the account is related to the beneficiary, he or she can set himself/herself up as the new beneficiary, regardless of age. The person can then spend that money on education in any form—like educational cruises, travel, and so forth. It will also cover education-related expenses of such jaunts, such as books and supplies, as long as the school is accredited. The money withdrawn for such purposes is not taxable, but the business owner cannot take his contribution as a tax deduction.[20]

Employer-Provided Child-Care Facilities Credit

This is another sleeper and an excellent tax break for business owners with children. The IRS allows a tax credit, up to 25 percent, of the cost of providing a qualified child-care facility for the business owner's children and those of the company's employees with a maximum of $150,000 per year. Unused credits can carry over to the next year for up to 20 years. Business owners can claim the credit even if they are paying an existing child-care facility, as long as it is licensed and meets all of the IRS requirements. Many states also offer similar credits, so it is wise to check and see what is available.[21]

Education

The owner's business may deduct the cost of all courses the owner or his or her staff take to increase the owner's professional or trade expertise related to the owner's business or industry. Management and business courses and seminars are deductible. A "C" corporation may reimburse the cost of the owner's education expenses for a degree along with those taken by other employees. However, the IRS does not allow the deduction to be taken by "S" corporations or other entities for the owner's reimbursement. Nevertheless, the owner may, of course, deduct the cost of specific seminars or workshops for his/her industry—just not the cost of courses leading to the degree. The owner's company, if eligible (i.e., a C corporation), may offer an education assistance plan, reimbursing employees for up to $5,250 of annual education expenses. As of January 1, 2002, graduate-level courses also qualify. However, there is no deduction if the degree is a requirement for the job, or if it is part of starting a new career altogether.[22]

Home Offices

This deduction can save you money and reduce your overall expenses and taxes. However, it's a red flag just asking for an IRS audit. We will take a look at various aspects of this deduction under the subtopic called Rent and Utilities.

Things You May Not Know but Ought To

There is a mixed bag of tax quirks for businesses that you may not know. Getting familiar with them can save you headaches down the line. Here are the most important ones.

1. As we discussed earlier, the owners of businesses can only participate in most "employee" fringe benefits if the business is organized as a C corporation. Even S corporation shareholders who own more than 2 percent of the company are excluded from most benefits. And the owners of self-employed business organizations (i.e., a sole proprietor, partners in a general partnership, or an owner of an LLC taxed as a general partnership or a sole proprietorship) cannot

take a *business deduction for their own* health insurance expenses and other "employee" fringe benefits (e.g., vacation, sick time, medical plans, various reimbursement plans for things like child care).[23]

2. Working shareholders of S corporations and officers of S corporations *must* receive wages with appropriate withholdings for Social Security and Medicare taxes. The Internal Revenue Service (IRS) has begun to crack down on owners of S corporations who do not pay themselves a reasonable wage. This means that the S corporation owners/employees must pay—through withholdings—the 7.65% combined Social Security and Medicare tax (i.e., 6.20% Social Security tax up to certain income limits and the 1.45% Medicare tax on the owner/employee's income to the maximum extent of his/her income). Additionally, the S corporation must also pay/match the 7.65% withheld from the S corporation owner/officer's wages as the S corporation must match each working employee's contribution.[24]

3. In contrast, self-employed owners, as that term is defined by the IRS (sole proprietors, partners, and those "otherwise in business for themselves"), are subject to a self-employment tax of 15.3% of their business profits from Schedule C or Schedule 1065-K-1.[25]

4. The self-employment tax is equal to the employer's and employee's portion of the Social Security and Medicare taxes that employers and employees pay on the employee's compensation when received as an employee. That amount is a total of 7.65% of the gross wages paid to the employee. The breakdown for the 7.65% is as follows— 6.20% for Social Security tax up to certain income limits and 1.45% Medicare tax on the owner/employee's income to the maxim extent of his/her income. The self-employed business owner must contribute 7.65% for each person he employs as an "employee" in his business from the income he receives from the business. The self-employment tax is a Social Security and Medicare tax primarily for individuals who work for themselves as sole proprietors or partners in a partnership. Business owners subject to the tax can deduct half (50%) in figuring their adjusted gross income. However, this deduction only affects their income taxes. It does not affect either their net earnings from self-employment nor the self-employment tax due.[26]

5. Only sole proprietorships and partnerships that have employees must report and pay the federal unemployment tax (FUTA). The FUTA tax is not withheld from the employee's pay. Additionally, sole proprietorships and partnerships don't pay the FUTA tax on the owner's compensation. If employers take part in state unemployment programs, they receive a tax credit that reduces the FUTA rate.

6. Finally, all tax experts emphatically state that business owners should not hide offshore income. To the IRS, "offshore" means "outside" the United States. That includes Canada, Mexico, and all those tempting tax-free havens such as the Caymans and the Bahamas. As a U.S. citizen or resident, your business is taxed on its worldwide income, not just domestic revenues. With the Internet, it's easy to open a bank account in another country without ever setting foot there. Business owners can deposit their offshore sales into that account and keep it as a secret nest egg until retirement. Alternatively, the business owner can have the bank issue him or her a debit card and the owner can spend the money here at home. Most people think that the IRS will never see a record of this money, but those people are incorrect in their assumption.

The world is becoming smaller. The IRS already has arrangements with Visa and MasterCard (your debit and credit cards) to audit their offshore accounts. Small countries often rely on U.S. financial assistance or tourism. When the U.S. government threatens to withhold those benefits, countries often elect to enter into treaties that effectively disclose information that they told the owner would remain secret. There are heavy fines, penalties, and even jail time if the business owner gets caught. The IRS is making a powerful effort to make the public aware of this—and paying rewards for information. There are legitimate ways to legally set up businesses and partnerships with people or businesses in other countries. If the owner's business is heading that way, he or she should definitely pursue that course of action. It's done all the time. However, the business owner should be sure to report all of his earnings in the business. When a business owner reaches this point in his business development, he should add an expert in international taxation to the business' advisory team. Otherwise, the business owner is likely to step on the toes of other countries' systems too.

Deductions That Only Business Owners Can Take

You'd be surprised at the number of "everyday" things that are universally deductible for business owners. They include the following:

Mixed Use Items

Things that many people use personally every day, such as computers, cell phones, cars, and so on, can be taken as business expense deductions by the business owner. The IRS refers to these items as "listed property." Most of the second page of Form 4562 deals with these items. Business owners can only claim depreciation deductions on the business use percentage of the value of the property. The main thing business owners need to know is that when the business use of the asset falls to 50 percent or less, the excess depreciation must be recaptured. The IRS defines excess depreciation as the amount of depreciation (including section 179 deductions) actually claimed in prior years, minus the amount of depreciation that would have been allowed using straight-line depreciation under the alternative depreciation system. Furthermore, the owner will not be able to use the General Depreciation System but must, thereafter, utilize the Alternative Depreciation System which results in a slower period of depreciation recovery.

Computers, video equipment, cameras, monitors, and beepers are no longer just luxury items. Cars, aside from real estate or a complete manufacturing plant, are likely to be the biggest one-shot expense to a small business. In the American economy, an owner's car is the key to his image. There are several effective ways to squeeze deductions out of it—whether you lease or buy.

First, there are two ways to report auto expenses—the mileage method and actual expenses. The actual expenses method, however, for leased vehicles and for purchased vehicles are not identical. Also, if business owners take advantage of any of the special depreciation methods, including the bonus depreciation or section 179 depreciation, they may not use the mileage method to deduct car expenses for the life of the vehicle.

Office Expenses

This category is often used as a catch-all for all general business expenses. However, the business owner should not take office expense deductions on items which should be depreciated. Similarly, the business owner should not deduct automobile expenses as office expenses.

Cost of Goods Sold

This deduction is generally for goods kept in stock for sale to customers. The cost of goods sold also includes labor costs, overhead, materials and supplies, depreciation, and administration expenses incurred in buying inventory or manufacturing inventory. When business owners are selling a product, wholesale or retail, the cost of the merchandise is captured and recorded as the cost of goods sold.

If the business involves putting on seminars, the cost of goods sold would include the fees to instructors or speakers, the cost of the facility, the cost of the refreshments the business provides, and the cost of handouts or books. However, some accountants feel that the proper way to account for these items would be to capture them as operating expenses. Additionally, to ease the recordkeeping burden for qualifying small taxpayers—that is, those with annual sales of $1 million or less—the IRS allows these qualifying taxpayers to use the cash basis of accounting and account for inventory as "incidental materials and supplies."[27]

Advertising, Marketing, and Publicity

These expenses are generally fairly straightforward and obvious. Rarely does the IRS take issue with them.

Commissions and Fees Paid

Business owners should issue 1099s to anyone they pay $600 or more a year. Many business owners fail to do this, however. The government exempts most payments to C corporations from this requirement. Some professional business codes prohibit commission payments to anyone not licensed in the business owner's field, so it is probably best to report this type of income as something other than commissions. On the other hand, even during an audit, one tax expert noted that "I haven't seen examiners question the legality of commission[s] paid by realtors to unlicensed individuals."[28]

Interest Expense

The law allows business owners to deduct the interest on a business loan. However, a business owner cannot deduct the interest on a personal loan. The owner should not list such loans on the books of the business.

Business owners who use a personal loan for the business may deduct the interest. However, the owner should keep proof of how the money was spent in a file that accompanies each year's tax return.

Business owners may also deduct credit card interest if they use all the money and products for the business. Again, the business owner should keep proof of how the money was spent in a file with each year's tax return.

The business owner may also deduct the interest arising from a vehicle loan, if the owner uses the vehicle for business purposes. However, the owner cannot deduct the portion of the loan interest attributable to personal use of the vehicle.

Rent and Utilities and Business Use of Part of a Home

The IRS expects that businesses will rent office space, or manufacturing space, or storage space. Such a deduction will not raise any red flags to the IRS. However, if the business owner is trying to deduct home office expenses, it becomes a much more complicated matter.

The IRS will only allow a business owner to deduct home office expenses to the extent that the business owner has a legitimate business with a profit motive and actually uses his or her house as the principal place of business. If the business owner does not own the dwelling, he or she must determine the business use percentage of the square footage of the dwelling. Thereafter the owner must multiply the business percentage times the total rent. The owner takes the deduction for this expense on line 20—other expenses—of form 8829. The IRS may limit the office-in-home deduction if the business shows a loss.

The business owner will need to take depreciation deductions if he or she owns the home. The owner is eligible to take business depreciation of the house over a period of 39 years. Also, the taxpayer must subtract from the total cost of the land the cost of that portion of the land on which the depreciable property is situated to determine the depreciable tax base.

The business owner can figure the deduction on his own even without a depreciation table. Here's an example: there are 468 months in 39 years (12 × 39). Therefore, the business owner must divide the depreciable cost by 468. The resulting figure gives the owner the depreciation per month. The owner, thereafter, must multiply the monthly amount by the number of months he or she used the space (square footage) for business in the relevant tax year. Business owners who use a designated portion of their homes as offices may also deduct utilities, Internet access, cable TV (business uses only), repairs and maintenance, property tax and interest, insurance, and household supplies stemming from the portion of the dwelling used for business purposes.

Insurance

Business owners may deduct business insurance premiums. This will typically include such items as property, casualty, malpractice, worker's compensation, inventory, liability, and overhead insurance. Additionally, business owners are able to deduct health insurance premiums within the parameters as set forth earlier in this book.[29]

Taxes and Licenses

The business owner may deduct taxes and licenses attributable to the operation of the business. This is fairly self-explanatory. However, owners cannot deduct estimated *personal* tax payments as a business expense.

Education

We have discussed this earlier under the subtopic Education. However, because business owners are entitled to deduct travel costs, it makes sense to take business-related courses in places the owners would really like to visit.

Travel, Transportation, and Lodging

Business owners may deduct general business-related travel, including travel to trade shows, meetings, workshops and seminars, or other educational events. However, owners cannot deduct the costs for family members who come along unless they are also employees of the business and have a bona fide business purpose for the travel.

Business owners have a choice in the way to deduct such expenses. They can keep receipts and records to deduct actual costs. The IRS also allows business owners to use per diem rates in lieu of actual expenses for meals, incidentals, and mileage. Business owners who are frugal may get a bigger deduction by utilizing the IRS's per diem rates.

Meals and Entertainment

With few exceptions, business owners can only deduct 50 percent of their expenses for meals and entertainment. Therefore, it is very important that business owners post their travel expenses properly. However, businesses owners who are also in the food service industry may take the full deduction.

Uniforms

There are other advantages to having uniforms in addition to the tax deduction. Uniforms create brand awareness and make your company name visible wherever the business owner and employees go. Uniforms may also give the owner and his or her staff a sense of pride. Business owners can turn anything into a uniform. The owner can accomplish this by sewing the company's logo onto his jackets, shirts, or other garments. By doing this, the owner can establish a particular look to enhance his or her image.

With the winds of change blowing hard on Capitol Hill since the election of Barack Obama, there may well be significant changes in business tax law. That is why it is so important to keep up with current law or have people around you who are "in the know." The recommended resource for this chapter is updated yearly, so you can be sure that you have the latest, accurate information as you plan and execute your tax strategies.

Recommended Resource

- *Small Business Taxes*, Barbara Weltman

Notes

1. Barbara Weltman. *Small Business Taxes* (Hoboken, NJ: Wiley & Sons, Inc., 2009), 377–78.

2. Robert W. Hamilton. *The Law of Corporations in a Nutshell* (New York: West Group, 2000), 28–39.

3. Ibid., 28–30.

4. Barbara Weltman. *Small Business Taxes* (Hoboken, NJ: Wiley & Sons, Inc., 2007), 24, 401.

5. Michael B. Kennedy, Mark T. Nash, Brittany B. Saks. *Pricewaterhouse-Coopers 2008 Guide to Tax and Financial Planning* (Hoboken, NJ: Wiley & Sons, Inc., 2007), 222.

6. Barbara Weltman. *Small Business Taxes* (Hoboken, NJ: Wiley & Sons, Inc., 2009), 377–78, and Eva Rosenberg, *Small Business Taxes Made Easy* (New York: McGraw-Hill, 2005), 182.

7. See IRS Publication 533, *Self Employment Tax* (2001), 9; see also Eva Rosenberg, 35, 156.

8. IRS Revenue Ruling 59–221.

9. IRS Publication 533, *Self Employment Tax*, 2, 4–5.

10. Ibid., 2.

11. Barbara Weltman. *Small Business Taxes* (Hoboken, NJ: Wiley & Sons, Inc., 2009), 254–55.

12. See IRS Publication 17.

13. www.irs.gov/businneses/small/article/0,,=102767,00.html (Accessed March 2009).

14. Eva Rosenberg, *Small Business Taxes Made Easy* (New York: McGraw-Hill, 2005), 158–59.

15. See IRS 1040 Forms and Instructions for taxable year. (This is the booklet the IRS send to help taxpayers prepare their taxes.)

16. Eva Rosenberg. *Small Business Taxes Made Easy* (New York: McGraw-Hill, 2005), 182.

17. David W. Meier. *Make Your Life Tax Deductible* (New York: McGraw-Hill 2006), 91–92, and Albert B. Crenshaw, "Workers' Family Coverage Reaches $10,880 Average," *Washington Post* (September 15, 2005), sec. D2.

18. Barbara Weltman. *Small Business Taxes* (Hoboken, NJ: Wiley & Sons, Inc., 2009), 377–78.

19. Ibid., 377–78.

20. Eva Rosenberg. *Small Business Taxes Made Easy* (New York: McGraw-Hill, 2005), 187–89.

21. Ibid., 184.

22. Ibid., 98.

23. Ibid., 181.

24. IRS Publication 533, Self Employment Tax, 9.

25. Ibid., 4–5.

26. Ibid., 2.

27. IRS Revenue Procedure 2001–10.

28. Eva Rosenberg. *Small Business Taxes Made Easy* (New York: McGraw-Hill, 2005), 96.

29. Ibid., 97.

CHAPTER 16

ESTATE PLANNING: SECURING YOUR FUTURE AND YOUR LEGACY

Part of the entrepreneurial mindset is looking to the future, not only the future of the business, but future security for you, your family, and your legacy within the larger community. In Chapter 11, you learned strategies for assuring the continuation of your business or for its transition into new hands. This chapter will delve more into things to consider in terms of extending your legacy and seeing to your health and financial needs and those of your family.

Accordingly, it is clear that a proper attention to estate planning matters is necessary for the would-be entrepreneur to successfully grow the business, to transfer ownership in the venture to future generations, and to strengthen the greater community as a result of the firm's operations.

In January, 2009, *Black Enterprise* magazine unveiled a new set of ten principles which it calls *the Wealth for Life Principles* to replace its decade old Declaration of Financial Independence. The magazine stated that it had created the new set of standards because "the dynamic of wealth building (and perhaps more importantly in these times, wealth preservation) have changed significantly."[1] The 10 Wealth for Life Principles as set forth by the magazine are as follows:

1. I will live within my means.
2. I will maximize my income potential through education and training.
3. I will effectively manage my budget, credit, debt, and tax obligations.
4. I will save at least 10% of my income.

5. I will use homeownership as a foundation for building wealth.
6. I will devise an investment plan for my retirement needs and children's education.
7. I will ensure that my entire family adheres to sensible money management principles.
8. I will support the creation and growth of minority-owned businesses.
9. I will guarantee my wealth is passed on to future generations through proper insurance and estate planning.
10. I will strengthen my community through philanthropy.[2]

Black Enterprise magazine has a monthly feature entitled the Black Wealth Initiative. The Black Wealth Initiative is essentially an estate planning tool designed to financially empower individuals and the entire black community. The monthly feature focuses on how well a featured individual or couple are adhering to the 10 Wealth for Life Principles established by the magazine in reaching their financial objectives.

Sharing Your Legacy: Ways to Give to the Community

Entrepreneurs can also give a portion of their assets derived from their firms to advance their favorite causes in a tax beneficial way. Accordingly, this subsection focuses on methods available to business owners to transfer their assets to worthy causes in a tax beneficial manner during their lifetime or upon death. Following are some suggestions based on *Black Enterprise* magazine's *Seven Ways to Give*.[3]

1. **Make Annual Gifts to an Established Charity.** Donors may contribute to a church, an educational institution, a fraternity or sorority, or other nonprofit organization. Donors should make sure that the organization has 501 (c) (3) legal status. If so, the donor can claim the appropriate tax deduction up to 50% of adjusted gross income for the year for cash and 30% for stock or property.

2. **Create a Trust.** A prospective donor may establish a *charitable remainder trust*. These trusts permit the creator/donor to take a charitable deduction for a gift in the year in which the trust is formed. The trust pays the donor income from the trust for life. Thereafter, the trust assets pass to a philanthropic fund or charity as the donor has designated in the trust instrument.

   A donor may, alternatively, establish a *charitable lead trust* to pay a regular, fixed amount to a fund or charities of the donor's choosing for a specific number of years. Thereafter, the remainder of the trust passes to the donor's designated heirs or other beneficiaries.

3. **Establish a Supporting Organization.** A prospective donor may wish to establish an organization that supports and funds a public charity with a mission compatible to the donor's values. The donor may have family members sit on the governing board and participate in the grant-making decisions. However, to qualify as a 501(c)(3) organization, the IRS requires that the organization must be (i) operated, supervised, or controlled by a publicly supported organization; (ii) supervised or controlled in connection with a publicly supported organization; or (iii) operated in connection with a publicly supported organization.[*]

4. **Create a Family or Private Foundation.** A business owner may also wish to establish a family or private foundation. The business owner and his or her family can retain control and flexibility over the foundation's distribution of its assets to specific organizations under this format. The business owner can establish the foundation as either a nonprofit corporation or as a charitable trust. The business owner is able to deduct *up to 30% of his or her annual adjusted gross income for cash donations* and *20% for gifts of stock or property.* Tax law, however, requires that private foundations pay out in annual grant funds an amount totaling 5% of their assets and pay a 1% to 2% excise tax on the foundation's net investment income.

5. **Establish a Giving Circle.** The business owner can find like-minded people with whom he or she can pool funds and then distribute the income and/or principal in the form of grants. Members can chip in anywhere from $100.00 to $2,500.00 or more. The funds may be held a public foundation or some other nonprofit or commercial entity that will invest the funds to earn income. This setup also saves individual donors the cost of setting up their own private foundations.

6. **Develop a Corporate Giving Program**. Many companies have an annual giving program to make grants (funded as part of their annual operating budget) and to match employees' cash gifts and volunteer time to nonprofits. Companies often make in-kind gifts of products to charities. The tax deduction for in-kind gifts is 10% of pretax profits. If the business is family-owned, the owners can establish a giving program or corporate foundation. Such giving programs typically start with a single donation that can become an endowment.

   The owners are usually the governing board, and the foundation is subject to the excise tax and minimum payout requirement.

7. **Develop a Donor-advised Fund Through a Public Charity.** A business owner may establish a donor-advised fund through a public foundation. Such funds are considered an alternative to

establishing a private foundation as there are no fees or complex paperwork. The business owner can designate one or more charities to benefit from the donation. The board of trustees of the public foundation managing the tax-exempt donor fund makes the decisions with regard to grant distributions to recipients.

General Thoughts on Securing Your Future

There are several important matters you should tend to early in the game. The earlier you consider and follow through with these matters, the better off you will be.

1. Make a will. Do not leave the disposition of your estate to the probate courts!

2. Consider whether to transfer some, if not all, of your assets through a living trust or an irrevocable trust to avoid the expense of a probate court supervising the transfer of the assets or for tax reasons.

3. Make a living will or advance directive if you do not want to be kept alive through heroic means when your conscious life has irrevocably terminated (e.g., if you are deemed by physicians to be in a persistent vegetative state). Be sure to update this document over the years so that it is timely. What might be appropriate when you are strong and fit in your 20s or 30s may not be appropriate if you are diagnosed with a terminal illness or are at the end of your natural life. An up-to-date document helps eliminate the possibility that your estate will be drained by expensive, nonbeneficial treatment or medical procedures. It also removes an enormous emotional burden from your family's shoulders. Be sure the document is readily accessible when it is needed.

4. Determine whether you should have a durable healthcare proxy and/or a durable power of attorney in the event that you become unable to take care of your affairs because of some health issue in the near future (e.g., approaching Alzheimer's disease, etc.). You may choose a durable or medical power of attorney as part of your living will/advance directive.

5. Consider whether to purchase a life insurance policy if you have dependents or expect to have dependents who rely on your income.

6. Adopt a written business continuation plan (buy-sell agreement) to determine the disposition of your equity stake in the business upon your death or retirement from the business.

7. Systematically invest some portion of your income every month.

Social Security and Medicare

A basic understanding of the workings of Social Security and Medicare is an integral part of your planning for the future. Both programs may undergo significant changes in the future, so you would do well to keep abreast of those changes. You can keep up with the most current information at the Social Security Web site http://www.ssa.gov and the Medicare Web site at http://www.medicare.gov. The bulk of the information in this section has been gleaned from those two sites unless otherwise noted.

Social Security

The underlying premise of Social Security, according to two notable experts in the field, has always been to provide just enough income to keep starvation at bay but not enough to guarantee a decent standard of living.[5] The self-employed individual who is also the sole breadwinner for a family should be aware of all programs that may be of potential benefit to him or her in the event of disability or death. Therefore, a rudimentary knowledge of Social Security benefits should be part of the entrepreneur's estate planning.

Social Security provides benefits to the following categories of persons who meet the eligibility requirements of the Act:

1. retired workers
2. certain dependents of retired workers
3. disability benefits for eligible workers under 65
4. surviving widows/widowers of eligible workers
5. surviving children of deceased workers
6. disabled surviving children of deceased workers
7. a $255.00 death benefit to the surviving spouse or family of deceased workers
8. a surviving ex-spouse (if married for 10 years and at least 60 years of age regardless of whether the spouse dies before age 62)
9. surviving parents of a deceased worker who are least 62, if the worker paid 50% or more of the parents support and expenses. The surviving parents can receive up to 75% of what the deceased worker would have been receiving.

To be eligible for Social Security, the worker must receive 40 credits over a 10-year period. This is the breakdown. In 2002, $870.00 of earnings by the worker/quarter = 1 credit. Thus, 4 quarters/year × 10 years = 40 quarters. Beginning in 1978, workers receive a credit for each fixed amount of earnings from covered employment regardless of the quarter in which the worker earned it up to four credits per year. In 2008, the amount needed to earn a credit increased to $1,050.[6] The amount to earn one credit increases yearly.

As of 2004, the average Social Security check for persons retiring at age 65 was $922.00/month. Persons retiring at age 62, on average, received a check of $722.00/month. Persons who retired at age 70, on average, received a check of $ 1,223 per month. As of 2004, the maxim amount per month was $1,825.00 per month. In 2008, the average retirement benefit for an individual who reached full retirement in 2008 was about $1,100 per month. And the maximum benefit in 2008 for someone first claiming benefits in 2008 was about $2,200 per month.[7]

Supplemental Security Income Benefits (SSI) guarantees a minimum level of income to financially hard-pressed older, blind, and disabled people regardless of work credits. Accordingly, SSI is a welfare benefit unconnected to eligibility for Social Security.

The following are illustrations of how Social Security operates in selected hypothetical situations. Assuming that a worker/retiree receives $1,000 in Social Security benefits per month, a nonworking spouse at age 65 will receive as her payment an amount equal to 50 percent of what the working spouse receives ($500.00/month). However, if the nonworking spouse begins to receive benefits at 62, the spouse will only receive as payment an amount equal to 37.3 percent of what the working spouse receives. But if the worker/retiree dies and the nonworking spouse waits until age 65 or older to begin receiving benefits, the nonworking spouse will get 100 percent of what the deceased worker/retiree would have received. Additionally, nonworking spouses are entitled to Medicare at age 65. One should also note that a surviving spouse who is entitled to benefits based on his/her own work record may elect survivors benefits based on the deceased spouse's work record if it produces a higher benefit.

A widow/widower of a worker can obtain survivor's benefits at age 60. A disabled widow/widower can receive benefits at age 50, and a widow/widower of a deceased worker can receive benefits at any age if he/she has children of the deceased under age 16. Children receive 50 percent but the maximum is 180 percent per family.

The government may tax some of a recipient's Social Security benefits depending on his or her total income. In determining total income, the IRS looks at what it refers to as the recipient's *combined income*. The *combined income* consists of three items: adjusted gross income, any nontaxable interest income, plus one-half of the recipient's social security benefits. As of 2002, if the recipient's combined income as an individual is between $25,000 and $34,000 (or for a couple filing jointly, between $32,000 and $44,000), the recipient may have to pay income taxes on 50 percent of his Social Security benefits. If the recipient's combined income is more than $34,000 ($44,000 for a couple filing jointly), the recipient may owe income taxes on up to 85 percent of his benefits. Publication 554, the "Older Americans' Tax Guide" explains this and numerous other tax rules applicable to older people. These standards have remained the same as of 2008.[8]

Medicare

Medicare consists of three parts: Part A and Part B and a new Part D. Medicare should not be confused with Medicaid, which is a welfare program in which the federal government matches state dollars to provide medical care for indigent persons. Indigent persons, for Medicaid purposes, are individuals with no more than $2,000.00 in assets as of 2002. The self-employed individual who is also the sole breadwinner for a family should, similarly, be aware of this program as part of the estate-planning process.

Like Social Security, eligibility for Medicare requires 40 credits of work. Medicare also covers nonworking spouses and dependent children under 16 years of age.

Part A of Medicare covers hospital visits. Days 1–60 (per year) are free after a $876.00 deductible. Days 61–90 are $ 219.00 per day and days 91–150 are $438.00/day. These were the applicable rates in 2004. The government increases the deductible every January 1. As of 2008, the days 1–60 deductible was $1,024, the days 61–90 deductible was $256.00 per day, and the days 91–150 deductible was $512 per day.

Part A also covers skilled nursing facilities. These are *not* nursing homes. Rather, they are facilities in which the patient can receive rehabilitative services. One can only enter a skilled nursing facility upon the recommendation of a doctor and with the approval of Medicare authorities. The first 20 days are free. Days 21–100 are at a cost of $109.50 per day. These figures reflect the costs as of 2004. In 2008, days 21–100 are at a cost of $128.00 per day. The amount goes up every year.

Medicare also covers Hospice Care. Hospice Care is not medical care. Rather, it is philosophy. One is eligible for Hospice Care if a doctor provides a Certificate of Terminal Illness that states that the patient is expected to die within 6 months. The purpose of Hospice Care is to (1) relieve pain, (2) provide comfort, and (3) provide psychological support for persons expected to die within a 6-month period.

Medicare also provides Respite Care. The purpose is to give caregivers a break for 7 days per year by providing for someone to relieve the care-taker of his/her care-taking responsibilities during the 7-day respite period.

Part B covers visits to the doctor. As of 2004, this benefit cost $ 66.60/month. Under current law, persons 65 and older are automatically enrolled in both parts A and B. Part B covers second opinions, laboratory tests, oral surgery based on medical necessity, and preventive care (glaucoma screening, prostate screening, etc.). As of 2008, the basic monthly premium was $96.40. However, the government charges an additional payment called a surcharge to people with higher incomes.

Medicare Part D provides a prescription drug program. Generally, Medicare Part D covers everyone who is age 65 or older, people under age 65 with certain disabilities, and people of all ages who have end-stage renal failure. Under the Medicare Prescription Drug Plan, enrollees must pay a separate monthly premium. There is a copayment or coinsurance and an annual deductible of $275 for prescription drugs.

A pharmacy must belong to the Medicare prescription drug network in order to fill the prescription. Otherwise, Medicare will not cover the cost. Participants in a Standard Medicare Prescription Drug Plan paid an average of about $32.00 per month for premiums in 2006.

Some participants have no other medical insurance and are covered solely by Medicare Plans A, B, and D. Other participants have Medigap policies that provide prescription and other benefits not covered by Medicare. Medigap policies—which the government authorized private companies to issue to cover "gaps" in Medicare coverage—do not provide the same benefits as Medicare. Persons with Medigap policies that include prescription drug coverage can keep their coverage through the plan if it provides better coverage. However, if the Medigap prescription plan does not provide better coverage, the individual may purchase a Medicare Prescription Drug Plan and a Medigap policy without a prescription plan.

Detailed information on the ins and out of each Medicare program can be found at the Medicare Web site http://www.medicare.com.

There is a lot to consider as you plan for the future of your business, your family, and your legacy. If you follow the leads given here, do your homework, and be sensitive to the winds of change in the marketplace and in Washington, you will be on the path to success and peace of mind.

Notes

1. Sheiresa Mcrae, "Wealth for Life: Following Our 10 New Principles Will Keep You on the Right Track for a Great Financial Future," *Black Enterprise* (January 2009): 60.

2. Ibid., used with permission.

3. Adapted from 7 Ways to Give Chart, Carolyn M. Brown, "America's Leading Black Philanthropists," *Black Enterprise* (August 2005): 118. Used with permission.

4. 501(c) (3) Organizations, http://www.irs.gov/charities/charitable/article/0,,id=96099,00.html, specific information via links within the opening text. Updated January 2009 (Accessed June 2009).

5. Joseph Matthews and Dorothy M. Berman. *Social Security, Medicare & Government Pensions* (Berkeley, CA: Nolo Press, 2002), 13.

6. Joseph Matthews and Dorothy M. Berman. *Social Security, Medicare & Government Pensions*, (Berkley, CA: Nolo Press, 2008), 24.

7. http://www.ssa.gov/retire (Accessed May 2009).

8. Joseph Matthews and Dorothy M. Berman. *Social Security, Medicare & Government Pensions* (Berkeley, CA: Nolo Press, 2008), 28.

CONCLUSION

Time for Action

The primary goal in writing this book has been to present both historical and practical information to inspire and assist all entrepreneurs and prospective entrepreneurs in launching, growing, and, ultimately, transferring ownership in a business venture to future generations.

Part II of this book focuses on the practical side. It furnishes important information that readers can use to improve their chances of achieving entrepreneurial success. But you must do more than merely read this book. Now is the time for you to begin your quest for business success. Drive and determination, not perfect abilities, will largely determine your success. Do not allow fear of failure or the belief that you need additional credentials to hinder pursuit of your entrepreneurial dreams.

It is not enough to have an excellent business plan; you must take concrete steps toward achieving your objective. This may initially mean taking baby steps. But even baby steps represent a movement forward. Avoid the stranglehold of analysis paralysis and begin seeking customers and clients today.

There will never be a perfect time to begin any new venture. The need for perfection often undermines the ability of individuals to either start or finish a project. Remember that even a lack of adequate resources is no excuse for doing nothing. An entrepreneurial mindset is a way of thinking that relies on a process of creativity, innovation, opportunity discovery, and risk evaluation to add value to situations, projects, activities, and organizations. Entrepreneurs, by definition, pursue opportunities even though they don't have all the funds they need and lack a full support network.

As we stated at the outset of Part II, you can dream all you want about the house you want to build but, at some point, you must get a design down on paper and start hammering nails. What better time to get started than now!

Appendix I

7(a) Loans—SBA Program Office

7(a) loans are the most basic and most used type loan of SBA's business loan programs. Its name comes from section 7(a) of the Small Business Act, which authorizes the Agency to provide business loans to American small businesses.

All 7(a) loans are provided by lenders who are called participants because they participate with SBA in the 7(a) program. Not all lenders choose to participate, but most American banks do. There are also some non-bank lenders who participate with SBA in the 7(a) program which expands the availability of lenders making loans under SBA guidelines.

7(a) loans are only available on a guaranty basis. This means they are provided by lenders who choose to structure their own loans by SBA's requirements and who apply and receive a guaranty from SBA on a portion of this loan. The SBA does not fully guaranty 7(a) loans. The lender and SBA share the risk that a borrower will not be able to repay the loan in full. The guaranty is a guaranty against payment default. It does not cover imprudent decisions by the lender or misrepresentation by the borrower.

Under the guaranty concept, commercial lenders make and administer the loans.

The business applies to a lender for their financing. The lender decides if they will make the loan internally or if the application has some weaknesses which, in their opinion, will require an SBA guaranty if the loan is to be made. The guaranty which SBA provides is only available to the lender. It assures the lender that in the event the borrower does not repay their obligation and a payment default occurs, the Government will reimburse the lender for its loss, up to the percentage of SBA's guaranty. Under this program, the borrower remains obligated for the full amount due.

All 7(a) loans which SBA guaranty must meet 7(a) criteria. The business gets a loan from its lender with a 7(a) structure and the lender gets an SBA guaranty on a portion or percentage of this loan. Hence the primary business loan assistance program available to small business from the SBA is called the 7(a) guaranty loan program.

A key concept of the 7(a) guaranty loan program is that the loan actually comes from a commercial lender, not the Government. If the lender is not willing to provide the loan, even if they may be able to get an SBA guaranty, the Agency can not force the lender to change their mind. Neither can SBA make the loan by itself because the Agency does not have any money to lend. Therefore it is paramount that all applicants positively approach the lender for a loan, and that they know the lenders criteria and requirements as well as those of the SBA. In order to obtain positive consideration for an SBA supported loan, the applicant must be both eligible and creditworthy.

What SBA Seeks In A Loan Application

In order to get a 7(a) loan, the applicant must first be eligible. Repayment ability from the cash flow of the business is a primary consideration in the SBA loan decision process but good character, management capability, collateral, and owner's equity contribution are also important considerations. All owners of 20 percent or more are required to personally guarantee SBA loans.

Eligibility Criteria

All applicants must be eligible to be considered for a 7(a) loan. The eligibility requirements are designed to be as broad as possible in order that this lending program can accommodate the most diverse variety of small business financing needs. All businesses that are considered for financing under SBA's 7(a) loan program must: meet SBA size standards, be for-profit, not already have the internal resources (business or personal) to provide the financing, and be able to demonstrate repayment. Certain variations of SBA's 7(a) loan program may also require additional eligibility criteria. Special purpose programs will identify those additional criteria.

Eligibility factors for all 7(a) loans include: size, type of business, use of proceeds, and the availability of funds from other sources.

Character Considerations

SBA must determine if the principals of each applicant firm have historically shown the willingness and ability to pay their debts and whether they abided by the laws of their community. The Agency must know if there are any factors which impact on these issues. Therefore, a "Statement of Personal History" is obtained from each principal.

Other Aspects Of The Basic 7(a) Loan Program

In addition to credit and eligibility criteria, an applicant should be aware of the general types of terms and conditions they can expect if SBA is involved in the financial assistance. The specific terms of SBA loans are negotiated between an applicant and the participating financial institution, subject to the requirements of SBA. In general, the following provisions apply to all SBA 7(a) loans. However, certain Loan Programs or Lender Programs vary from these standards. These variations are indicated for each program.

http://www.sba.gov/services/financialassistance/sbaloantopics/7a/.

Appendix II

Micro-Loans—SBA Program Office

The Microloan Program provides very small loans to start-up, newly established, or growing small business concerns. Under this program, SBA makes funds available to nonprofit community based lenders (intermediaries) which, in turn, make loans to eligible borrowers in amounts up to a maximum of $35,000. The average loan size is about $13,000. Applications are submitted to the local intermediary and all credit decisions are made on the local level.

Terms, Interest Rates, and Fees

The maximum term allowed for a microloan is six years. However, loan terms vary according to the size of the loan, the planned use of funds, the requirements of the intermediary lender, and the needs of the small business borrower. The maximum loan amount is $35,000, however, the average loan amount is around $13,000. Interest rates vary, depending upon the intermediary lender and costs to the intermediary from the U.S. Treasury. Generally these rates will be between 8 eight percent and thirteen percent.

Collateral

Each intermediary lender has its own lending and credit requirements. However, business owners contemplating application for a microloan should be aware that intermediaries will generally require some type of collateral, and the personal guarantee of the business owner.

Technical Assistance

Each intermediary is required to provide business based training and technical assistance to its microborrowers. Individuals and small businesses applying for microloan financing may be required to fulfill training and/or planning requirements before a loan application is considered.

How to Apply

Small businesses that are interested in applying for a microloan should contact a microlender in their area.

Microlenders (Intermediaries) are located in 46 of the 50 states, the District of Columbia and Puerto Rico. Alaska, Rhode Island, Utah and West Virginia are the only states without an Intermediary. Rhode Island is currently being serviced by South Eastern Economic Development out of Taunton, MA and a portion of West Virginia is being serviced by Washington County Council on Economic Development out of Washington, PA. For an intermediary lender in your area click on the link [at the end of this article].

SBA Microloan Intermediaries

Information For Non-Profit Entities Seeking To Become Intermediary Lenders Applying to become an Intermediary—Organizations interested in becoming Intermediaries should contact SBA for information on the application process, but generally applicants must meet three general criteria:

- An applicant must be organized as a non-profit organization, quasi-governmental economic development corporation, or an Agency established by a Native American Tribal Governement;
- An applicant must have made and serviced short-term fixed rate loans of not more than $35,000 to newly established or growing small businesses for at least one year; and
- An applicant must have at least one year of experience providing technical assistance to its borrowers.

Applications should contain supporting information describing:

- The types of businesses assisted in the past and those the applicant intends to assist with Microloans;

- The average size of the loans made in the past and the average size of intended Microloans;
- The extent to which the applicant will make Microloans to small businesses in rural areas;
- The geographic area in which the applicant intends to operate, including a description of the economic and demographic conditions existing in the intended area of operations;
- The availability and cost of obtaining credit for small businesses in the area;
- The applicant's experience and qualifications in providing marketing, management, and technical assistance to small businesses;
- Any plan to use other technical assistance resources (such as counselors from the Service Corps of Retired Executives) to help Microloan borrowers.

http://www.sba.gov/services/financialassistance/sbaloantopics/microloans/index.html.

Appendix III

CDC/504 Program—SBA Program Office

The CDC/504 loan program is a long-term financing tool for economic development within a community. The 504 Program provides growing businesses with long-term, fixed-rate financing for major fixed assets, such as land and buildings. A Certified Development Company is a nonprofit corporation set up to contribute to the economic development of its community. CDCs work with the SBA and private-sector lenders to provide financing to small businesses. There are about 270 CDCs nationwide, with each covering a specific geographic area.

Typically, a 504 project includes a loan secured with a senior lien from a private-sector lender covering up to 50 percent of the project cost, a loan secured with a junior lien from the CDC (backed by a 100 percent SBA-guaranteed debenture) covering up to 40 percent of the cost, and a contribution of at least 10 percent equity from the small business being helped.

Maximum Debenture

The maximum SBA debenture is $1,500,000 when meeting the job creation criteria or a community development goal. Generally, a business must create or retain one job for every $50,000 provided by the SBA except for "Small Manufacturers" which have a $100,000 job creation or retention goal (see below). The maximum SBA debenture is $2.0 million when meeting a public policy goal.

The public policy goals are as follows:

- Business district revitalization.
- Expansion of exports.
- Expansion of minority business development.
- Rural development.
- Increasing productivity and competitiveness.
- Restructuring because of federally mandated standards or policies.
- Changes necessitated by federal budget cutbacks.
- Expansion of small business concerns owned and controlled by veterans (especially service-disabled veterans)
- Expansion of small business concerns owned and controlled by women.

The maximum debenture for "Small Manufacturers" is $4.0 million. A Small Manufacturer is defined as a small business concern that has:

Its primary business classified in sector 31, 32, or 33 of the North American Industrial Classification System (NAICS); and All of its production facilities located in the United States.

In order to qualify for a $4 million 504 loan, the Small Manufacturer must 1) meet the definition of a Small Manufacturer described above, and 2) either (i) create or retain at least 1 job per $100,000 guaranteed by the SBA [Section 501(d)(1) of the Small Business Investment Act (SBI Act)], or (ii) improve the economy of the locality or achieve one or more public policy goals [sections 501(d)(2) or (3) of the SBI Act].

What funds may be used for

Proceeds from 504 loans must be used for fixed asset projects such as: purchasing land and improvements, including existing buildings, grading, street improvements, utilities, parking lots and landscaping; construction of new facilities, or modernizing, renovating or converting existing facilities; or purchasing long-term machinery and equipment.

The 504 Program cannot be used for working capital or inventory, consolidating or repaying debt, or refinancing.

Terms, Interest Rates and Fees

Interest rates on 504 loans are pegged to an increment above the current market rate for five-year and 10-year U.S. Treasury issues. Maturities of 10 and 20 years are available. Fees total approximately three (3) percent of the debenture and may be financed with the loan.

Collateral

Generally, the project assets being financed are used as collateral. Personal guaranties of the principal owners are also required.

Eligible Business

To be eligible, the business must be operated for profit and fall within the size standards set by the SBA. Under the 504 Program, the business qualifies as small if it does not have a tangible net worth in excess of $7.5 million and does not have an average net income in excess of $2.5 million after taxes for the preceding two years. Loans cannot be made to businesses engaged in speculation or investment in rental real estate.

http://www.sba.gov/services/financialassistance/sbaloantopics/cdc504/index.html.

BIBLIOGRAPHY

Articles and Book Chapters in Multiauthored Books

Alexander, Bill. "The Black Church and Community Empowerment," in *On the Road to Economic Freedom, An Agenda for Black Progress.* Washington, DC: Regnery Gateway, 1987.

Alexander, Koteles. "Adarand: Brute Political Force Concealed as a Constitutional Colorblind Principle." *Howard University Law Journal* 39, (1995): 367, 380.

Allen, Walter R. and Jewell, Joseph O. "The Miseducation of Black America: Black Education Since an American Dilemma," in *An American Dilemma Revisited: Race Relations in a Changing World.* New York: Russell Sage Foundation Publications, 1996, 181

Barras, Jonetta Rose. "United We Stood, but Divisions Now Show; Cosby Ignited a Debate About Class. We Need to Keep Talking." *Washington Post* (June 27, 2004), sec. B.

Benjamin, J. H. "The Supreme Court Decision and the Future of Race-Conscious Remedies." *Government Financial Review* (Apr. 1989): 21.

Bernstein, Aaron. "An Inner City Renaissance." *Business Week* (Oct. 27, 2003): 364.

Birnie, C. W. "The Education of the Negro in Charleston, South Carolina, Prior to the Civil War." *Journal of Negro History* 12, (1927): 13.

Bolick, Clint. "Rule of Law: So Far, Clinton Can't Kick His Quota Addiction." *Wall Street Journal* (June 12, 1996), sec. A.

Brown, Carolyn M. "America's Leading Black Philanthropists." *Black Enterprise* (August 2005): 118.

Butler, John Sibley. "Myrdal Revisited: The Negro in Business, the Professions, Public Service, and Other White Collar Occupations," in *An American*

Dilemma Revisited, Race Relations in a Changing World. New York: Russell Sage Foundation, 1996.

Butler, Sana. "Black Wealth Initiative: The Coleman's Tap Multiple Income Streams." *Black Enterprise* (June 2008): 81.

Cherry, Robert. "The Culture of Poverty Thesis and African Americans: The Work of Gunnar Myrdal and Other Institutionalists." *J. Econ. Issues* 12, (1995): 1119.

Cohn, D'Vera. "D.C. Gap in Wealth Growing: Uneducated Suffer Most Study Shows." *Washington Post* (July 22, 2004), sec. A.

"Coming of Age," Vol. 2 *The Volume Library.* Nashville, TN: The Southwestern Company, 1995.

Crenshaw, Albert B. "Fear, Greed the Players in Pension Debate: Middle Ground Could Prove Elusive as Congress Considers Reforms After Enron." *Washington Post* (Feb. 8, 2002), sec. E.

Crespi, Gregory S. "Market Magic: Can the Invisible Hand Strangle Bigotry?" *Boston University Law Review* 72, (1992): 991, 1002.

Cunningham, Christi. "Identity Markets." *Howard University Law Journal* 45, (2002): 491, 494–95.

Days, Drew S. III. "Fullilove." *Yale Law Journal* 96, (1987): 453.

Derbyshire, John. "Attack of the Wealth Eaters." *National Law Review* (Sept. 25, 2000): 39, available at 2000 WL 11593985.

Dingle, Derek T. "B.E. 100's 26th Annual Report on Black Business." *Black Enterprise* (June 1998): 93.

———. "B.E. 100's Overview." *Black Enterprise* (June 2000).

———. "B.E. 100's 31st Annual Report on Black Business." *Black Enterprise* (June 2003).

———. "B.E. 100's Overview, Only the Strong Survive." *Black Enterprise* (June 2004).

———. "B.E. 100's Flashback," *Black Enterprise* (June 2007): 176

———."B.E. 100's: Report on the Nation's Largest Black-Owned Banks," *Black Enterprise* (June 2008): 174.

———. "Bob Johnson's Second Act," *Black Enterprise* (June 2007): 200.

Donahue, John J. III. "Advocacy versus Analysis in Assessing Employment Discrimination Law." *Stanford Law Review* 44, (1992):1583, 1593.

Engardio, Peter. "Nice Dream If You Can Live It." *Business Week* (Sept. 13, 2004).

Farhi, Paul. "Feeding the Beast: The Greed That Lives (and Seems to be Thriving) in Us All." *Washington Post* (Mar. 3, 2002), sec F.

Fletcher, Michael A. and Hockstader, Lee, "U-Mich. Rulings Spur Strategic Scramble: Affirmative Action's Backers and Foes Ponder Response to High Court's Decision." *Washington Post* (June 25, 2003), sec. A9.

Gaiter, Dorothy J. "Black Entrepreneurship: A Special Report, Short-Term Despair, Long-Term Promise: As Traditional Black-Owned Businesses Lose Ground, Hopes Rest on a New Generation of Entrepreneurs." *Wall Street Journal* (Apr. 13, 1992), sec. R.

Golden, Frederick. "Albert Einstein, Person of the Century." *Time,* (Dec. 31, 1999): 62, 80-81.

Goldsmith, Marshall. "We're All Entrepreneurs." *Business Week*, (August 25, 2008): 46.

Hamblin, Seth and Stanton, Laura. "Remembering the Fallen." *Washington Post* (May 26, 2003), sec. A.

Harris, Hamil R. "Some Blacks Find Nuggets of Truth in Cosby's Speech, Others Say D.C. Remarks About Poor Blacks Went Too Far." *Washington Post* (May 26, 2004), sec. A.

Hayman, Robert L. and Levit, Nancy. "The Constitutional Ghetto." *Wisconsin Law Review* 3, (1993): 627.

Hockstader, Lee and Fletcher, Michael A. "U-Mich. Rulings Spur Strategic Scramble: Affirmative Action's Backers and Foes Ponder Response to High Court's Decision." *Washington Post* (June 25, 2003).

Jackson, Lee Ann. "Not Just for a Rainy Day, Getting African Americans to Start Saving One Dollar at a Time." *Black Enterprise* (Jan. 2003).

Kane, Gregory. "High Court's Gore Ruling Far from Its Worst." *Baltimore Sun* (Dec. 24, 2000).

King, Colbert I. "Happy Talk on Holiday." *Washington Post* (July 12, 2003).

Lane, Charles. "Affirmative Action for Diversity Is Upheld, in 5 to 4 Vote, Justices Approve U-Mich. Law School Plan." *Washington Post* (June 24, 2003), sec. A.

———. "Highlights of the Decisions in *Grutter v. Bollinger* and *Gratz v. Bollinger*." *Washington Post* (June 24, 2003).

———. "Affirmative Action for Diversity is Upheld: Court Backs Affirmative Action but Envisions Its End." *Washington Post* (June 24, 2003), sec. A.

———. "In Court's Ruling, a Nod to Notion of a Broader Elite." *Washington Post* (June 25, 2003), sec. A.

Lee, Elaine. "Do Good, Get Rich." *Black Enterprise*, (May 2008): 73.

Loury, Glenn C. "Making it All Happen" in *On the Road to Economic Freedom, An Agenda for Black Progress*. Washington, DC: Regnery Gateway, 1987.

Marshall, Thurgood. "The Constitution: A Living Document." *Howard University Law Journal*, Vol. 30, (1987): 623.

McKinney, Jeffrey. "The Perils of Being Public." *Black Enterprise* (April 2001).

Moreno, Sylvia. "As Release Nears, These Inmates Are All Business (Street Smarts Are Put to Good Use in Tex. Program)." *Washington Post* (November 3, 2006), sec. A3.

Mtima, Lateef. "African American Economic Empowerment Strategies for the New Millennium—Revisiting the Washington–Du Bois Dialectic." *Howard University Law Journal* 42, (1999): 391, 400.

Mongkuo, Maurice and Rice, Mitchell F. "Did Adarand Kill Minority Set-Asides?" *Public Administrative Review* (Jan/Feb., 1998)): 82.

Pearlstein, Steven. "Pixar Stock Offering a Hit for Steve Jobs." *Washington Post* (Nov. 30, 1995).

——— "Farewell to Free- Market Capitalism: Wave Goodbye to the Invisible Hand." *Washington Post* (August 1, 2008), sec. D1 and 8.

Rice, Mitchell F. "Government Set-Asides, Minority Business Enterprises, and the Supreme Court." *Public Administrative Review* (Mar./Apr. 1991): 114.

"Reconstruction," in *The Volume Library*. Nashville, TN: The Southwestern Company, 1995.

Rucker, Philip. "Megachurches Migrating to Charles: Boon Mirrors Population Growth." *Washington Post* (December 12, 2006), sec. A1 and A4.

Saddler, Jeanne. "Black Entrepreneurship: The Next Generation, Young Risk Takers Push the Business Envelope." *Wall Street Journal* (May 12, 1994), sec. B.

Shulman, Robin. "After Success in Poor Nations, Grameen Tries New York." *Washington Post* (March 10, 2008), sec. A3.

Singletary, Michelle. "Many Marriages Would Benefit From Sound Family Financial Plans." *Washington Post* (Apr. 25, 2002), sec. E.

Stanton, Laura Stanton and Hamblin, Seth. "Remembering the Fallen." *Washington Post* (May 26, 2003), sec. A.

Steele, Charles, Jr. "The Color of Credit." *Washington Post* (June 23, 2008), sec. A15.

Taifa, N. "Criminal Sentencing." *University of Memphis Law Review*, Vol. 12, (1996): 158, 160.

Walker, Juliet E. K. "Racism, Slavery, and Free Enterprise." *Business History Review* 364, (Autumn 1986): 60.

Ward, James D. "Response to Croson." *Public Administrative Review* (Sept./Oct. 1994): 483.

Williams, Krissah. "Radio One Branches out So Blacks Will Tune In." *Washington Post* (Feb. 5, 2003).

———. "Church Reaches Out Through Small Businesses." *Washington Post* (March 2, 2004), sec. E1,

Wilson, M. "Set-Asides of Local Government Contracts for Minority-Owned Businesses: Constitutional and State Law Issues." *New Mexico Law Review* 17, (1987): 337–59.

Wiltz, Teresa. "BET a Case of Selling Out or Selling Up? But Has the Network Sold a Bit of its Soul?" *Washington Post* (Nov. 4, 2000).

Zimmer, Michael J., Sullivan, Charles A., and Richard, Richard F. "Are Antidiscrimination Laws Necessary?" in *Cases and Materials on Employment Discrimination*, 5th ed. New York: Aspen, 2000): 35, 35–55.

Articles

"Black Entrepreneurs: Have Capital Will Flourish." *Economist* (Feb. 27, 1993).

"The Jobless Recovery." *Washington Post* (Jan. 27, 2004).

"The Typical Federal Worker." *Washington Post* (Sept. 1, 2003).

Scholarly and Other Books

Andrews, Marcellus. *The Political Economy of Hope and Fear: Capitalism and the Black Condition in America*. New York: NYU Press, 1999.

Barringer, Bruce R. and Ireland, R. Duane. *Entrepreneurship*. Upper Saddle River, NJ: Pearson Prentice Hall, 2006.

Becker, Gary. *The Economics of Discrimination*. Chicago: University of Chicago Press, 1971.

————. *Human Capital: A Theoretical and Empirical Analysis, with Special Reference to Education*. New York: Columbia University Press, 1975.

Bell, Derrick. *Race, Racism, and American Law*. New York: Aspen Law and Business, 2001.

Bennett, Lerone Jr. *Before the Mayflower*. New York: Penguin Books, 1982, 6th Revised Edition, 1993.

Berman, Dorothy M. and Matthews, Joseph. *Social Security, Medicare & Government Pensions*. Berkeley, CA: Nolo Press, 2002.

Berman, Dorothy M. and Matthews, Joseph, *Social Security, Medicare & Government Pensions*. Berkley, CA: Nolo Press, 2008.

Bernstein, Peter W., ed. *The Ernst & Young Tax Guide 1998*. New York: John Wiley & Sons, Inc. 1998.

Butler, John Sibley. *Entrepreneurship and Self-Help Among African Americans, a Reconsideration of Race and Economics*. New York: State University of New York Press, 1991.

Carmichael, Stokley and Hamilton, Charles V. *Black Power: The Politics of Liberation*. New York: Harper and Row, 1985.

Cary, William Lucius and Eisenberg, Melvin Aron. *Cases and Materials on Corporations*. New York: Foundation Press, 1995.

Clayton, Obie, ed. *An American Dilemma Revisited: Race Relations in a Changing World*. New York: Russell Sage Foundation Publications, 1996.

Conard, Alfred F., Knauss, Robert L. and Siegel, Stanley. *Agency Partnerships*. New York: Foundation, Press, 1987.

Curley, Michael T. and Walker, Joseph A. *Stockbroker Examination, Series 7*. Hauppauge, New York: Barron's Educational Series, Inc., 2000.

Delaney, Martin A. *Condition, Elevation, Emigration and Destiny of the Colored People of the United States*. Ithaca, NY: Cornell University Library, 1852.

D'Souza, Dinesh. *The End of Racism: Principles for a Multiracial Society*. New York: Free Press, 1995.

Du Bois, W. E. B. "The Talented Tenth," in *The Negro Problem: A Series of Articles by Representative Negroes Today* (1903), reprinted in Leslie H. Fishel and Benjamin Quarles, *The Negro American*, 1967.

Dukeminier, Jesse and Krier, James E. *Property*. New York: Aspen Law, 2000.

Dunnan, Nancy. *Dunn and Bradstreet's Guide to Your Investments 1999: Chapter 29—Social Security, Retirement, and Pensions*. New York: Harper Perennial, 1999.

Earle, Jonathan. *The Routledge Atlas of African American History*. New York: Routledge, 2000.

Eisenberg, Melvin Aron. *Corporations and Other Business Organizations, Cases and Materials*. New York: West Publishing Company, 1995.

Emmanuel, Stephen E. *Constitutional Law.* New York: Emmanuel Publishing Corp., 1997.

Epstein, Richard A. *Forbidden Grounds: The Case Against Employment Discrimination Laws.* Boston, MA: Harvard University Press, 1995.

Fishel, Leslie H. and Quarles, Benjamin. *The Negro American.* New York: William Morrow and Company, 1967.

Frazier, E. Franklin. *Black Bourgeoisie.* New York: Simon & Schuster, 1997.

Freeman, Richard B. *Black Elite: The New Market for Highly Educated Black Americans.* New York: McGraw-Hill, 1976.

Hall, Kermit L. (Editor), Benedict, Michael Les (Contributor). "Slaughter- House Cases." *The Oxford Guide to United States Supreme Court Decisions* New York: Oxford University Press, Inc. 1999.

Hamilton, Robert W. *The Law of Corporations in a Nutshell.* New York: West Group, 2000.

Harris, Abram L. *The Negro as Capitalist.* Chicago: Urban Research Press, Inc., 1992, originally published in 1936 by the American Academy of Political Science.

Heilbroner, Robert and Thurow, Lester. *Economics Explained.* New York: Simon & Schuster, 1998.

Hernstein, Richard and Murray, Charles. *The Bell Curve: Intelligence and Class Structure in American Life.* New York: Free Press, 1994.

Hynes, Dennis J. *Agency, Partnership and the LLC in a Nutshell.* New York: West Publishing Company, 2001.

Glazer, Nathan. *Affirmative Discrimination: Ethnic Inequality and Public Policy.* New York: Basic Books, 1975.

Johnson, Hannibal B. *Black Wall Street—From Riot to Renaissance in Tulsa's Historic Greenwood District.* Austin, TX: Eakin Press, 1998.

Kennedy, Michael B., Nash, Mark T., and Saks, Brittany B. *PriceWaterhouseCoopers 2008 Guide to Tax and Financial Planning.* Hoboken, NJ: Wiley & Sons, Inc., 2007.

Kiyosaki, Robert T. *Before You Quit Your Job: Ten Real Life Lessons Every Entrepreneur Should Know About Building a Multimillion-Dollar Business.* New York: Warner Business Books, 2005.

Levy, Leonard W. "Cruikshank." *Encyclopedia of the American Constitution.* New York, 1986.

Little, Jeffrey B. and Rhodes, Lucien. *Understanding Wall Street.* Blue Ridge Summit, PA: Liberty House, 1987.

Low, Peter W. and Jeffries, John C. Jr., *Federal Courts and the Law of Federal State Relations* 923. New York: Foundation Press, 1998.

McEvoy, J. P. and Zarate, Oscar. *Introducing Quantum Theory.* London: Icon Books, 1999.

McJohn, Stephen M. *Intellectual Property.* New York: Aspen Publishers, 2003.

McWhorter, John H. *Losing the Race: Self-Sabotage in Black America.* New York: The Free Press, 2000.

Meier, David W. *Make Your Life Tax Deductible.* New York: McGraw-Hill 2006.

Midgett, Edwin W. *An Accounting Primer.* New York: Mentor, 1974.

Myrdal, Gunnar. *An American Dilemma: The Negro Problem and Modern Democracy.* New York: Harper & Brothers, 1944, in 1998 reprinted edition.

Rifkin, Jeremy. *The European Dream: How Europe's Vision of the Future is Quietly Eclipsing the American Dream.* New York: Penguin Group (USA), 2004.

Rosenberg, Eva. *Small Business Taxes Made Easy.* New York: McGraw-Hill, 2005.

Schwartz, Bernard. *Statutory History of the United States: Civil Rights.* New York: McGraw-Hill, 1970.

Sherman, Andrew J. *Raising Capital.* New York: Kiplinger, 2000.

Slavin, Steve. *Economics: A Self Teaching Guide.* Hoboken, NJ: Wiley & Sons, Inc., 1999.

Steingold, Fred B. *The Employer's Legal Handbook.* Berkeley, CA: Nolo Press, June 1999.

Sullivan, Charles A. and Zimmer, Michael J. *Cases and Materials on Employment Discrimination.* New York: Aspen Publishers, 2000.

Thernstrom, Abigail and Thernstrom, Stephen. *America in Black and White, One Nation Indivisible.* New York: Simon and Schuster, 1997.

Tribe, Laurence H. *Constitutional Law Treatise.* New York: West Publishing Company, 2000.

Wallace, Robert L. *Black Wealth Through Entrepreneurship.* New York: Duncan & Duncan, 1997.

Wallace, Robert L. *Black Wealth, Your Road to Small Business Success.* Indianapolis, IN: Wiley Publishing, Inc., 2002.

Wessels, Walter J. *Economics.* New York: Barron's, 1987.

Wilson, William Julius. *The Declining Significance of Race.* Chicago: University of Chicago Press, 1978.

Weltman, Barbara. *Small Business Taxes.* Hoboken, NJ: Wiley & Sons, Inc., 2007.

Woodson, Robert L. *On the Road to Economic Freedom, An Agenda for Black Progress.* Washington, DC: Regnery Gateway, 1987.

Zimmer, Micheal J., Sullivan, Charles, A., and Richard, Richard F. *Cases and Materials on Employment Discrimination,* 35–55. New York: Aspen, 2000.

Reference Books and Miscellaneous

African American Desk Reference. New York: Stonesong Press and New York Public Library, 1999.

Black's Law Dictionary. New York: Thomson West, 1983.

Restatement (Third) of Agency Sec. 1. New York: Lexis Nexis, 2001.

The African American Almanac. Farmington Hills, MI: Gale Research Inc., 1997.

The Nuts and Bolts of Business Plans. Syracuse University, Department of Entrepreneurship and Emerging Enterprises, 2005.

U.S. Small Business Administration. *SBA Office of Business Development Report to Congress on Minority Small Business and Capital Ownership Development for Fiscal Year.* Washington, DC: 2001.

The Volume Library. Nashville, TN: The Southwestern Company, 1995.

Wall Street Journal Almanac 1999. New York: Dow Jones & Co., 1998.

The World Almanac and Book of Facts 1998. New York: The Rosen Group, 1998.

The World Almanac and Book of Facts 2003. New York: The Rosen Group, 2003.

SEC, Q & A: Small Business and the SEC Concerning the Private Offering Exemption 14–15 (1993).

Legal Cases

Adarand Constructors, Inc. v. Peña, 515 U.S. 200 (1995).

Bolling v. Sharpe, 347 U.S. 497 (1954).

Brown v. Board of Education, 347 U.S. 483 (1954).

Chrysler Corp. v. Silva, 118 F.3d 56, 58 (1st Cir. 1997).

City of Richmond v. J.A. Croson Co., 488 U.S. 469 (1989).

Civil Rights Cases, 109 U.S. 3 (1883).

Colbert v. Hennessey, 217 N.E. 2d 914 (Mass. 1966).

Colo. Anti-Discrimination Comm'n v. Cont'l Airlines, Inc., 372 U.S. 714 (1963).

Corning v. Burden, 56 U.S. 252, 267 (1853).

Craig v. Boren, 429 U.S. 190 (1976).

Diamond v. Chakrabarty, 447 U.S. 303 (1980).

Dred Scott v. Sandford, 60 U.S. 393 (1856).

Donahue v. Rodd Electrotype, 328 N.E.2d 505, 511 (Mass. 1975).

Fullilove v. Klutznick, 448 U.S. 448 (1980).

Galler v. Galler, 203 N.E.2d 577 (Ill. 1964).

Gateway Potato Sales v. G.B. Inv. Co., 822 P.2d 490 (Ariz. 1991).

Griggs v. Duke Power Co., 401 U.S. 424 (1971).

Grutter v. Bollinger, 539 U.S. at 306 (2003).

Hall v. De Cuir, 95 U.S. 485 (1878).

Jones v. Alfred H. Mayer Co., 392 U.S. 409 (1968).

Kahn v. Lynch Comm. Sys., Inc., 638 A.2d 1110 (Del. Sup. Ct. 1994).

Loving v. Virginia, 388 U.S. 1, 9 (1967).

McCallum v. Rosen's Diversified, Inc., 153 F.3d 701 (8th Cir. 1998).

McQuade v. Stoneham, 189 N.E. 234 (N.Y. 1934).

Metro Broadcasting v. FCC, 497 U.S. 547 (1990).

Monroe v. Pape, 365 U.S. 167 (1961).

Plessy v. Ferguson, 163 U.S. 537 (1896).

United States v. Price, 383 U.S. 787 (1966).

Prigg v. Pennsylvania, 41 U.S. 539 (1842).

Regents of the University of California v. Bakke, 438 U.S. 265 (1978).

Reves v. Ernst & Young, 294 U.S. 56 (1990).

Ringling Bros.–Barnum & Bailey Combined Shows v. Ringling, 53 A.2d 441(Del. Sup. Ct. 1947).

Runyon v. McCrary, 427 U.S. 160 (1976).

SEC v. W.J. Howey Co., 328 U.S. 293 (1966).

Shapiro v. Thompson, 394 U.S. 618 (1969).
Slaughter-House Cases, 83 U.S. 36 (1873).
Sutton v. Sutton, 637 N.E.2d 260 (N.Y. 1994).
Two Pesos v. Taco Cabana, 505 U.S. 763(1992).
United States v. Cruikshank, 92 U.S. 542 (1876).
United States v. Guest, 383 U.S. 745 (1966).
United States v. Hall, 26 F. Cas. 82 (C.C.S.D. Ala. 1871).
United States v. Reese, 92 U.S. 214 (1876).
United Steel Workers v. Webber, 443 U.S. 193 (1979).
Virtual Works, Inc. v. Volkswagen of America, Inc., 238 F.3d 264 (4th Cir. 2001).
White v. Consumers Fin. Serv., Inc., 15 A.2d 142 (Pa. 1940).
Wilkes v. Springside Nursing Home, 353 N.E.2d 657, 663-64 (Mass. 1976).
Williamson v. Lee Optical of Oklahoma, 348 U.S. 483 (1955).
Wygant v. Jackson Bd. of Educ., 476 U.S. 267 (1986).

Selected Legal Statues

Legal Statutes Civil Rights Acts of 1866.
Civil Rights Act of 1870.
Civil Rights Act of 1964, 42 U.S.C. § § 2000a-2000h (2002).
Delaware General Corporation Law, 8 DEL. CODE ANN. 141(b).
REV. UNIF. PARTNERSHIP ACT of 1997, § 401(i), 6 U.L.A. 133 (2001)(pt. II).
REV. UNIF. PARTNERSHIP ACT § 202(a), 6 U.L.A. 92 (2001).
REV. UNIF. PARTNERSHIP ACT § 202(c), 6 U.L.A. 92-93 (2001)(pt. I).
REV. UNIF. PARTNERSHIP ACT § 401 (i), 6 U.L.A. 133 (2001)(pt. I).
The Securities and Exchange Act of 1934.
UNIF. PARTNERSHIP ACT of 1914, § 18(g), 6 U.L.A. 101 (2001)(Part II).
UNIF. PARTNERSHIP ACT § 6, 6 U.L.A. 313 (2001)(pt. I).
UNIF. PARTNERSHIP ACT § 7(4), 6 U.L.A. 418 (2001)(pt. I).
UNIF. PARTNERSHIP ACT § 18(g), 6 U.L.A. 101 (2001) (Pt. II).
Section 8 (a) of the Small Business Act, 15 U.S.C. § § 631-37, at § 637.
Voting Rights Act of 1965, 42 U.S.C. § 1971, 1973 to 1973bb-4 (2002).
Civil Rights Acts of 1866, 42 U.S.C. § § 1981, 1982 (2000).
The Community Reinvestment Act of 1977.
18 U.S.C. § 241 (2000).
18 U.S.C. § 1985 (c) (2000).
The SBA's Small Business Development Centers
The SBA's Section 7(a) Loan Guaranty Program
The SBA's Microloan Program
The SBA's Section 504 Certified Development Company Program
HUD's Community Development Block Grant Program
HUD's Renewal Communities, Empowerment Zones, and Enterprise Community
    Programs
The New Markets Tax Credit Program

Web sites

The Black Entrepreneur's Hall of Fame, www.blackentrepreneurship.com.

The Black Wall Street, Wikipedia, http://en.wikipedia.org/wiki/TheBlackWall
    _Street,1 (3-27-07).

Jeff Cornwall, "Growing Firms in the Entrepreneurial Economy," *Entrepreneurial
    Mind*, October 25, 2007, http://www.drjeffcoenwall.com (search growing
    firms).

Davey D's Hip Hop Corner, Black Wall Street, http://www.daveyd.com/blackwall
    politic.html, 3 (3-27-2007).

http://www.cnn.com/casualties/SPECIALS/2008/Iraq/forces/casualties.

Key Business Needs Insurance, Cape Insurance Education, http://www
    .capeschool.com/md_ins/md_download_welcome_1.html (August 7, 2008),
    18–22.

Medicare Part D, Cape Insurance Education, http://www.capeschool.com/
    md_ins/mddownload_welcome_1.html (August 7, 2008).

Russell Simmons, http://en.wikipedia.org/wiki/Russell_Simmons (July 30,
    2008).

SBA Office of Advocacy, "How Important are Small Businesses to the U.S. Econ-
    omy?" See Frequently Asked Questions, http://www.sba.gov/advo/stats/
    sbfaq.pdf.

Tulsa Race Riot: A Report by the Oklahoma Commission to Study the Tulsa Race
    Riot of 1921, 45, available at http://www.ok-history.mus.ok.us/trrc/freport
    .pdf.

Vinnie Johnson, http://www.pistongroup.com/profiles/vjohnson.html.

Code of Federal Regulations

3 C.F.R. § 339 (1965).
3 C.F.R. § 230 (1978).
41 C.F.R. § 60 (1980).

Executive Orders

Exec. Order No. 11,246.
Exec. Order No. 12,086.

INDEX

Note: page numbers followed by *t* indicate that the citation may be found in a table.

About the Author

W. SHERMAN ROGERS is Professor of Law at Howard University. He has published a number of articles in professional and legal journals, authored five instructional manuscripts, written numerous federal appellate court briefs, and argued cases before various United States Federal Circuit Courts of Appeal.